# LOYALIST RESOLVE

# LOYALIST RESOLVE

*Patient Fortitude*
*in the English Civil War*

Raymond A. Anselment

**DELAWARE**

Newark: University of Delaware Press
London and Toronto: Associated University Presses

Associated University Presses
440 Forsgate Drive
Cranbury, NJ 08512

Associated University Presses
25 Sicilian Avenue
London WC1A 2QH, England

Associated University Presses
P.O. Box 488, Port Credit
Mississauga, Ontario
Canada L5G 4M2

The paper used in this publication meets the requirements of the American National Standard for Permanence of Paper for Printed Library Materials Z39.48-1984.

**Library of Congress Cataloging-in-Publication Data**

Anselment, Raymond A.
  Loyalist resolve.

  Bibliography: p.
  Includes index.
  1. English poetry—Early modern, 1500–1700—History and criticism   2. Great Britain—History—Civil War, 1642–1649—Literature and the war.   3. Politics and literature—Great Britain—History—17th century.
  4. Charles I, King of England, 1600–1649, in fiction, drama, poetry, etc.   5. Royalists—Great Britain—History—17th century.   6. Monarchy in literature.
  7. Philosophy in literature.   8. Ethics in literature.
  I. Title.
  PR435.A57   1988      821'.4'09358        87-40514

  ISBN 0-87413-338-6 (alk. paper)

PRINTED IN THE UNITED STATES OF AMERICA

For Jessica

# Contents

Acknowledgments   9

Introduction   13

1   The Caroline Circle of Peace   21

2   William Cartwright and the "Gather'd Mind"   46

3   George Daniel and the "Onlie True Content"   69

4   Richard Lovelace and the "Gallant Thorough-made
    Resolve"   97

5   Alexander Brome and "the Safe Estate"   127

6   Abraham Cowley and the "Soule Compos'd of th'Eagle
    and the Dove"   155

Notes   185

Select Bibliography   211

Index   225

# Acknowledgments

A sabbatical leave from the University of Connecticut provided the opportunity to read in the extensive seventeenth-century holdings at Cambridge University Library; a grant from the University of Connecticut also supported a summer at the British Library and numerous trips to Yale's Beinecke and Sterling Memorial libraries. Some of this research was developed initially in different form in *Philological Quarterly, Modern Language Studies, Essays in Literature,* and *Renaissance and Reformation;* the ideas appear in this book with the permission of these journals' editors.

The following chapters are indebted to the historians of the Caroline decades acknowledged in the notes as well as to several colleagues at the University of Connecticut. As they have on other occasions, William E. Sheidley and David Sonstroem found time in their busy schedules to share their reactions and suggestions. Bill's thorough, carefully reasoned reading of the completed manuscript proved invaluable direction for the revisions; and Dave's painstaking response to the final draft encouraged greater clarity. C. David Benson also read the manuscript, responding to the general approach, and at various stages Samuel F. Pickering, Jr. gave both professional advice and support. But the largest debt, once again, is to my wife Carol who offered sensitive criticism of the initial arguments and their expression.

# LOYALIST RESOLVE

# Introduction

WHEN Harry Coningsby published Boethius's *The Consolation of Philosophy* in 1664, his translation included a lengthy biography of his own father and a poetic version of Lipsius's *Of Constancy*. The younger Coningsby remembers his father Thomas as a resolute individual who "lived and died *Honest,* preferring his Conscience and Loyalty to his Life, Liberty and Estate."[1] Thomas Coningsby of North Mimms had been the high sheriff of Hertfordshire until his arrest in 1643, when the parliamentarian supporters sequestered his estate and imprisoned him in the Tower. Seven years later his son succeeded in obtaining his father's freedom, but the physically weakened Coningsby continued to protest the deprivation of his property and was soon arrested again. Before he died in 1654, "disdaining in the whole story of his Life to submit his native and gallant Freedom to the frowns of any that were but his Fellow-subjects,"[2] Thomas Coningsby sought solace in translating *Two Bookes of Constancy.* Inspired perhaps by his father's example and "considering the Person and Fate of our most Gracious *Sovereign,*"[3] Harry Coningsby also attempted to "recreate himself" and to offer his own translation of *The Consolation.* Together the two Stoic works are left to posterity as a testimony to the "Honest Mind" and a remembrance of the "unhappy Times." In the patient fortitude that consoled Boethius as he faced death and that sustained Lipsius when he confronted war, Thomas and Harry Coningsby found their own courage to endure "the giddy roulings of Fortune" and to "Loyal stand."[4] Though both are now little more than minor figures in the history of England's civil war, the Coningsbys represent a timeless suffering and spirit. Within the seventeenth-century context of a nation torn apart by conflict, theirs is a loyalist resolve.

The essence of this resolve is the self-sufficiency found in a long tradition of Stoic humanism. The tranquillity, wisdom, and patience valued among these classical and Christian writers reflect the self-possession Seneca emphasizes in *"De Vita Beata."* "The happy life," this essay concludes, "is to have a mind that is free, lofty, fearless and steadfast—a mind that is placed beyond the reach of fear, beyond the reach of desire, that counts virtue the only good, baseness the only evil, and all else but a worthless mass of things."[5] Boethius writes that the serene man can fearlessly accept an uncertain fortune because his "ordered" life enables him to stand above the onslaught of fate.[6] In Joseph Hall's version, the patient man "hath so conquered himselfe, that wrongs cannot conquer him."[7] The wise man, he adds in another common image, "stands like a center unmoved, while the circumference of his estate is drawne above, beneath, about him."[8] All agree with Lipsius that constancy, the offspring of patience, is deeply rooted in right reason or "A true sense and iudgement of thinges humane and diuine."[9] The steadfast individual possesses the virtue and integrity Cicero construes as the Stoic doctrine of "'living conformably to nature': . . . we are always to be in accord with virtue, and from all other things that may be in harmony with nature to choose only such as are not incompatible with virtue."[10]

This commitment to virtue was readily associated in the Renaissance with the traditions of Stoicism. Throughout the Middle Ages the writing of Boethius and the essays of Seneca offered a repository of Stoic ideas, and by the end of the fifteenth century, major editions of Cicero and Seneca ensured a widespread understanding of Stoicism among the Renaissance humanists.[11] Editions of Diogenes Laertius, Epictetus, Plutarch, and Marcus Aurelius appeared in the next century; and by the time Thomas Lodge published *The Workes both Morall and Naturall of Lucius Annaeus Seneca* (1614), most of the major Stoic writers had been translated into English. By then Justus Lipsius's neo-Stoic *De Constantia* (1584) and Guillaume Du Vair's *La Philosophie Morale des Stoiques* (ca. 1586) had also been translated, and the "English Seneca," Joseph Hall, had written *Heaven vpon Earth* (1606) and *Characters of Vertves and Vices* (1608).[12] "The allure of unshakable self-sufficiency," Gordon Braden's recent study of Seneca cautions, "remains in European literacy at a deep level, prior to any specific revival of interest in Seneca or Stoicism"; but as his chapter on "Stoicism and Renaissance" indicates, Stoic attitudes are central to the period's literature.[13] Classical and neo-Stoic ideas influenced the drama of the Elizabethan and Jacobean theater, the verse satires of the 1590s, as well as the prose style of the seventeenth century; and modern scholars continue to stress the Stoic traditions in writers as diverse as Shakespeare, Jonson, and Donne.[14] Though Renaissance contemporaries, mindful of a dangerous arrogance and independence in the classical philosophy, wrestled unsuccessfully with the distinction between Stoic self-possession and Christian patience,[15] they were often drawn toward the promise "Thou shalt be a king indeed free indeed, only subiect vnto God, enfranchized from the seruile yoke of Fortune and affections."[16] A Stoic emphasis on "things indifferent" and "morally indifferent" minimized the importance of events external to the self with the assurance "we can doe no more but vndertake a matter with wisedome, pursue it with hope, and be readie to suffer whatsoeuer shall happen with patience."[17] Indifference to fortune and commitment to virtue attracted especially Renaissance humanists preoccupied with their own uncertain role in the state.

Their ambivalence about the obligation of the humanist to the state is unmistakable in the two central classical writers, Cicero and Seneca.[18] The

Roman orator and philosopher who embodied the ideals of humanism for many in the Renaissance eloquently expresses the importance of engagement. "If wisdom is the most important of the virtues, as it certainly is," Cicero contends, "it necessarily follows that that duty which is connected with the social obligation is the most important duty. And service is better than mere theoretical knowledge, for the study and knowledge of the universe would somehow be lame and defective, were no practical results to follow. Such results, moreover, are best seen in the safe-guarding of human interests."[19] While Cicero in *De Officiis* has no doubt that the great soul indifferent to fortune also naturally responds to a moral and social obligation, Seneca among others less readily agrees with him that "the whole glory of virtue is in activity."[20] Seneca's essays and epistles on the subject of leisure wrestle in particular with the temptation to stand unmoved outside of society as well as above fortune. "If the state is too corrupt to be helped," he suggests in "On Leisure," "if it is wholly dominated by evils, the wise man will not struggle to no purpose, nor spend himself when nothing is to be gained."[21] In the midst of peril, "On Tranquillity of Mind" further counsels, the virtuous will not conceal their abilities. "But if you should happen upon a time when it is not at all easy to serve the state, your necessary course will be to claim more time for leisure and for letters, and, just as if you were making a perilous voyage, to put into harbour from time to time, and, without waiting for public affairs to release you, to separate yourself from them of your own accord."[22] This pragmatic view leads Lipsius in the second book of his treatise *Of Constancy* to retreat from the tumult of war into the quiet of the garden. The model is Solon, the Athenian lawgiver who saw the futility of defending liberty and withdrew to his home.[23]

The private state Lipsius commends affords for many in the Renaissance an attractive yet troubling alternative to the public state. The dilemma for the humanist is inherent in Guillaume Du Vair's Stoic recognition, "the good & happines of man consisteth in the right vse of reason, and what is that but vertue, which is nothing els but a constant disposition of will, to followe that which is honest and conuenient."[24] Neither the Renaissance translation of Du Vair's *"honneste & convenable"* nor the modern version "honorable and appropriate" resolves the tension between personal and social obligations. The movement inward implicit in Stoic indifference assumes that self-sufficiency is not confused with self-indulgence and that personal integrity does not entail social compromise. Unwilling to concede the possibility of irresponsible escapism, Stoic proponents attempt to unite action and contemplation. "It is of course required of a man," even Seneca insists, "that he should benefit his fellow-men—many if he can, if not, a few; if not a few, those who are nearest; if not these, himself."[25] Ideally, withdrawal into the garden and into the self offers both recreation and re-creation. Within the garden, safety and quiet provide undisturbed leisure conducive to meditative study; within the self, such contemplation further cultivates the personal integrity—the "honest" and the "honorable"—that encourages confident and responsible action.[26] This is the ideal Harry and Thomas Coningsby modestly fulfill through their translations of Boethius and Lipsius; their goal is a creative and self-sufficient life also characteristic of other civil war contemporaries.

The withdrawal from society and the movement inward have not, of course, gone unnoticed among the literary discussions of the seventeenth century. Although the pattern of Stoic influence has not been established with any precision,[27] Stoicism unmistakably shapes the midcentury search for the happy life. Two of the seminal works on the period, Maren-Sofie Røstvig's *The Happy Man* and Earl Miner's *The Cavalier Mode from Jonson to Cotton*, sensitively delineate the Stoic characteristics of the good life sought in the years of growing crisis.[28] The *beatus ille* philosophy Røstvig traces and the *vir beatus* Miner explores often seem explicitly Horatian in their inspiration, but the tendency toward rural retirement and the sense of *integer vitae* they describe commonly suggest the Stoic wisdom of the individual "*sapiens, sibi qui imperiosus.*" "The quality that above all distinguishes the 'Stoic' element in Horace," they propose, "is a self-sufficiency involving self-knowledge and wisdom, living a life relying on oneself, and refusing to be distracted by the baubles of the world." "Not only self-sufficiency but sanity in a mad world and freedom among people self-enslaved are required."[29] The nature of these studies, however, necessarily subordinates the writers to a fundamental concern with detailing the evolution of a theme or describing the development of a mode; observations about specific poets are not intended to substitute for extended discussion, and a tendency toward generalization is inherent in the approach. By shifting the focus to a series of representative authors and exploring their changing responses to the national upheaval, the following study develops a sustained analysis of their attempts to find a meaningful resolve.

It does so out of the conviction that England's civil war is less simple than the conflict between Cavaliers and Roundheads evident in the traditional literary view. Recent historical scholarship has reconsidered the tragedy of the "accidental war," the "unnatural war," the "war that nobody wanted."[30] General agreement now exists among historians that most of the English favored a constitutionally balanced or mixed monarchy and that few thought the nation would resort to armed conflict.[31] Before the war reached its bitter end, almost a quarter of the country's men would bear arms, but their allegiances were not always undivided. The majority of the nation, in fact, was not eager to fight, and expressions of neutrality and desire for accommodation were particularly apparent at the outset of the war and again in 1645.[32] The roles played by the rising or falling gentry and aristocracy are also less certain than historians once argued, and considerable skepticism

now exists about the polarization of the country and the court or of Presbyterians and Independents.[33] The current wealth of local and specialized
studies simply contradicts easy generalizations about monolithic identities
and values. Strong religious and political beliefs certainly determined some
allegiances; economic and military realities influenced many others.[34] Those
who could not or would not remain neutral committed themselves to an
internecine war that they themselves often viewed with more complexity than
the heritage of Whig historians has led some to believe.

The following chapters analyze this multiplicity in a group of writers
chosen to represent a social and chronological spectrum encompassing the
Caroline years of peace, war, defeat, and restoration. William Cartwright
(1611–43) is foremost among the poets who developed at Oxford a new
English commemorative verse, and the occasional poetry he wrote in the
1630s and early 1640s offers an important complement to the Whitehall
masques and the courtier praise. George Daniel (1616–57) has no apparent
links with either court or university, yet from his modest estate at Beswick
this obscure Yorkshire gentryman remained remarkably attuned to the royalist fortunes in the growing military conflict. Richard Lovelace (1618–57), on
the other hand, has long been considered the quintessential Cavalier courtier
whose romantic vision of wine, women, and royalism explores not only the
struggles but also the defeat of the king's supporters. Alexander Brome
(1620–66), a successful London lawyer who also responds to the end of the
monarchy and the uncertainty of the 1650s, expresses in various voices an
often critical and deliberately detached response to the rise and fall of
monarchy's opponents. Finally Abraham Cowley (1618–67) draws together
in his distinguished poetic career much that is central to the other loyalists.
Among the university and court poets in the decade before the war and at
Oxford with the royalists during the first important battles, Cowley joined
the exiled monarchists in defeat, returned to live under an Interregnum rule,
and then welcomed the Restoration promise.

His and the other poets' reactions to the national crisis reveal an understanding of Stoic humanism and a sense of political realities at odds with
common literary assumptions about the Caroline culture and the civil war
allegiances. Although all these poets are identified with the losing cause, none
succumbs to the uncritical and self-indulgent adulation that one provocative
scholar believes vitiated the world of Charles I.[35] They also do not lapse into
the unrelieved disillusionment another critic senses in a movement forced to
go on the defensive.[36] Theirs is not a failure to sustain an "unequivocal moral
and intellectual vigour," and they are not guilty of an allegedly pervasive
"self-absorption and hollowness."[37] Their poetry expresses in surprising and
rewarding range the hopes and fears of a generation of writers forced to
reexamine traditional values and personal commitments.

Hence the title *Loyalist Resolve*. Though each of the poets supports Charles

I and all are often considered royalists in this book, the term "loyalist" more precisely distinguishes their political values. As Anthony Fletcher suggests in his important study *The Outbreak of the English Civil War,* "in a real sense everyone was a royalist in 1641." Before royalism emerged as a political position consciously opposed to the parliamentarian view, "the concepts of duty and obedience which rested in the last resort on the Tudor theory of the godly prince were taken for granted."[38] When the king raised his standard and forced many to take sides, loyalism offered an alternative to the embattled opposition. The anonymous author of *The foure Ages of England: Or, The Iron Age* describes the "loyall Subjects" in his 1648 poem as Englishmen who are wary of religious innovation and weary of military conflict:

> They love the *King* in earnest, and believe,
> His presence doth a perfect essence give
> To *Parliaments;* which though they don't adore,
> They duly honour, and do wish for more,
> Though not for such.[39]

Not all the writers discussed in the following chapters are as moderate in their loyalties, but their reactions to changing political fortune confirm a shift from the less-troubled allegiances of the 1630s to the more complicated commitments of the 1640s and 1650s. More important, they are loyalists in the sense that they never completely sacrifice thought and sensitivity to blind ideology.[40]

Their resolution emerges from the aura of peaceful royalism that embues the 1630s with a distinctive halcyon quality. Charles and his court consciously stressed the bountiful blessings of his pacifist policies, and the first chapter examines the vision of peace that persisted long after the outbreak of war had made it only a memory. Drawing on the work of revisionist historians,[41] this chapter's discussion of the decade before the political crisis emphasizes the interaction between myth and history. When the period is considered without the hindsight of the civil war and without the assumption that the conflict was inevitable, the real benefits of the king's peace cannot be easily dismissed. England had not become embroiled in the Thirty Years' War that ravaged Europe, and she had reason to heed the Whitehall declarations of the gratitude she owed her ruler. The court masques of the 1630s and several central poems by Thomas Carew lend substance to a vision too often deemed extravagant flattery. Carew's long, thoughtful defense of Charles's position and his important contribution to the celebration of the monarchy in particular reveal that the royalist supporters understood the political necessity of developing an alternative to the traditional image of martial heroism. But the "active" and "heroic" virtue they associate with the pacifist king changes as the later pieces confront the threat of disturbance. By the time the last of the court masques is produced, Charles appears a patient, long-suffering ruler who has accepted the wisdom of a decidedly Stoic nobility. At the same time, outside the enclosed world of Whitehall, Thomas Carew retreats from the harsh fact of the First Bishops' War into the "capacious circle" of the country estate Wrest Park. Later writers caught up in the tempestuous events of the years that followed would recall often wistfully the calm England had once enjoyed; many would also turn both away and inward in search of meaning.

The five poets analyzed in the following chapters suggest in their different poetic modes the complexity of this quest. Following the lead of Ben Jonson and the Roman moralists, William Cartwright stresses in his commemorative verse the integrity and fortitude that enable both monarch and commoner to stand unmoved in purposeful courage and bound in a mutual sense of duty and sacrifice. When the king appears to lose the wonder, mystery, and force that the court masques and university panegyrics ascribe to the royal personage, George Daniel turns first to the re-creation Boethius and Lipsius find in meditative leisure and then to the "true and rightfull countrey" of heaven[42] ultimately found in classical and Christian Stoicism. Imprisonment and defeat forced Richard Lovelace to draw away from a threatening reality toward the light and reverie symbolized in Lucasta and made possible in the country estate among the conviviality of friends; but as the sense of loss becomes with time more oppressive, Lovelace confronts his own troubled feelings and paradoxically realizes that the undaunted spirit can achieve triumph in defeat. In spite of a satiric vein and a pragmatic disposition seen in none of the previous writers, Alexander Brome also manages to overcome a skeptical and even cynical detachment with a faith in those who patiently and unselfishly make the business of daily living easier. Abraham Cowley, in turn, ambitiously celebrates a more heroic dimension of nobility in his own growing understanding of the patient fortitude and the providential forces that lead him to the hope of a restored national well-being and the promise of the Stoic life of solitary leisure.

Circularity and inwardness do not similarly define the direction all the contemporary poets follow, but the writers analyzed in this work represent the sensibilities of this period more accurately than the conventional impressions of civil war loyalties. Despite the rueful recognition, "a warlike, various, and a tragical age is best to *write of,* but worst to *write in,*"[43] they uphold the humanist tradition in their attempts to understand these decades of monumental change. Together the loyalist poets suggest if not a microcosm at least a better sense of midcentury poetry, and the extended discussions of their works reveal the directions and accomplishments of not only representative but often diverse poets who are interesting in their own right. Cartwright's prominence at Oxford, Lovelace's importance among the Cavaliers, and Cowley's significance at the centers of royalist activity are obvious in the contemporary tributes as well as in the literary judgments their works have inspired. Though Caroline and later assessments have not accorded Daniel and Brome comparable poetic stature, their extensive writings offer more than valuable cultural documents of similar complex allegiances among the lesser country gentry and the professional urban class. All five poets illuminate at length and in detail the political and artistic struggles of a tragic generation.[44] While none of the writers in the following pages ever rises to the level of Milton or Marvell, each contributes to a greater awareness of the complex loyalties and qualified nobility possible even in the throes of revolution.

# 1
# The Caroline Circle of Peace

I N his meditation on the ill-fated months of 1642, when he had fled London, had been repulsed at Hull, and was faced with a nation armed against him, Charles I plaintively asks, "Are the hazards and miseries of civil war in the bowels of my most flourishing kingdom the fruits I must now reap after seventeen years living and reigning among them with such a measure of justice, peace, plenty, and religion as all nations about either admired or envied?"[1] The king's insistence in *Eikon Basilike* upon this unrivaled national well-being might be dismissed as still another instance of the "evasion of political realities" and the "mood of make-believe" that literary, historical, and art scholars commonly find "characteristic of Caroline culture" and its "legend of the calm and happy 1630's."[2] But Charles's understanding of his reign is not simply the delusion of a monarch who had isolated himself and his court. Despite the special pleading of *Eikon Basilike,* the king's perception of the Caroline decades cannot easily be separated from the reality. Contemporary histories of the years before the war commonly lend support to Charles's vision of this peace, and modern research has given new credibility to their accounts of an unprecedented Caroline prosperity. The reactions to the civil war explored in the following chapters often reflect the uncertain blend of fact and fiction surrounding Charles's monarchy. Their sense of the peace once possessed and then lost shares, however, more than the king's nostalgic esteem for the past decades.

The changing fortunes of Charles's reign forced these loyalist poets to redefine the limits of an exalted Caroline peace. The historical and political realities of the 1630s, this chapter suggests, had encouraged the king and his supporters to celebrate the halcyon calm England alone enjoyed among the European countries ravaged by the Thirty Years' War. Charles and his supporters understood how easily the present peace could be disturbed, and they deliberately emphasized the heroic virtue that sustained the nation's unrivaled tranquillity. Historical fact blurred in the mythic interpretations promulgated at length in the Caroline masques, as the nation was reminded of the prosperity that radiated outward from the Whitehall world. But as the remote destruction of the European religious war threatened to become the immediate chaos of an English civil war, the realm of peaceful fulfillment celebrated in the 1630s and remembered by the later writers was transformed into an inner, Stoic peace of the soul. The transformation appears in the movement inward this chapter traces: the circle that delimits the secure realm narrows to the court world and then becomes coextensive with a country-house refuge. In the process the peace found not in Europe but in England comes to exist ultimately not in the nation but in the mind and heart. Charles realized this truth first in the later masques and then in *Eikon Basilike;* it is a reality each of the loyalist poets in this study confronts. Central to their experience is a pervasive sense of loss.

To be sure, critical contemporary accounts of the so-called personal rule between 1629 and 1640 insist upon the "Principles of *Misery,* and seeds of *Diseases* in the *Body politique*" and detect a "horrid tempest" underneath the "calme and smooth surface,"[3] but their unsympathetic voices do not dispel a more common emphasis upon the enviable tranquillity England had enjoyed. Foremost among the histories written in the aftermath of the civil tragedy are the remarkably similar characterizations offered by Edward Hyde, earl of Clarendon, and Sir Philip Warwick. Both in *The Life of Edward Earl of Clarendon* and in the *History of the Rebellion,* Clarendon insists that "*England* enjoyed the greatest Measure of Felicity, that it had ever known" and "the greatest calm and the fullest measure of felicity that any people in any age for so long time together have been blessed with."[4] In the *Memoires Of the reigne of King Charles I,* Warwick independently contends, "from the year 1628, unto the year 1638, I believe England was never Master of a profounder peace, nor enjoy'd more wealth, or had the power and form of godlines more visibly in it."[5] The justice, wisdom, wealth, and godliness they see in abundance are also found to varying degrees in the less well-known histories. While not all share the unreserved praise in William Sanderson's *A Compleat History of the Life and Raigne of King Charles* (1658), the diverse accounts in David Lloyd's *Memoires* (1668), John Davies's *The Civil Warres of Great Britain and Ireland* (1661), and Hamon L'Estrange's *The Reign of King Charles* (1656) all give considerable credence to the notion of a nation flourishing in "an Universal peace on every side."[6] Surprisingly, their laudatory views have not been entirely rejected in current reevaluations of a decade "extraordinarily difficult to assess."[7]

Revisionist interpretations of Charles and his policies have begun to suggest that he is a far more complicated monarch than the ruler portrayed by Whig historians and that the years between the 1629 Parliament and the Short Parliament are less troubled than the fashionable tag "eleven years tyranny" suggests.[8] The biases of royalists or Whigs notwithstanding, modern scholars are also beginning to accept the Venetian ambassador's view of the economic advantages England enjoyed during this time.[9] Analysis of Charles's eleven-year rule between parliaments is still incomplete, and even the most basic questions about the economy are difficult to resolve, but study of his early reign suggests he was not in conflict with a disaffected nation. Rising inflation and a growing population had stabilized; the always troublesome revenue seemed in better control; and the administration of laws ensured a less restive nation.[10] Contrary to present popular impression, the king was not unalterably opposed to the institution of Parliament, nor was the country completely unwilling to go along with his ship-money levies; in reality a monarch faced with a number of difficult problems did not shirk them: "In peacetime, his regime was perhaps stronger than has been thought."[11] When Charles and his contemporary historians, therefore, extol a halcyon time, they may not have hopelessly confused myth or legend with history. Their insistence, however, upon an unbounded prosperity reflects in its extremeness a reaction to the immediate experience of civil war.

*Eikon Basilike* clearly conveys the same dismay Charles's contemporary historians express in response to their own loss. While much of Europe had been consuming itself in the devastating Thirty Years' War, an England "enviously set off" from the continent as "the garden of the world" and "the happiest People under Heaven" appears in their accounts blind to her own good fortune.[12] Lloyd's recognition that "we were not sensible either of our Happiness or of the use of it" and Warwick's concession that "if men would but have reflected . . . or compared themselves with their neighbours" affirm the irony Clarendon underscores: "But all these blessings could but enable, not compel, us to be happy: we wanted that sense, acknowledgment, and value of our own happiness which all but we had, and took pains to make, when we could not find, ourselves miserable."[13] Central to these reactions seems to be the Virgilian lament that climaxes Clarendon's autobiographical description of the peaceful years preceding the war, *"O fortunatos nimium, sua si bona norint!"*[14] John Davies's parenthetical allusion "(had they known and been sensible of it)" pointedly stresses in his adaptation of the lines from the *Georgics* the bitter truth "Oh happy, (if his Happiness he knows)."[15] War had taught Charles and the others, it would seem, to value a world "Free from th' Alarms of Fear, and the storms of Strife,"[16] a knowledge poignantly shared by the loyalist writers in this study who confront the political revolution and its aftermath. And yet, paradoxically, their bitter realization is not at all surprising, for many in the 1630s already understood the timelessness of Virgil's lines. However much the civil war led to an exaggerated impression of England's lost happiness, the sense of her unique peace had been well established before the outbreak of armed conflict. Charles and his contemporary historians, in fact, recount an inseparable blend of myth and history fashioned in the context of international and not civil war. Political necessity as well as historical reality shaped this view.

The Caroline emphasis on peace reflects the Stuart legacy of neutrality in the Thirty Years' War. Along with his father's famous label "The Peace-Maker," Charles had inherited from the self-styled *Rex Pacificus* a reluctance to support the militant Protestant view of the continental religious struggles. James had little religious sympathy for this vision of apocalyptic confrontation with a papal Antichrist, and he refused to accept the idea of a Europe polarized simply along Catholic and Protestant lines. Attracted toward an alliance with the Hapsburgs, the king pursued through marriage negotiations and diplomatic avenues the "Peace of all Christendom."[17] The marriage he arranged between his daughter Elizabeth and the Elector Palatinate threatened to upset his efforts, however, when his son-in-law Frederick claimed the crown of Bohemia and embroiled Europe in the Thirty Years' War. While many of James's Protestant subjects welcomed the conflict as part of a providential plan to destroy the Antichrist, the king held to the belief that he could mediate a settlement. Before James's death in 1625, Frederick's failures on the battlefield, Charles's abortive marriage alliance with Spain, and Buckingham's blundering involvement with France offered little support for the funeral eulogies of *Great Britains Salomon* and *The Peace-Maker: Or, Great Brittaines Blessing*. The peacemaker's son Charles was left to flounder with the consequences of Buckingham's disastrous wars with Spain as well as with France, and in the first years of his reign, he confronted in recalcitrant parliamentarians the continued Protestant desire for involvement on the continent. But by the end of the decade and the last of the parliaments, the young king became, in the words of the Venetian ambassador, a ruler who is "pacific, but by necessity."[18] Charles had learned from his struggles with the parliaments he was compelled to call that their apparent sentiments for the Protestant cause did not always have the necessary will or means to pursue a successful military venture. At this time Charles wrote his sister Elizabeth, "one of my chiefest ambitions is to do you real service"; and on another occasion he also pledged "The entire restitution of his brother and nephew to their dignities and patrimony"; but the restoration of the Palatinate remained only a hope. With neither adequate funding nor political support, the king had to make a virtue of necessity; he had learned the wisdom of his father's efforts to avoid military entanglements.[19]

The negotiations he concluded with the Spanish in November 1630 established the peaceful tenor of his personal rule. Formally, the treaty between Charles I and Philip IV committed Spain to support Frederick's Palatinate claim and drew England closer to the Hapsburg alliance James had desired;[20] informally, the diplomacy also asserted the paramount importance of peace. During the course of the negotiations in England on Spain's behalf, the emissary Peter Paul Rubens observed, "This Island . . . seems to me to be a spectacle worthy of the interest of every gentleman, not only for the beauty of the countryside and the charm of the nation; not only for the splendor of the outward culture, which seems to be extreme, as of a people rich and happy in the lap of peace."[21] The observation is not merely the tact of a diplomat eager to acknowledge the Stuart motto *Beati Pacifici* or to promote a successful end to the military conflict. Rubens had lived through the devastation of the European war, and like the speaker in Virgil's *Georgics,* he could see the happiness not all English could appreciate. Later he would complete for the Banqueting House the magnificent canvases that epitomize the Caroline vision of peaceful bounty, but when he left London in March 1630, Rubens presented Charles with a smaller expression of the same theme. In his painting *War and Peace,* a nursing mother and several children under the protection of Minerva draw the viewer's attention away from Mars and toward maternal bliss. The triumph of wisdom, love, and peace expresses the life-affirming hope that Charles and his supporters nurtured during the personal rule.[22]

In the years between parliaments, the king developed a distinctive image of the peaceful monarchy. Unlike his father Charles was, as many have noted, "formal and reserved"; his court was also more "refined and wholesome" than the often-scandalous Jacobean milieu. Others have suggested the roles his visit to Spain and his exposure to the European culture played in shaping his preoccupation with grandeur, splendor, and gravity. The Orders for Conduct at Court, the restoration at Windsor of the rituals of the Garter and St. George, and a reemphasis on knighthood further attest to the king's desire for deference, order, and ceremony.[23] Less commonly emphasized are the domestic and administrative reforms Charles pursued in lieu of a vigorous foreign policy. The Book of Orders, which he promulgated in 1630 and 1631 as the "cornerstone of his regime's paternalism," reveals Charles's concern for the welfare of the poor and for the efficiency of local government.[24] Laws requiring the gentry to remain on their estates and new powers assumed by the Privy Council are also part of the administrative reformation easily overlooked in the attention historians commonly give to his ecclesiastical policies on behalf of uniformity. Despite a system of revenue badly outmoded by years of inflation, Charles also addressed the financial issues that constrained his government, and he appears to have been quite successful. On the whole, England was in fact "probably as 'well-governed' as any country in Europe";[25] and it owed its good fortune, the king and his supporters insisted, to the wise, benevolent, and peaceful policies of his personal rule.

Within a year of the last parliament, Ben Jonson's complementary masques *Love's Triumph through Callipolis* and *Chloridia* established the official view that dominated the Banqueting House in the 1630s. The only masques Jonson wrote for Charles and Henrietta Maria depart from his and the other Jacobean productions in their celebration of an extraordinary royal love.[26] The queen appears in the masque the king presented to her on 9 January 1631 as the wondrous source of beauty and the "Pure object" of "heroic love and regal respect."[27] A month later in the masque composed for her husband "The beauties of the spring, / Founts, rivers, everything" sing "The honours of his Chloris to the King" (2:422). Both performances praise in the triumph of love the power of the king and queen to displace the rebellious factions that threaten harmony and goodness. Thus in the first masque the "certain sectaries, or depraved lovers" who break away from the torturous "wheel of love" to dance an antimasque in the guise of "the four prime European nations" are displaced by the "true sphere of Love" created through the "right affection of the mind" and the "circle of the will" that inform the mutual love reflected in the monarchs. Jonson avoids any direct commentary on the world outside the masquing hall, but the political implications of the chaotic antimasquers in *Love's Triumph* and the rebellious Cupid in *Chloridia* are evident. The circles the masques laud and the "space" they form are part of "public spectacles" meant "To Make the Spectators Understanders" (1:405) of the bountiful peace they alone enjoy. Overshadowing the fashionable trappings of Neoplatonism and the rituals of mutual compliment is a remarkable sense of marital fulfillment and fecundity. At the ends of both masques, when the spectacle traditionally involves the court spectators in a communal celebration of its ideals, the goddess of marriage dominates. Juno's presence along with that of Hymen and Venus, in fact, transforms *Love's Triumph* into a "holy nuptial" ending with the disappearance of the throne and the sudden appearance of a palm tree rooted in roses and lilies and topped with an imperial crown:

> Beauty and Love, whose story is mysterial,
> In yonder palm tree and the crown imperial,
> Do from the rose and lily so delicious
> Promise a shade shall ever be propitious
> To both the kingdoms. But to Britain's genius
> The snaky rod and serpents of Cyllenius
> Bring not more peace than these, who so united be
> By Love, as with it earth and heaven delighted be.
>
> (1:407)

Charles and Henrietta Maria "historify" the emblem of peace. Through the bounty of Juno and actions "virtuous, great and good," their world surpasses Rubens's vision of peace; it indeed becomes in *Chloridia* a heaven on earth.

The "mirrors of man's life" Jonson creates in the masques visualize a love and peace seen not only "by the mind's eye." Though the Caroline masques have often been criticized as extravagant attempts to withdraw into a narrowly circumscribed world,[28] these court productions are no more blindly self-congratulatory than earlier royal representations. In celebrating the monarch's fruitful and happy marriage, Jonson stresses a reality no other British ruler in the last one hundred years could claim. Once Charles and Henrietta Maria overcame their initial difficulties, a marriage of political convenience gradually grew into a devotion that far surpassed the estranged relationship of James and Anne. With the birth of Prince Charles in May 1630, the English could further celebrate for the first time since the early Tudors a royal offspring with unquestioned right to the throne. The new prince also frustrated the militant Protestant hopes that the crown might revert to the children of Charles's sister, Elizabeth;[29] and each of his six brothers and sisters lengthened the dynastic line that ensured a stability England had not always enjoyed. The outpouring of poems occasioned by these nativities lapses into perfunctory and even obligatory performances, but the sheer number is a tribute to the country's wishes for the well-being of both the royal family and the nation. Even though the reserved, decorous king and the foreign, Catholic queen remained at times remote from their subjects, their marriage may have been as meaningful for the 1630s as Elizabeth's virginity had been in the 1580s. In the tempestuous Europe of the Thirty Years' War, England's peaceful island and its rulers' bountiful love seemed one.

Those who see "with the eyes of understanding," the next masque to be presented at court insists, will appreciate the blessings of the king's peace policy. The king's arms and an imperial crown now first catch the eyes of the audience invited in *Albion's Triumph* to "see" and "feel" a triumph "heroic" as the monarch's mind, "Just as his actions, glorious as his reign, / And like his virtues, infinite in train" (2:454). Aurelian Townshend's re-creation of the Roman ceremony celebrating the reestablishment of peace envisions the monarch as "brave Albanactus Caesar," an imposing leader cast in the tradition of a Roman emperor who commands his own passions as well as his enemies. The king's greater triumph, however, comes after he is "subdued" by the chaste love of the goddess Alba. When Charles assumes his place next to the queen and the scene changes in this Twelfth Night masque of 1632 to a prospect of his Whitehall palace and London city, Caroline triumph surmounts that of Rome. Innocency, Justice, Religion, Affection to the Country, and Concord underline the reality: through the royal love they are the means to Peace, an "Imperious" figure crowned with olive and bearing the traditional palm. Her victorious reception by the five companions stresses the pacifist philosophy Charles embraces:

> 'Tis not the laurel tree that brings
> Annointing oil for sacred kings;
> Those princes see the happiest days
> Whose olive branches stand for bays.
>
> (2:457)

Nevertheless the triumphant return of peace has an insistent, almost defensive quality that reveals some Caroline unease. The richly attired and symbolically suggestive Peace descends on a cloud, "proclaiming her large benefits and the world's ingratitude"; she is greeted by the gods Neptune, Plutus, Bellona, and Cybele, "complaining of ease and plenty" and asking in their song "Why should this isle above the rest / Be made (great gods) the halcyon's nest" (2:457)? The answer to their question is of course apparent to all: Peace need only command Neptune and Bellona to guard the nation while Cybele and Plutus increase its bounty. Through the spectacle of Inigo Jones and the poetry of Aurelian Townshend, celestial and Roman worlds come together in an expression of love and virtue that allays any misgivings about a supine royal pacifism and redefines imperial triumph.

The celebration of heroic nobility appears as much a conscious response to the imperialism of the Thirty Years' War as it does an assertion of Caroline autocracy.[30] *Albion's Triumph* and the two earlier Jonson masques may indeed offer the royal alternative to the martial heroism so apparent in Gustavus Adolphus, the brilliant Swedish general whose mounting successes on the battlefield challenged Charles's peace policies. For many followers of his victories, Gustavus was "one of the Iewels of the *Protestant* Princes," whose "matchlesse and imparalell Heroike Acts and Expeditions" seized contemporary imaginations. Hailed the "*Lyon* of the North" and the "Northern star," the Swedish king appears to writers of the early 1630s as the "Divine future operation" foretold in the new star discovered in 1572.[31] Successive triumphs detailed at great length in the weekly accounts of Butter, Bourne, and the other writers of corantos rekindled the militant desire to destroy the triple crown of popedom; and eulogists of the warrior-king's piety, magnanimity, courage, and valor proclaimed Gustavus the new Joshua, Josiah, or Moses, who would lead the Protestant nations to their promised destiny.[32] Charles needed little reminder of these heroic exploits, for he had tried unsuccessfully to win Gustavus's support for Frederick's thwarted right to the Palatinate.[33] When the general's victories made his own neutrality seem unattractive to some of his subjects, the king through the Star Chamber even imposed a censorship on all news of the continental war.[34] He undoubtedly also used the talents of Inigo Jones and his collaborators to justify through the 1631 and 1632 masques the royal policy of nonintervention in the Thirty Years' War.

The death of Gustavus Adolphus at the battle of Lutzen in November 1632 prompted another supporter of Charles I to enlist his poetical talents on the king's behalf. Thomas Carew responded to the disbelief and grief that swept England at the news that "the Lords Annointed, whose right hand the Lord hath holden to subdue nations before him," was dead.[35] At court Charles and Henrietta Maria were reported to have changed into clothes of mourning; and throughout the nation, Simonds D'Ewes recorded in his diary, "Never did one person's death in Christendom bring so much sorrow to all true Protestant hearts."[36] Among the unusually large number of poetic tributes to the fallen warrior, a poem addressed to "Tom Carew" by the author of *Albion's Triumph* pressed the need to elegize the Protestant hero. Carew's response "In answer of an Elegiacall Letter upon the death of the

King of *Sweden* from *Aurelian Townsend,* inviting me to write on that subject"
has until recently struck most readers as a reflection of "cultural self-consciousness" masking, perhaps, a "sense of false security" or as the "ignoble
passivity" of "silken dalliance."[37] Carew's refusal to disturb "Our *Halcyon*
dayes" and to heed the alarms of the continental war should not, however, be
faulted outright as another instance of the "pusillanimous hedonism" typical
of a "narrow snobbery and an effete indulgence."[38] Like Francis Quarles,
who has none of his links with the court, Carew realizes in the history of
Gustavus the value of England's peace. He shares Quarles's Virgilian recognition,

> what happiness have wee,
> The last, and dregs of Ages, thus to see
> These hopefull Times; nay more, to sit beneath,
> Beneath our quiet Vines, and think of death
> By leisure, when Spring-tides of blood o'rewhelms
> The interrupted peace of forain Relms![39]

He also shares Quarles's awareness that England was fortunate to have "A
Prince, that (briefly to characterize him) / Wants nothing, but a People, how
to prize him."[40] In the context of the 1630s, Carew's poem appears a
thoughtful and seminal defense of the king's policy and the court celebration.

Both issues are tactfully yet insistently raised in Townshend's suggestion
that Carew put aside his lyric devotion to Celia and compose a suitable
memorial for "the dead conquering king."[41] Townshend's request contains
neither the abrasiveness nor the stridency of John Saltmarsh and of John
Russell when on the same occasion they deride "those soft *Poets,* who have
dipt their brains / In am'rous humours" and they challenge those "gen'rous
spirits, in whose manly breasts / An ardent love of *Fame* and *Honour* rests."[42]
Townshend also avoids the chiding present in Dudley North's similar rebuke:

> Is brave *Gustavus* of too solid stuffe,
> His great exploits, for your sleight vein too tuffe?
> That like poor falsifyers you despair,
> To profit from a piece so rich and fair:
> Whil'st from more trivial subjects you will drive
> A trade, shall make your reputation thrive.[43]

Townshend appeals, instead, to "a speritt that full mans it all," and he alludes
to Carew's elegy on Donne, encouraging his friend to produce still another
poetic triumph and offering a long, somewhat forced version of the tribute
Carew might render Gustavus Adolphus. But even though the request does
not overtly raise the issues of poetic seriousness pressed in poems such as
Dudley North's "Incentive to our Poets," it implies that the heroic elegy is
more substantial inspiration for the muse than is the lyric.

With characteristic lightness and grace, Carew disarms this tacit criticism of his poetic subjects and defends the Caroline commitment to love rather than to war. Structurally and thematically the queen displaces Gustavus Adolphus.[44] She becomes, as Carew addresses her in another poem, the

> great Commandresse, that doest move
> Thy Scepter o're the Crowne of Love,
> And through his Empire with the Awe
> Of Thy chaste beames, doest give the Law.

(p. 90)

As in the masques in which she figures so prominently, the transformation depends largely upon perspective. The first forty-four lines of the answer draw the martial heroism of Gustavus into realistic focus, and the next forty-four oppose this reality with the ideals embodied in Henrietta Maria. Rhetorically, the poem's dialectical thesis and antithesis, like the antimasque and masque, move toward acceptance of the peaceful prosperity envisioned in the previous Caroline masques. Once again Carew implicitly extends their invitation to see with the masques' "eyes of understanding" the "peace and plenty, which the blessed hand / Of our good King gives this obdurate Land" (ll. 47–48, p. 75).

Acknowledging the achievements celebrated in other elegies and adopting much of their tribute, the poem's initial movement subverts its conventional disavowal of all attempts to praise Gustavus Adolphus. The mock modesty in the opening lines' concern about profaning the dead king with "humble" and "low verse" is admittedly less evident in Carew's contention that no poet

> Could a just Poem to this subject fit,
> His actions were too mighty to be rais'd
> Higher by Verse, let him in prose be prays'd,
> In modest faithfull story, which his deedes
> Shall turne to Poems.

(ll. 14–18)

In other poems Carew remains somewhat skeptical about the power of poetry, but the reservations he may have about the poet's ability to capture truth do not necessarily imply doubt about Gustavus Adolphus. Outwardly refusing to grieve for Gustavus Adolphus, Carew actually expresses qualified praise when he entrusts the "grave Chronicler" with Gustavus's "too-briefe storie" and asserts

> his Journals may
> Stand by the *Cæsars* yeares, and every day
> Cut into minutes, each, shall more containe
> Of great designement then an Emperours raigne.

(ll. 27–30)

Contemporary news reports, sermons, and elegies devoted to the Swedish king seldom miss the opportunity to discuss the anagram Gustavus/Augustus, and they often proclaim at great length how Adolphus in less time, against stronger enemies, and with higher ideals surpassed even the greatest of ancient military rulers. They concur, moreover, with Carew that "Hee / Gain'd after death a posthume Victorie" both in mortal and in heavenly reward.[45]

Differences arise only when Carew places Gustavus at greater distance. In the first of a series of imperatives designed to alter the focus, the poem proposes an alternative to Townshend's elaborate memorial:

> And (since 'twas but his Church-yard) let him have
> For his owne ashes now no narrower Grave
> Then the whole *German* Continents vast wombe,
> Whilst all her Cities doe but make his Tombe.
>
> (ll. 31–34)

Carew buries the monarch with wit, decorum, and grim humor. Gustavus's greatness was, after all, achieved through terrible devastation, and Carew refuses to obscure this reality. His recognition that the vitality of Gustavus and the fecundity of Germany are now ashes implies a futility underscored in Carew's view of "supreame providence." While other elegies on the death of Gustavus Adolphus routinely attribute his destiny to the inscrutable designs of providence, the fate of Gustavus and the course of the Thirty Years' War illustrate for Carew the folly in believing that a single man or faction can triumph. Certain that "Divine wisedome would not leave the Land / Subject to any one Kings sole command" (ll. 41–42), Carew finds the choice between warring sides immaterial. The momentum of the passage's logic and syntax gives forcefulness to the final imperatives:

> Then let the Germans fear if *Cæsar* shall,
> Or the Vnited Princes, rise, and fall,
> But let us that in myrtle bowers sit
> Vnder secure shades, use the benefit
> Of peace and plenty.
>
> (ll. 43–47)

Carew recognizes limitations in Gustavus's greatness that none of the other poems admits, and he refuses to obscure "the benefit / Of peace and plenty" in a glorification of military grandeur. Indeed, his assessment of the ill-fated attempt to wage religious war seems to anticipate the modern judgment that Gustavus's death marks the end of an era in which religion could unify large areas of the continent.[46] The suggestion of the overreacher tacit in Carew's criticism of the doomed attempt to defy "Divine wisedome" and to establish "sole command" may also reflect the moderate criticism of Gustavus found outside the many published tributes. In a letter written to Henry Vane hinting at the Swedish monarch's arrogance and ambition, the courtier Toby Matthew voices an attitude current beyond the court as well. Diaries and letters of the period record that Gustavus "was tax'd to be over-ventrous and headstrong" and that he had become "puffed up too much with his own victories."[47] Carew's own reservations about Gustavus's purpose and the poem's refusal to romanticize the realities of his victories, in any case, value peace far more than any military venture. Fundamental to the poem is the hope expressed a year earlier in "A New-yeares gift. To the King,"

> Circle with peacefull Olive bowes,
> And conquering Bayes, his Regall browes.
> Let his strong vertues overcome,
> And bring him bloodlesse Trophies home:
> Strew all the pavements, where he treads
> With loyall hearts, or Rebels heads;
> But *Byfront*, open thou no more,
> In his blest raigne the Temple dore.

(p. 90)

The desire for the "great continued festivall" possible in Charles's reign if the doors of war remain shut is not a conventional and isolated New Year's wish. The insularity Carew advocates surely reflects the bitter experience of England's recent military fiascoes, and he will not obscure this lesson in a conflict that at a distance appears attractive. An England at peace, quite simply, promises much more than an England at war, and Carew proposes to celebrate this potential in the revels considered in the poem's second movement.

When he urges his friend to forget "Fames trumpet" and to pick up his "past'rall pipe," encouraging Townshend to capture in "sweetly-flowing numbers" the beauty of *The Shepheards Paradise,* Carew defends the masque as a serious art form especially suited to the Caroline world and the cause of peace. Controversy about the extent to which Carew bases his comments upon Townshend's *Tempe Restored* or upon the poet's masque version of Walter Montague's *The Shepheards Paradise* need not obscure the qualities the poem admires.[48] Unwilling to concede Francis Bacon's criticism "These things are but toys," Carew argues that the masque illuminates a "misterious fable" through "rich fancie, and cleare Action." Again, as in his poems on John Donne and William Davenant, he acknowledges the power of poetic fancy, and he emphasizes the poet's obligation to seize the "soule, and sense" with "Knowledge and pleasure." He agrees in principle with Bacon's essay "Of Masques and Triumphs" that "those things which I here set down are such as do naturally take the sense, and not respect petty wonderments";[49]

but in practice Carew believes the "strong and manly" elegance Bacon desires demands the same poetic skill displayed in the best contemporary poetry.

Throughout the poem's flattering account of Townshend's earlier courtly entertainment, Carew stresses the wondrous meaning and not the elaborate mechanics of the spectacle. Fancy, action, sense, and style "dispence / Knowledge and pleasure, to the soule, and sense" (ll. 75–76). The power of the masque to seize the aesthetic and even spiritual wonder of its audience lies most obviously behind the final tribute Carew pays to Townshend's creativity:

> But when the Queene of Beautie did inspire
> The ayre with perfumes, and our hearts with fire,
> Breathing from her celestiall Organ sweet
> Harmonious notes, our soules fell at her feet,
> And did with humble reverend dutie, more
> Her rare perfections, then high state adore.
>
> (ll.83–88)

A manifestation of her power to liberate human potential from its Circean bonds of lust, the Queen of Beauty also embodies the transcendent position both Townshend and Carew accord Henrietta Maria: she is in the mythology of the 1630s a guarantor if not a creator of "Our *Halcyon* dayes." Carew need not recall the royal relationship figured in the union of Divine Beauty and Heroic Virtue; to anyone familiar with the masques, the queen's triumph is the inspiration for "our good King." Through their love and virtue, the poem implies, theirs is the greater conquest, for they create the harmonious fulfillment that eludes even the greatest of war's disciples.

In overbalancing the lines on Gustavus with those on the revels of Caroline peace, the poem does not escape into an impossible idealization. Charles and his court, it is true, had continued James's trend away from the pageantry and spectacle staged in the years of Elizabethan glory; and the Stuarts were less committed than their predecessor to promoting the royal presence in popular culture.[50] But the suggestion that the Whitehall world of art fails somehow to command the assent elicited by its Elizabethan counterpart merits reconsideration.[51] Recent studies of the occasions and intentions of the masque lend credibility to Carew's description of its affective power, and revisionist historians offer valuable correctives to the common literary tendency to dismiss as superficial or artificial the period and its literature. While England may not have been "the Garden of the world" or Charles "the most indulgent to his Subjects, and most solicitous for their Happiness and Prosperity,"[52] Carew still had reason to celebrate the peaceful rule "our good King gives this obdurate Land." Thus the inspiration of Townshend's previous poetry is, he can conclude, "proper to our clyme":

> Tourneyes, Masques, Theaters, better become
> Our *Halcyon* dayes; what though the German Drum
> Bellow for freedome and revenge, the noyse
> Concernes not us, nor should divert our joyes;
> Nor ought the thunder of their Carabins
> Drowne the sweet Ayres of our tun'd Violins.
>
> (ll. 95–100)

Underlying his insistence on the value of their "harmelesse pastimes" are both the refusal to glorify a war that had destroyed much of Europe and a reaffirmation of the contented life:

> Beleeve me friend, if their prevailing powers
> Gaine them a calme securitie like ours,
> They'le hang their Armes up on the Olive bough,
> And dance, and revell then, as we doe now.
>
> (ll. 101–04)

The casualness and even disdain with which Carew turns a deaf ear to military glory are meant to be provocative. Certain that the "Rowte" and "vulgar trade" of this "sullen Age" cannot appreciate anything beyond the superficial, he often encourages his friends to draw together and ignore misguided criticism. This appeal to the "wiser world," so memorably apparent in his poem to Ben Jonson, explains his scorn for the "Bellow for freedome" and his smugness about "calme securitie." Rhetorically the provocative conclusion also challenges Townshend and any other reader not to ignore the choice others would surely take if given the chance. Behind the encouragement to enjoy "Our *Halcyon* dayes" may well be the Horatian "air of confident and well-contented modernity"[53] seen in the Roman odes' celebration of *pax Augusta*. The Virgilian eclogues' criticism of war may give further weight to Carew's voice,[54] and the wisdom of the *Georgics* must also be heeded. One of the few Englishmen of the 1630s who did not lack the "sense, acknowledgment, and value of our own happiness," Thomas Carew attempts to illuminate these values for others in his answer to Townshend.

The scope of Carew's understanding and artistry is further apparent in his own contribution to "harmelesse pastimes," *Coelum Britannicum*. The longest and greatest Caroline masque, this Shrove Tuesday production of 1634 confirms the high seriousness of the form Carew praises. Its glorification of unbounded peacefulness and prosperity depends again upon the talents of Inigo Jones, but the poet assumes a supremacy unmatched in other court productions. The verve and imagery of the masque's long descriptive passages, its witty dialogue and ingenious arguments, and the cynical as well as idealistic dimensions of its tone characterize the best Caroline poetry. For the performance at Whitehall, Carew develops an Italian work of Giordano Bruno into an impressive vision of British grandeur. Surpassing the celebration of royal love, law, and justice staged two weeks earlier in the Inns of Court's spectacular production of James Shirley's *The Triumph of Peace*, he allies the ideals of Jonson and Jones in a celebration of the monarchy and its policy of peace that does, indeed, "dispence / Knowledge and pleasure, to the soule, and sense."

Its success depends, paradoxically, upon a self-conscious realism that tempers the masque's celebration.[55] In triumphant hyperbole Carew redefines the position of those "Bright glorious Twins of Love and Majesty," Henrietta Maria and Charles. Reversing the traditional movement toward apotheosis, the opening image of the king and queen anticipates the final vision: they are the end to which everything celestial and temporal aspires. The flattering description of the first one hundred lines is not, however, unqualified. With the entrance of Momus, Carew introduces a satiric voice. Momus immediately acknowledges the artificiality of the occasion, and his long lament about the new reforms in heaven parodies both specific Caroline reforms and the masque's basic conceit. The urbane manner with which Carew mocks his own hyperbole in slightly ludicrous accounts of the gods' attempts to become Charles and Henrietta Maria appears even more obvious in his ridicule of the notion that mortals will displace the gods. Again Momus breaks the illusion of the masque and asks his audience, "Doe not you faire Ladies acknowledge your selves deeply engaged now to those Poets your servants, that in the height of commendation have rais'd your beauties to a parallell with such exact proportions, or at least rank'd you in their spruce society" (11. 308–13, p. 161)? And later he promises any "Lady not competently stock'd" with virtue "shall not on the instant utterly despaire, if shee carry a sufficient pawne of handsomenesse; for however the letter of the Law runnes, *Jupiter* notwithstanding his Age and present austerity, will never refuse to stampe beauty, and make it currant with his owne Impression" (ll. 318–24). Carew, quite obviously, has no illusions about the poetic game played for the entertainment of the court, yet despite this sophistication, or perhaps because of it, he succeeds in adding dimension to the masque's conventions.

The idealization of the peaceful Caroline era, in fact, derives much of its impact from the masque's triumph over a pervasive sense of realism. Momus brings to the world of masquing lords and ladies political comment and topical satire, but the major threat to the vision of a celestial Britain remains the contenders for the places vacated when the constellations are purged of their former occupants. The rival claims of Riches, Poverty, Fortune, and Pleasure advanced in the middle section of the masque tax the wit and logic of both Momus and Mercury with a seriousness unusual in traditional antimasque figures. Although Mercury assures his audience that their "forc'd reasons, and strain'd arguments, / Vrge vaine pretences," the four figures press their arguments for domination and will not be dismissed out of hand with Mercury's rejoinder, "but we advance / Such vertues onely as admit excesse" (ll. 659–60). These ideals of magnificence, prudence, magnanimity, and "Heroicke vertue" become the proper focus of the masque only when Riches, Poverty, Fortune, and Pleasure are shown to possess none of the substance the masque demands.

Once they are driven from the stage, the poetry and spectacle of *Coelum Britannicum* manifest true worthiness in the magnificent metamorphosis of the masque's conclusion. In contrast to the vociferous arguments of the four contenders, the king has no need to break his silence; his "Actions" have already established "that secure fix'd state . . . to which the labouring world, / Wading through streams of blood, sweats to aspire" (ll. 853–55). Charles, as the embodiment of England's greatness, is the center of a vision of past, present, and future glory whose changing songs and scenes involve all the senses in celebration. In the wonder of the final movement, self-consciousness about the artificiality of the occasion disappears and everyday reality is forgotten. Through the magic of Jones's mechanical illusions and the power of Carew's poetical ones, the masque gives immediacy to its emblem of England's Genius, "a young man in a white embroidered robe, upon his faire haire an Olive garland with wings at his shoulders, and holding in his hand a Cornucopia fill'd with corne and fruits" (ll. 893–95).

The kingdoms, druids, and rivers called forth by this Genius of England and the group of ancient heroes who emerge from the rock upon which the three kingdoms sit help confirm an alternative to the destructiveness of war. Visually and poetically Charles and his wife are the focus of the audience and design; gone is the masque's opening scene of ancient Roman or British ruins: "In the firmament about him, was a troope of fifteene starres, expressing the stellifying of our British Heroes; but one more great and eminent than the rest, which was over his head, figured his Majesty. And in the lower part was seene a farre off the prospect of *Windsor* Castell, the famous seat of the most honourable Order of the Garter" (ll. 1080–86). Surrounded by his subjects on the masquing floor of Whitehall and the six allegorical representations of his reign, Charles literally and figuratively embodies England's civilizing forces. Emblematically, the troop of stars and the prospect of Windsor Castle insist upon the heroic magnitude of his efforts to realize a harmonious, prosperous government where "Religion, Truth, and Wisdome" can flourish. The greatest of the stars, greater even than Arthur or St. George, he is visually placed in a tradition of heroism symbolized in the Order of the Garter and its commitment to the greatest religious and national ideals of England. The chivalric king of Rubens's *Landscape with St. George and the Dragon* and of Van Dyck's *Charles I on Horseback* becomes in Carew's conception the heroic defender of Caroline civilization.

This vision is surpassed only in the magnificent ceiling paintings that displaced the masques in the Banqueting House. Completed and sent to England by the autumn of 1635, the nine Rubens canvases capture the essential world of the masques, which would now no longer be performed beneath the Banqueting House ceiling "lest this might suffer by the smoke of many lights."[56] The focus of the ceiling, the oval center panel depicting the apotheosis of James I, epitomizes the canvases' triumphant celebration of the first Stuart's reign. The rectangular paintings on either side commemorating the union of Scotland and England and the rejection of Mars visualize along the center of the ceiling the victories of "Our Solomon," a ruler who had made a united England "*Beth-salem,* the house of Peace."[57] In transforming the Banqueting Hall into another house of peace, however, Rubens also defines the essence of Charles's reign, for the paintings are ultimately a statement of the king who commissioned them.[58] Their emphasis on Minerva and Mercury is still another expression of the wisdom and understanding the Caroline writers value in the son who had also refused the crown Mars offers and gained the laurel of peace and plenty. The heroic and active virtue particularly lauded in the masques finds further expression in the four oval corner paintings, tentatively identified as the victories of Hercules and Minerva over rebellious Envy and Ignorance and as the triumphs of Liberality and either Temperance or Reason over Avarice and Immoderation. Flanking the center of the ceiling, two panels proclaim in a decidedly less awesome tone the bounty of a pacific reign. The fruit-laden chariots and the numerous putti caught up on one side in the overflowing cornucopia of fruit and on the other side astride the wild animals they control express the joyous exuberance and abundance Carew and others could see in the son's blessings. Together above the Banqueting House, the nine panels assert the majestic, heroic, and festive realities that constitute the Whitehall vision of Caroline rule.

Outside the imaginary world depicted in the artistry of Rubens and in the court poets, the promise of peace was still very real. Although the death of Frederick V soon after the loss of Gustavus had diminished the Palatinate issue, nevertheless militant voices continued to urge Charles to sound the alarm and "vindicate the wrong / Of thy deare Sister, and her Children young."[59] With the death in 1635 of the lord treasurer Richard Weston, a major opponent of military expenditures was silenced, and in the next two years the Palatinate became a further rallying point for an anti-Spanish faction interested in promoting the Protestant cause and their own financial interests.[60] In this altered atmosphere, the Venetian ambassador reports, another party arose "which balances every other opinion, and shows how useful and opportune it is to stand and look on at the tragedy of others as spectators and enjoy peacefully that blessedness which God has chosen to grant to these realms amid such universal calamities."[61] Commercial interests lent their support, for during this period of "perfect quiet and security" a neutral England exploited the shipping and trade advantages peace had given the nation. Not all his subjects were happy with Charles's attempts to raise revenue and to determine religious policy, but contemporary and modern historians alike recognize the success of the king's peace in the mid-1630s. While revisionist interpretations eschew the hyperbole found in seventeenth-century descriptions of "present repose and unique tranquility," they contend in particular that Charles enjoyed the country's support and that he may have been in 1637 more firmly in control than he was ten years earlier.[62] Certainly among the numerous tributes that regularly greeted the royal couple and their growing family, none found occasion to liken England to the "unfortunate Europe" Rubens depicts in *The Horrors of War* as a "grief-stricken woman clothed in black, with torn veil, robbed of all her jewels and other ornaments . . . who, for so many years now, has suffered plunder, outrage, and misery."[63]

Neither the Scottish resistance to the Laudian prayer book nor the legal challenge to ship money could dispel in early 1638 the royal confidence reasserted in Davenant's revival of the court masques *Britannia Triumphans* and *Luminalia: The Queen's Festival of Light*. The performances at Whitehall in "a new temporary room of timber" do not match, however, the splendor of the Banqueting Hall triumphs. The celebration of the royal "wisdom, valour, and piety" in the first masque and its "gentle, wise and just" policy in the second turn upon the now familiar recognition of the "wonder of his virtue" and the "beauties of her mind." In *Luminalia* the "magnificent virtues" of the king and queen create in the peaceful island of Britanides another garden "not inferior in beauty to that of the Hesperides" (2:706). More pointedly, in *Britannia Triumphans* the figures of Naval Victory and Right Government on the proscenium arch and the view of the British fleet in the final scene assert the justness of Charles's ship-money levies and his foreign policy designed to maintain England's maritime strength. Once again the wonder the masques evoke depends upon an awakening and opening of the senses. When Bellerophon, or Heroic Virtue, allies with Action to dispel the arch-magician Merlin and Imposture, the "misty clouds of error clear" and Fame can then appropriately invite all to experience the "universal wonder," Britanocles or Charles I. Similarly in *Luminalia* the dazzling illumination emanating from the Queen of Light and Beauty appears when the Queen of Night and her illusory realm are vanquished. Perhaps more so than in the earlier productions, both masques reveal a Caroline sensitivity to the threat posed by ignorance and lethargy. Fame is commanded in *Britannia Triumphans,* "if there can be any maliciously insensible, awake them from their pretended sleep, that even they with the large yet still increasing number of the good and loyal may mutually admire and rejoice in our happiness" (2:662). The chorus of *Luminalia* also sounds the Virgilian note in its assurance,

all this isle their triumphs now express
Not to beget, but show their happiness;

A precious sign, they know their own estate,
And that makes nations chiefly fortunate:
For it alike should often valued be
To know, and to deserve felicity.

(2:707)

This insistent, almost hortatory quality disappears in the final song, where the obligatory well-wishes to the king and queen express the awareness:

Yet you by such a human difference raise
Your virtue more because 'tis conjugal.

Be long expected on your thrones above!
And stay on earth until our judgements know
The noble use of that we so much love;
Thus heaven still lends what we would ever owe.

(2:709)

Though the degree of intentional irony and even wistfulness here eludes precise determination, events would soon give this understanding a resonance only the experience of civil disruption could impart.

A year later Charles was involved in an unsuccessful war, and a decade of peaceful, personal rule was in jeopardy. The First Bishops' War began with considerable royalist confidence that the Scots could be defeated, but by the time the Pacification of Berwick was signed in June 1639, it was apparent that the enthusiasm and personal fortunes of royalists such as John Suckling could not implement the king's will. Charles was the first monarch in some three hundred years to take the nation to war without securing parliamentary support, and he soon faced the possible disintegration of his authority.[64] A financial system successfully suited to policies of pacifism collapsed when both the gentry and the common citizenry resisted the taxation necessary to fund the military venture, and dissatisfaction with an unpopular war was soon apparent in the communities as well as in London. Fearful of a rumored Catholic conspiracy and resentful of the threats to their well-being, the English nevertheless had no thought of revolution.[65] The nation's unsettled, troubled mood in the months before the Short Parliament and the Second Bishops' War is apparent at least to some degree in the last formal celebrations of peace, the Lord Mayor's show on 29 October 1639 and the Twelfth Night masque of 21 January 1640.

To commemorate the installation of Henry Garway, the Society of Drapers commissioned Thomas Heywood to write *Londoni Status Pacatus,* a pageant lauding "A peaceable and blest estate, in which our Soveraigns Royalty hath a correspondence with *Saturnes* Reigne, which was cald the golden world."[66] Performances staged for the Lord Mayor's show traditionally justified the city's commercial interests,[67] and not surprisingly, the five scenes in the

procession from Westminster to the Guildhall warn against all who seek to
disrupt the harmony of peaceful commerce and prosperous trade. The final
show, however, presents a scene of war and peace unusual among the earlier
London fêtes. Along with a symbolic ship of commerce, an "artificiall Archi-
tecture" gives visual form to the triumph's title: "In one part thereof are
exprest to the life, the figures of *Death, Famine, Sicknesse, strage*, &c. in the
other *Prosperity, Plenty, Health, Wealth*, but especially the free and frequent
Preaching of the Word and Gospell."[68] The scene's emphasis on honor,
government, concord, and unity has a frequent parallel in the court productions. A long speech by the Genius of the City describing the horrors of war
"As lately in Germany" also culminates in the depiction of the reality royalist
supporters had until now pressed less forcefully,

> And such a time is *War*, and such the throwes
> Our *neighbour Nations* travell *now* in; woes
> Quite desperate of delivery: whilst *calme Peace*,
> *Prosperity*, and *Plenty*, with *increase*
> Of all concatinated *Blessings* smile
> With cheerefull face on this *sole-happy Isle*.
>          Let then our *gratitudes* and *Pious cares*
> Strive to *entaile them* to *Us*, and our *Heires*:
> Lest that too late, (having sterne *Warre* accited)
> We wish that *Peace*; which (whilst we had) we slighted.[69]

Three months later a Whitehall audience witnessed the dangers of ingratitude in the last Caroline masque, *Salmacida Spolia*. Charles now appears
as the embattled monarch Philogenes, the lover of his people, endowed with
a "secret power" and a "secret wisdom." Though the unknown virtue remains
as mysterious as the waters of Salmacis, which magically subdued the barbaric fierceness of all who tasted them, its possessor has the similar ability to
transform the threatening tempest. An explication of the masque's subject
explains at length that the victory achieved at Salmacis "without blood or
sweat" prefigures the triumph Charles realizes through his prudence, mercy,
and clemency. Fated to govern in an "adverse" and "sullen age," he must deal
with the fury Discord, who arises in the tempestuous first scene from the
conflagration of the earth and is "grieved the world should everywhere /
Be vexed into a storm, save only here! / Thou over-lucky, too-much-happy isle"
(2:731). More stridently than in the previous masques, Concord and the
Good Genius of Great Britain chide a nation that has only "slowly understood" the blessings it has long enjoyed yet seldom valued. Suitably chas-
tened, the audience can then identify with the Chorus of Beloved People who
are led to see "with instructed eyes" the way to comfort and honor. The sight
of Charles and Henrietta Maria seated with a prospect of London in the
background and surrounded by the eight spheres and numerous deities

descended from above appeals to a faith in monarchy that defies the history of the moment. They are the unvanquished center of the universe and the source of all order:

> All that are harsh, all that are rude,
> Are by your harmony subdued;
> Yet so into obedience wrought,
> As if not forced to it, but taught.
>
> (2:734)

Though less spectacularly, the king also manifests another dimension of himself not seen in the previous masques. Before he is united with the queen, Charles appears on his throne an emblem of peace and honor; he is praised, however, for his ultimate wisdom:

> If it be kingly patience to outlast
> Those storms the people's giddy fury raise
> Till like fantastic winds themselves they waste,
> The wisdom of that patience is thy praise.
>
> (2:733)

Earlier masques often laud the king's ability to control and tame; now his heroic and active virtue assumes new meaning:

> Since strength of virtues gained you Honour's throne,
> Accept our wonder and enjoy your praise!
> He's fit to govern there and rule alone
> Whom inward helps, not outward force, doth raise.
>
> (2:733)

More than a consciously crafted apology for Charles's inability to change events he could no longer control, the premium given to patience and the inward life initiates a redefinition of the regal nature. When later the nation was forced against its will into armed conflict, Charles would show on the battlefield the bravery if not the success of Gustavus Adolphus, but he would not be remembered in later years as another St. George or warrior king. As the royal fortunes declined in the next decade, he was increasingly seen as the monarch of *Eikon Basilike*, the self-possessed and long-suffering man who prayed, "Teach me the noblest victory over myself and my enemies by patience, which was Christ's conquest and may well become a Christian king."[70]

The patience and inner fortitude that inspired the king and his loyal subjects in the coming crisis are one expression of a crucial movement inward; the other and often complementary dimension is apparent in Carew's alternative understanding of the masques' development. Although "To my friend *G. N.* from *Wrest*" is an important contribution to the genre of country-house poetry, Carew's last poem also consciously adapts the masque and its celebration of peace to his personal response to the national unrest.[71] The epistle, written in early 1640 or late 1639, confronts the threatening times from the safety of Wrest Park, where Carew found a haven after his service the previous summer in the Scottish campaign:

> I Breathe (sweet *Ghib:*) the temperate ayre of *Wrest*
> Where I no more with raging stormes opprest,
> Weare the cold nights out by the bankes of Tweed,
> On the bleake Mountains, where fierce tempests breed,
> And everlasting Winter dwells.
>
> (ll. 1–5, p. 86)

Carew understands firsthand the tempestuous world Inigo Jones designed for the opening scene of *Salmacida Spolia,* and he is more strongly drawn to the ideals of the Caroline masque. The "cold," "sterill," and "wilde North" has no place in the Bedfordshire estate praised for its warmth, hospitality, and fecundity. Here in the natural beauty of the manor the traditional figures of the masque are at home:

> *Amalthea's* Horne
> Of plentie is not in Effigie worne
> Without the gate, but she within the dore
> Empties her free and unexhausted store.
> Nor, croun'd with wheaten wreathes, doth *Ceres* stand
> In stone, with a crook'd sickle in her hand:
> Nor, on a Marble Tunne, his face besmear'd
> With grapes, is curl'd uncizard *Bacchus* rear'd.
>
> (ll. 57–64)

Gathered around the bountiful table of Lord and Lady de Grey, their friends form a "capacious circle" at the center of Wrest Park; outside the estate the river circumscribes a still-larger circle:

> till they twice surround
> This Island Mansion, which i' th' center plac'd,
> Is with a double Crystall heaven embrac'd,
> In which our watery constellations floate,
> Our Fishes, Swans, our Water-man and Boate,
> Envy'd by those above, which wish to slake
> Their starre-burnt limbes, in our refreshing lake,
> But they stick fast nayl'd to the barren Spheare,
> Whilst our encrease in fertile waters here
> Disport, and wander freely where they please
> Within the circuit of our narrow Seas.
>
> (ll. 78–88)

In celebrating this miniature replication of England, Carew may not have been familiar with the final image of *Salmacida Spolia,* but the universe he imagines obviously plays with a conceit central to *Coelum Britannicum* and the other Caroline masques.[72] Like the creators of the Whitehall masques, the builders of the estate employed "the worke of Art" to shape their own microcosm; they diverted the natural flow of the river to encircle a space that both epitomizes and excludes the world without.

Within the closed circle Carew celebrates a life that is more immediate and yet paradoxically more isolated than that of the masquing world. The Wrest Park he describes to his friend G. N. has an animated vitality not characteristic of the masques' emblematic poses:

> The Lord and Lady of this place delight
> Rather to be in act, then seeme in sight;
> In stead of Statues to adorne their wall
> They throng with living men, their merry Hall.
>
> (ll. 31–34)

The virtuous action so insistently emphasized in the royal tributes is to be seen everywhere in the estate's purposefulness. The manor has a "usefull comelinesse"; its unpretentious walls are erected for "reall use"; and all appears "fit for service." The comfort and security afforded by this ordered life depend upon an aristocratic responsibility commonly associated with the royalist ideal, but they evoke none of the awe, mystery, or wonder of the masques. Initially the poem assaults the senses with a teeming sensuousness; at the end its exaltation of Ceres and Bacchus conveys urgency. In moving toward the edge of the estate's encircling waters, the poem culminates its undercurrent of sexuality in the description of a decidedly libertine world where Vertumnus and Zephyr pursue their loves and Ceres appears to swell with the god of wine. The garden world of tactile delight ends the poem with sensuous revivification so intense that the final lines seem anticlimactic:

> Thus I enjoy my selfe, and taste the fruit
> Of this blest Peace, whilst toyl'd in the pursuit
> Of Bucks, and Stags, th'embleme of warre, you strive
> To keepe the memory of our Armes alive.
>
> (ll. 107–10)

The conclusion brings the poem full circle as it underscores the reality Carew had refused to ignore in his earlier answer to Townshend. Now that England faced the threat of war, withdrawal into a golden world is becoming increasingly attractive.

The events of the decade had, in sum, modified the Caroline vision of peace. In the Whitehall days of glory, the masques proclaimed that all of

England prospered in the love and benevolence of a royal couple who wisely eschewed traditional martial heroism and nurtured their country's tranquillity. Among the cardinal Stoic virtues celebrated in these court performances, prudence, justice, and temperance ensure the ordered, responsible government that appears to transform the nation into the envy of the gods. When the ever-present fear of war threatens peace, the imperial triumph diminishes and the fourth Stoic virtue of fortitude assumes greater importance. Narrowed to the confines of the country estate and the self-possessed individual, the realm of peaceful security still encompasses for many the essential sense of nobility. Later years of civil war challenged yet reconfirmed the Stoic and humanist belief in the responsibility each has, in the words of Seneca, to "benefit his fellow-men—many if he can, if not, a few; if not a few, those who are nearest; if not these, himself."[73]

Carew did not live to see the Short Parliament, the Second Bishops' War, and the Long Parliament; others who saw England move into civil crisis would consider at greater length the value of nobility and the attractiveness of the enclosed, inward life. The writers examined in the next five chapters illustrate the complexity of these responses. None abandons the Caroline emphasis on a heroic, active virtue, and two of them seek epic glory in the war that divided the nation, but even they are drawn toward a greater understanding of self-containment and peace. Running throughout all the works is an appreciation of the patience and fortitude Charles would come to embody. Theirs is not the "forc'd / Falsly exalted passive Fortitude" Mercury derides in *Coelum Britannicum*. Rooted in a Renaissance humanism variously indebted to classical and Christian Stoicism, their patience offers them the means to confront unhappy times. Some are attracted to the rural existence Carew offers Townshend and G. N. in the pastoral and country-house worlds, and at times their celebrations of the convivial circle formed upon friendship and wine tend toward cynicism and indulgence. Nevertheless the diverse group of poets who lift their cups in Bacchic tribute to their cause or rise in meditative solitude above the tumult do not succumb to the suffering, disillusionment, and despondency of war. In all their complicated moods, the writers never abandon their faith in the potential of human integrity and in the promise of peace.

In analyzing the struggle to affirm a purposeful existence, the following pages stress the importance of this faith. Although the focus remains on the five writers' redefinitions of nobility, the sense of Caroline peace they expressed cannot be ignored. When John Gauden preached to the assembled members of the House of Commons on 29 November 1640, his cadenced voice reverberated in the parliament: "Your populous *Cities and Townes,* your stately houses, your fruitefull fields, your pleasant gardens, your costly cloathes, your plentiful tables, your ancient *liberties* and Noble immunities, wherewith *above all subjects in the world* you are invested and honour'd, all

joyne in this voyce, *O love the truth and peace:* which affords you all these
sweete enjoyments and Noble ornaments of life."[74] Three years later Henry
Glapthorne imagines an empty Whitehall that recalls "Brave *Charles*" and
"*Maria Henrietta* his deare Bride,"

> Who with a numerous progeny has blest
> The British Kingdom; which in peace and rest
> Was pregnant with felicity, untill
> Like torrents falling from some lofty hill,
> Or like some sudden storme out of a cloud
> Mischief came thundering from the North.[75]

The sense of loss, the feeling "O those were Golden dayes," contributes to the
rueful and occasionally nostalgic tone apparent in the next decades.[76] None
of the writers in this study communicates Marvell's or Milton's poignant
awareness of a fallen world; among them, however, even those who do not
help fashion or perpetuate the Caroline mixture of myth and history betray
their yearning for a lost peace. While each of the five poets, this chapter
suggests, tends to turn inward in search of peace, for those who live through
the aftermath of the war, the future also assumes new promise. In the
patience and inner fortitude of Charles's son, they would come to see the
means through which an even greater Caroline peace could be restored.

Long before the Restoration, the nature of this resolve is apparent in the
poetry of William Cartwright, the focus of the next chapter. The occasional
verse Cartwright began publishing in the 1630s celebrates a virtue tempered
in the early years of war. At first his many contributions to the commemorative volumes Oxford University published reaffirm the expectations of the
court poets: the actions of the monarch and the births of the royal children
are occasions to praise the bountiful blessings of the Caroline peace. But
Cartwright also reveals his indebtedness to the Stoic humanism Jonson had
earlier admired, and his portraits of Charles, Henrietta Maria, and other
contemporary worthies begin to stress a characteristic self-sufficiency. In
appropriating the Stoic symbol of the circle, Cartwright defines an ideal
founded on the classical belief that virtue and nobility are synonymous. When
the civil crisis transformed Oxford into an armed royalist camp, Cartwright
helped others discover the heroic virtue of people able to stand unmoved in
the face of adversity and death.

# 2

# William Cartwright and the "Gather'd Mind"

UNLIKE Ben Jonson and John Donne, with whom he has some affinities, William Cartwright is identified with an "age of panegyric," a
world characterized as self-absorbed in flattering tributes devoid of "moral
imagination"; and it is easy to dismiss him as one of the "dutiful University
wits, most commonly anxious to versify and glamourise official ideology."[1]
His poetry is prominent among the many volumes Oxford issued in celebration of the royal couple, and Cartwright's poems frequently appear in the
collections gathered outside the university to praise recent publications or to
mourn sudden deaths. Examined in their own right, however, Cartwright's
poems of praise and commemoration reveal a wit, gracefulness, and high
seriousness at odds with the prevalent descriptions of his poetry and his age.
From 1633 until his death some ten years later, these occasional pieces trace
Cartwright's increasingly serious response to a decade of promise that ended
in crisis. The expectation in the earlier ceremonial poems changes as the
hopes of a bountiful royal blessing wane, but the growing emphasis on self-
sufficiency and inner nobility does not diminish the celebration. In the tradition of the Stoic humanists, his poetry lauds an active virtue that binds the
nation's ruler and his loyal subjects together in a community of responsible
service. Wealthy aristocrats, established poets, and obscure countrymen unselfishly stand with the royal family in mutual obligation and purposeful
resolve. Their constancy, integrity, and courage form the circle of virtue that
Cartwright celebrates as the essence of true nobility and the basis of society.

His contributions to Oxford's celebrations of the royal family suggest the
direction of his evolving attitudes. Although one of his Latin poems appears
in the volume hastily published by the university in the summer of 1630 to
celebrate the birth of Prince Charles, Cartwright first significantly influences
Caroline congratulatory poetry in 1633. That year the king's recovery from
an illness, his journey to Scotland, and the birth of his son James occasioned
separate tributes from the university. Cartwright composed Latin verses for
each of the three publications, but he is also prominent among the writers in
these volumes who wrote English poems. Of the 108 poems on the king's

illness, the four by William Cartwright, Jasper Mayne, Jeremy Terrent, and Thomas Lockey mark the first time since Oxford initiated the commemorative publications in 1587 that a group of university writers expressed themselves in English.[2] Sixteen others would join Cartwright in similarly greeting Charles's return to England, and nineteen English poems were added to the birthday wishes. Each of the ten Oxford publications from 1633 to 1643, in fact, contains an often increasing number of English encomiums. From the outset the poets insist that they have abandoned their Latin "Mother tongue" and "translate some of our joyes" for the benefit of the queen, "to tell our meanings, which you here may reade / In the same Dialect in which you breed."[3] Cambridge would also resort to the same pretext when its wits belatedly followed suit and included ten English poems in *Voces Votivae* (1640), but the queen's inability to read Latin seems at best a convenient justification for the trend toward using English. At Oxford the traditions of Christ Church and the presence of William Cartwright undoubtedly shaped the emergence of praise addressed in English for the most part to the king and not the queen.

Cartwright flourished at the center of a creative environment that gave new immediacy to the humanist emphasis on the poet as a public spokesman and that offered him, he reportedly said, "three advantages: . . . great spirited Tutors, choice Books, and select Company."[4] When Cartwright was elected to the college in 1628, Jeremy Terrent became his tutor, but the vice-chancellor of the university, Brian Duppa, appears to have been the major influence on his education and his early publications. Humphrey Moseley acknowledges Duppa's significance as the young man's "Patron," and the chancellor renowned for "the pleasant Instructions of the choicest wits in the University" probably encouraged Cartwright's contributions to each of the 1633 publications Duppa headed.[5] Within the "knot of the choicest *Oxford* Wits always together" and presumably often drawn together by Duppa, Cartwright formed an especially close bond with Jasper Mayne, the other mainstay of the Oxford commemorative verse; both appear to have also fallen under the influence of Duppa's friend and former resident at Christ Church, Ben Jonson. Though Cartwright never numbers himself among the sons of Ben or identifies with the courtiers of their London coterie, from the outset his poems justify Jonson's approving judgment, "My Son Cartwright writes all like a Man."[6] Distinct from the lifeless, predictable homage all too common in the more than 250 English poems the university wits produced for the royal family, Cartwright's poems provide a significant academic counterpart to the masques at Whitehall. Unrivaled among his Oxford peers, Cartwright creates a mode of praise that successfully uses the traditions of university poetry to support the monarchy in both its triumphant and troubled moments.

His poems to Charles and Henrietta Maria "On His Majesties Return from Scotland. 1633" celebrate Cartwright's central vision of the Caroline reign. Along with the other Oxford poets who take their cue from the book's title and the rhetorical commonplaces of the occasion, Cartwright's welcoming addresses in *Solis Britannici Perigaevm* develop the imagery of light to establish the traditional tone of joy.[7] His distinction between the triumphant spectacle commonly accorded the "haughty Power" and the joyous upwelling spontaneously given the king also establishes the ideal conduct traditional in such panegyric; but unlike Jasper Mayne, Cartwright does not follow Jonson's example in "A Panegyre, on the Happy Entrance of Iames . . . March, 1603" and insist at length upon the regal virtues that ensure popular loyalty. Instead, piety and love are the essence of the reunion that makes the nation "a people now againe":

> Your pious Raign secur'd your Throne, your Life
> Was guard unto your Scepter: no rude strife,
> No violence there disturb'd the Pompe, unlesse
> Their eager Loue, and Loyalty did presse
> To see and know, whiles lawfull Majesty
> Spread forth its Presence, and its Piety.
>
> (p. 449)

Although he is well aware of the discord rulers must in fact recognize, both in this poem and in the companion piece to the queen, Cartwright asserts the inseparable presence of love and loyalty. When he repeatedly assures Henrietta Maria that the university poets share her longing for the king and proclaims that their happiness "will be try'd by Yours," the lines are neither presumptuous nor disrespectful. These are poems of unity reminiscent of the Caroline attitude Jonson celebrated two years earlier in *Love's Triumph* and *Chloridia*. The complementary masques' emblem of the crowned palm tree entwined with roses and lilies symbolizes the reality of peaceful bounty Cartwright shares with both Jonson and Carew. Thus he can conclude his welcome with the appropriate and unstrained exaltation: "Cry we a second HYMEN then, and sing, / Whiles You receiue the Husband, Wee the King" (p. 450).

Love, peace, and unity also inform the next poem Cartwright wrote, "On the Birth of the Duke of *York*." The birth of Prince James two months after the king's return from Scotland occasioned the first of the five volumes with English poems Oxford published to congratulate the growing royal family. Their often similar praise of the queen's fecundity and the nation's blessings observes the prescriptive rhetorical and poetic precedents of the genethliacon or nativity poem. In Puttenham's representative formulation, poets were required to show their "duetie and ciuilitie" to their rulers through "ioyfull songs and ballades, praysing the parentes by proofe, the child by hope, the whole kinred by report, & the day it selfe with wishes of all good successe,

long life, health & prosperitie for euer to the new borne."[8] While too often
the Oxford poets fulfilled their duty with a combination of conventional
gesture and ingenious wit, Cartwright for the most part fashions the *topoi* of
the genethliacon into thoughtful tribute. His promise of the future, moreover, never forgets the realities of the present and the need for heroic
nobility.

As the praise in his first poem moves from the nativity day and the newly
born duke of York through wishes for the future and back to the royal family,
Cartwright develops a suitably formal and public expression that tempers
obligatory praise with wit and seriousness both intimate and personal. At the
outset the comparison between the unnatural premonitions accompanying
some births and the uneventful calm attending that of James subverts convention with the assurance that a wondrous child needs no further signs of
wonder. Even in this early poem, the speaker assumes, most clearly in his
prayer to nature, the classical and Renaissance obligation of the poet-orator:

> let it be
> My pray'r, that Shee'll be modest, and that Hee
> Have but the second honour, be still neere;
> No imitation of the Father here.
> Yet let him, like to him, make Pow'r as free
> From blot or scandall, as from poverty;
> Count Blood and Birth no parts, but something lent
> Meerely for outward grace, and complement;
> Get safety by good life, and raise defence
> By better forces, Love, and conscience.
>
> (p. 451)

Underlying the wishes for the king's second son is the humanist premise that
"no other way of correcting a prince is so efficacious as presenting, in the
guise of flattery, the pattern of a really good prince."[9] The tacit instruction in
the idealized image held before the son recalls in part Jonson's insistence
"That bloud not mindes, but mindes did bloud adorne: / And to liue great,
was better, then great borne";[10] indeed, the entire prayer expresses not only a
Jonsonian but a classical and decidedly Stoic understanding of nobility
fundamental to all of Cartwright's commendatory verse. His poetry recognizes, though less stridently than Jonson and the Roman moralists,[11] that the
uncertainties of daily living demand the "good life" he wishes the prince and
sees in the king, a life dependent upon inner nobility nurtured through
"conscience" and "Minde" and confirmed in action. Though the inauspicious
birth signifies that "'tis a Sonne of mirth, / Of peace and friendship,"
Cartwright understands that an era of peace also depends upon the willingness to use the sword. A passing reference to some possible future time of
"unfil'd people" and the other allusions to the manner in which James's father
Charles came to the throne and his grandfather Henry IV lost his life temper

the unrestrained praise without dispelling its festive tenor. Appropriately, the final lines exhibit little fear and considerable wit in their direct request to the king to "show / You can be tender too, in this one thing / Suffer the Father to depose the King" (p. 452); and they end with the "welcome Trouble" of the queen who "Strives to divide the Mother" equally among the three children. This domestic note confirms the poem's opening words, "The State is now past feare." The final impression evokes without its extravagant visual trappings the same ideal expressed to the king and queen a year earlier at a Whitehall masque:

> may your virtuous minds beget
> Issue that never shall decay,
> And so be fruitful every way.
> May plenty Proteus-like appear,
> Varying your pleasures every year.[12]

The births of the princesses Elizabeth on 28 December 1635 and Anne on 17 March 1637 fulfill the wishes that the king and queen "may perpetuate themselves by a royal posterity." In praising the two girls as copies and mirrors of their parents, Cartwright joins the other Oxford poets in lauding the nation's bountiful blessings. The unbounded love and creativity of Charles and his queen now assume for many an imperial dimension, and Cartwright too exclaims, "Your Sonnes, Great Sir, may fix your Scepter here, / But 'tis this sexe must make you raigne elsewhere" (p. 505). Though his poem to the king on the birth of Anne cryptically alludes to the "disloyall envy" of those who complain at the loss of some gold, this apparent reference to the ship-money levies serves mainly to accentuate further the plenitude and selflessness of the monarchy. Political realities are not allowed to disrupt the happiness that attends the children's births; and no one could foresee, in any case, the disastrous consequences of the crown's policies. A sense of unity again emphasizes the close relationship or "Linkt Dependance" that binds subject and ruler, and a feeling of joy emerges from the traditional poetic exercises. At his best, when he describes the cupids who seem to appear before the infant Anne, Cartwright sustains a delicate and graceful lyricism that rivals the Banqueting House performances:

> These Venus eyes (says one) these are
> Our mothers sparkes, but chaster farre:
> And Thetis Sylver feete are these,
> The Father sure is Lord o' th' seas.
> Faire one (saith this) we bring you flowrs;
> The Garden one day shall be Yours:
> Wear on your Cheekes these, and when you doe
> Venture at words, you'll speake 'em too.
> That veyle that hides great Cupids eyes

(Saith that) must swath Her as shee lyes:
For certaine 'tis, that this is shee,
Who destind is to make Love see.

(p. 510)

State concerns intrude along with personal sorrow in the series' next poem, "To the Queen after her dangerous Delivery. 1638." On the eve of the First Bishops' War, the death of Princess Catherine within hours of her birth on 29 January 1639 prompted from Oxford an outpouring of consolation. Cartwright's poem on the infant's ill-fated nativity and the queen's safety transforms the tragedy of death into the solace of a double birth, "Halfe unto Heaven, Halfe unto the Earth." In dispelling the aura of elegy with the reminder of Catherine's salvation and the queen's renewed life, the wit offers decorous comfort. But Cartwright is most effective, as he often is, in striking an apt resolve. The example he offers the queen of the king's own behavior gives immediacy to a classical image of nobility:

> See how Your Great Iust Consort bears the Crosse!
> Your Safeties Gaine makes him oresee the Losse:
> So that, although this Cloud stand at the Doore,
> His Great Designes goe on still as before.
> Thus stout Horatius being ready now
> To Dedicate a Temple, and by Vow
> Settle Religion to his God, although
> 'Twas told his Child was dead, would not let goe
> The Post o'th' Temple, but unmov'd Alone
> Bid them take care o'th'funerall, and went on.

(pp. 530–31)

Horatius's refusal to let news of his son's death stop his dedication of the temple to Jupiter appears in Livy's account ambiguous: "Whether he did not believe the news to be true, or possessed great fortitude, we are not informed with certainty, nor is it easy to decide."[13] Cartwright, however, has no doubt about the resoluteness with which "stout Horatius" and the "Great Iust Consort" Charles bear their burdens. The tactful allusion to the king's troubled religious policies in Scotland recognizes not only the importance of the "Great Designes" but also the selfless dedication Cartwright considers among the hallmarks of Charles's virtue.

This royal magnanimity stands out in the birthday poem written for the last of the nativity collections, *Horti Carolini Rosa Altera*. Once again Cartwright stresses the bounty added to the Caroline garden with the birth of Prince Henry on 8 July 1640, but he now expresses indignation at the nation's unwillingness to appreciate its Edenic existence. "These Your Constant Tributes to the State," he assures the queen, "Might make us stand up High, and trample Fate; / We might grow Bold from Conscience of just

Good, / Had it the fortune to be Understood" (p. 535). The lines that echo
the Virgilian lament *"O fortunatos nimium, sua si bona norint"* had been
voiced earlier the same year in the 1640 productions of the last Caroline
masque, *Salmacida Spolia;* and the resolve seems much the same in both
Davenant's masque and Cartwright's poem. The king, who becomes in the
court production Philogenes, the lover of people, armed with a "kingly
patience to outlast / Those storms the people's giddy fury raise,"[14] also stands
in Cartwright's view "our Great Guide, carelesse of Common Voyce, / As
Good by Nature rather, then by Choyce":

> And, like the Unmov'd Rock, though it doth heare
> The Murmurs of Rude Waves, whose Rage breakes there;
> He still gives Living Gemms, and doth present
> To Froward Nations Wealth, and Ornament.
>
> (p. 536)

Steadfast in the midst of the raging flood that would engulf the nation,
Charles also appears constant in his willingness to give of himself in these
"Thanklesse" times. His children now more than ever hold the promise of the
splendor and harmony the court had recently seen in the mechanical magic of
Inigo Jones and the patterned songs of William Davenant. The masque's
desire is the hope that also climaxes Cartwright's wishes for the newborn
Henry:

> But if He be, by Milder Influence, borne
> The Sonne of Peace, the Rose without a Thorne;
> What Once his *Grand-sires* Ripe Designes did boast,
> And Now His Serious Father labours most,
> Hee, as a Pledge sent to Both Nations, doe;
> And cement Kingdomes, now againe call'd Two.
>
> (p. 536)

The Stuart patrimony of peaceful and prosperous unity idealized in the
Rubens paintings on the ceiling of the Banqueting House as well as in the
court masques often staged in this Whitehall building remains essential to
Cartwright's nativity poems. Though the last of them ends with a fanciful
blend of fable and history, Cartwright has no illusions about the prospects
that "This Floating Island" will be "setled" by the birth. These poetic rites
and celebrations are part of a communal expression, which like the masque
"may be taken as a kind of mimetic magic on a sophisticated level, the attempt
to secure social health and tranquillity for the realm by miming it in front of
its chief figure. The frequency of prayer as a rhetorical mode in the masques is
hence not accidental."[15] The poems, of course, are not mime, and they have
no assurance of the king's audience, but through their publication they reach
beyond the community of Oxford scholars and the court. Poems of royal love

and creativity, they extol the generosity Charles and Henrietta Maria manifest without regard for their own suffering; and like the masques they encourage a similar generosity from readers who share with Cartwright an appreciation of this bounty and who understand with him the unstinting nobility that makes it possible.

Following the traditions of humanism and the example of Jonson, the other celebrations of both happy and troubled occasions also proclaim that "*Good men* are the Stars, the Planets of the Ages wherein they live, and illustrate the times."[16] Throughout this poetry images of light, astronomy, and fruition continue to affirm the virtue seen in the individuals Cartwright praises, but he is not deceived about the growing darkness and sterility. Although he lacks Jonson's bleak vision of human vanity, Cartwright agrees that the poet, "the neerest Borderer upon the Orator," must possess "exact knowledge of all vertues, and their Contraries; with ability to render the one lov'd, the other hated, by his proper embattaling them."[17] The ideals his poems commend are often set against their opposites, and like the nativity verses these tributes increasingly recognize the threatening realities of dissident subjects unhappy with the Laudian church and the personal rule. The luminaries in the poems stand out as guides for all who see their light; at the same time they may be encouraged to shine more brightly. This illustrious gathering of lords and commoners radiates the nobility most clearly seen in the important group of congratulatory and New Year's poems written largely to Cartwright's friend and patron, Brian Duppa.

The appointment of the dean of Christ Church as royal tutor to the Prince of Wales first gave Cartwright the opportunity to congratulate his patron and to commend his friend's new responsibilities. Regret about the darkness Oxford must now suffer in his absence yields after rather forced analogy to Cartwright's main purpose, a variation on the themes seen in Renaissance treatises on the education of princes. His recognition that the nation owes "The Son unto our King, the Prince to You" exalts the responsibility of Duppa to shape the mind of young Charles and thereby "instruct a future Common-Wealth." The man Cartwright values as the soul or informing spirit of the college assumes with this new role as surrogate father a status comparable to the honor Jonson reserves for William Camden:[18] both are learned teachers whose friends and countrymen alike are indebted to their integrity and dedication. In contrast to the superficial education most princes receive, the poem assures the dean "you will Dictate wholesome grounds, and sow / Seeds in his Mind, as pure as that is now" (p. 454). Cartwright in effect sets ideals before Duppa and the young prince. The poem's didactic tenor leaves no doubt about the real tutor, the poet, but neither its dictates nor its wishes become obtrusive. Cartwright maintains a secondary position, ending his praise modestly, "let this be / Your sole Ill-luck, that Good is wisht by me" (p. 454); and throughout the poem he insists that Duppa's future success depends upon the teacher's ability to recreate himself in his pupil, making the prince "the true / Resemblance of your Worth." Nurtured in the heir apparent, Duppa's moral strength and goodness promise a virtuous self-reliance that will unify "Faith and Policy" in a pious reign of love and harmony.

Wishes turn to prophecy as the hopeful relationship between tutor and prince is developed at greater length in the New Year's poem "To the Right Reverend Father in God, *Brian,* Lord Bishop of *Chichester.*" The pastoral setting and the speakers of this piece, which Cartwright probably wrote in 1638, emulate the mode Jonson chose for his "A New-yeares-Gift sung to King *Charles,* 1635"; but the innocent shepherds and their simple wishes mask a new urgency not evident in Jonson. When Cartwright emphasizes the theme of peace traditionally associated with Janus and the New Year, the poet's misgivings are unmistakable:

> He labours that we may
>     Not cast our Pipes away;
> That Swords to Plowsheares may be turn'd,
> And neither folds, nor Sheep-coats burn'd;
>     That no rude Barbarous Hands
>     May reap our well grown Lands,
> And that, sweet Liberty being barr'd,
> We not our Selves become the Heard.
>
>                                    (p. 523)

His fear of the unruly and grasping multitude underlies the wishes for unity and peace that the shepherds Syringus and Ergastus bring the royal tutor and his charge. The "one great Spring" they hope the prince and his subjects will always enjoy promises none of the thistles pointedly identified with Scotland. Theirs is a future that longs for "one Mind" yet recognizes an all too threatening discord:

> May he not have a Subject look,
> To please with murmuring, as the Brook,
> And let the Serpent of the year
> Not dare to fix his sharp Teeth here.
> May his Guide pull them out, and so
> Sow them that they never grow,
> Or if in furrows Arm'd they spring,
> Death to themselves their Weapons bring.
>
>                                    (p. 525)

Though the shepherds would wish away dissent and make their vision of peace a reality, Cartwright understands the impossibility of gardens without serpents and seasons without change. He does not, however, undercut the heartfelt motives that prompt the shepherds' New Year's gift. Like the poem's alternating wishes for the bishop and the prince, its gesture of giving expresses the mutual devotion and communal spirit Cartwright believes are easily lost when a nation consumes itself with selfish interests and forgets "Who e'r bestows, he still returns him more" (p. 524).

Confronted with the growing unrest of the late 1630s, Cartwright also asserts with greater conviction his belief that unwavering virtue will ultimately triumph. The steadfast mind apparent in the actions of the king and in the character of the royal tutor is defined most explicitly in "To Mrs *Duppa*, sent with the Picture of the Bishop of *Chichester* (her Husband) in a small peece of Glass." The poem written sometime between 1638 and 1641 accompanies the picture with a portrait of the bishop drawn by the poet in the familiar form of wishes intended for Duppa's birthday or perhaps for the New Year. Fears about the unsettling times and their disconcerting omens repeatedly yield to the recognition that the "Times to your Vertues will submit." The clamor about religious reformation prompts, for example, the understandable desire,

> I was about to pray,
> The years good in this day;
> That fewer Laws were made, and more were kept,
> The Church by Church-men swept.
>
> (p. 507)

But Cartwright's dismay at religious innovations that tear out the "seeming" ills and force changes under the guise of justice proves unnecessary: "But I am taught firme Minds have firmly stood / And good-wils work for good unto the Good" (p. 507). From the behavior of Bishop Duppa, Cartwright continually affirms that "solid" and "pious Minds" can weather undisturbed the "raging Tide" of a people threatening to sweep away the church's hierarchy. In a recognition fundamental not only to the poem but to all his poetry, Cartwright realizes:

> And you my Lord are he
> Who can all wishes free,
> Whose round and solid Mind knows to Create
> And fashion your own Fate;
> Whose firmness can from Ills assure success
> Where Others do but guess;
> Whose Conscience holy Calms enjoys
> 'Mid'st the loud Tumults of State-Noise;
> Thus gather'd in your self, you stand your own,
> Nor rais'd, by giddy changes, nor cast down.
>
> (p. 508)

The ideals of Stoic self-sufficiency recall Horace's celebration of the rounded individual and Jonson's justification of the gathered self. Cartwright praises in Duppa the "wise man" whom the Stoics deem "free" because he is, in Horace's words, "wholly contained in himself, well rounded, / Smooth as a sphere on which nothing external can fasten, / On which fortune can do no harm except to herself."[19] The description of the bishop in terms very reminiscent of Jonson's epigram to Sir Thomas Roe recaptures the classical vision of the centered self. Cartwright too admires individuals who possess a moral integrity and inner firmness that enable them to "stand" forth in tumultuous times, and he too values the "good mind" and "conscience" that in Jonson's noble figures defeat time and chance.[20] Mindful of the Stoic and humanist reservations about withdrawing from a hostile world, Cartwright also shares Jonson's reluctance to countenance isolated inactivity. The obligation to action, lauded elsewhere as the "Royal marke," and the promise that virtuous nobility will ultimately triumph lend support to Jonson's similar hope that the noble will thrive. The inner beauty expressed in the flourishing royal family and in the fruits of the learned teacher finds parallel expression in the church and in the name Duppa upholds. Following Jonson's tendency to depict the inner form in architectural terms,[21] Cartwright's conclusion compares the bishop to his cathedral. Like the virtuous people who rise figuratively as columns in Jonson's poems "to shew the times what you all were,"[22] Duppa surpasses the many pillars of his church: "The Strength yet, and the Beauty of that frame / Lies not in them so much as in your Name" (p. 508). Though he does not use names with Jonson's discriminating sense of praise and blame,[23] Cartwright appreciates the power of naming, and he understands the force names can assume. Duppa, he assures the bishop, has created "A Name above all Praise, that will stand high / When Fame it self shall dye" (p. 508); and those who value all that it represents will both perpetuate and share the Stoic virtue it defines.

The volume's final poem to Duppa affirms this creativity. "A New-years-gift to *Brian* Lord Bishop of *Sarum,* upon the Author's entring into holy Orders, 1638" stresses the circular nature of the virtue that emanates from the noble individuals Cartwright admires. Though he attempts to fulfill the conventions of the New Year by bringing the bishop both a poem and a "new man," once he admits that "I who thus present my self as New, / Am thus made New by You" (p. 529), Cartwright realizes the futility of traditional gift-giving and resolutions. Distinctions between giving and receiving disappear in the gracious conclusion:

> Who thus with your fire burns
> Now gives not, but Returns;
> To Others then be this a day of Thrift
> They do receive, but you Sir make the Gift.

(p. 530)

The gift of new life initially claimed as the poet's own creation and defined in the body of the poem offers the stability and moderation Cartwright dissociates from the "Common Throng" and finds in the established traditions. His later translation of Grotius's elegy on Arminius seems to imply that Cartwright sympathizes with the Arminian beliefs then current at both Oxford and Cambridge, but neither the elegy nor the New Year's poem espouses theological positions. Both are sensitive to the religious dissent that endangers Grotius's world and soon threatens the Laudian church, but theirs is not "an over-anxious" commitment that ignores moderation and charity. From his friend and spiritual creator, Cartwright has learned not "to search out for New Paths,"

> where
> Nor Tracks nor Footsteps doth appear,
> Knowing that Deeps are waies,
> Where no Impression staies,
> Nor servile thus, nor curious, may I then
> Approve my Faith to Heaven, my Life to Men.
>
> (p. 529)

By entering the church's service and accepting its *via media*, Cartwright both completes and begins anew the cycle of giving whose value he urges in the other two poems written for the New Year.

"A New-years-gift to a Noble Lord. 1640" again commends the "large Mind" that refuses to distinguish between personal and public welfare. The unnamed lord and "Just Patriot" stands above the "distemp'red Many" as one of the few lustrous worthies in a darkening era who are "still Blessing, and still Bless'd." While others succumb to pride or immoderation, the noble lord exhibits the dispassionate restraint and selfless devotion the other poems praise:

> an unbiass'd Breast,
> Discharg'd of all Self Interest;
> From Square, and solid Actions without flaw,
> That will in time themselves grow Law,
> Actions that shew you mean
> Nought to the Common Scene,
> That you'l ne'r lengthen power by Lust,
> But shape and size it by your Trust.
>
> (p. 533)

The nobleman's gains are also the nation's, although the poem is specifically concerned with the church. As a member of its clergy, Cartwright understandably decries zealots determined to destroy the established religion, but he never resorts to sweeping recriminations. His list of possible causes for the unrest considers along with the standard explanations of ambition, mistrust, and pride the possibility of unspecified "true Crimes"; and he further recognizes that "Want of Moderation" may exist "Both in the Ill, and Remedy."

Despite his obvious fears about the stormy times, Cartwright maintains a semblance of the unbiased and moderate judgment he praises in the man the poem addresses, and he never lapses into a defensive or despondent pessimism. Though he yearns for the calmness of the earlier golden days, Cartwright realistically confronts the storm and hopes the sacred ark will "rise higher with the Floud." The fulfillment of the biblical type depends explicitly upon patriotic nobility, but the church's future also lies in the moderate and compassionate understanding the poet displays.

Praise and well-wishes bind subject, poet, and country together more closely in the last example of the New Year's poem, a piece simply entitled "A New-years Gift." Cartwright's modern editor tentatively identifies the poem's recipient as King Charles, but the individual addressed in the piece has only the identifying characteristics of the ideal type. A man of conscience caught up in the unnatural and divisive times, he too stands apart as a moderate devoted to the nation. Foremost among his and the poet's concerns is the peace now so poignantly missed:

> He wishes Peace, that Publike Good,
>    Dry Peace, not bought with Bloud,
> Yet such as Honour may maintain,
>     And such the Crown
>     Would gladly own.
> Wish o'r that Wish to him again.
>
>                     (p. 527)

Speaker and subject seem to merge into one as the poem voices the common desire for the "one fix'd Calm" that would dispel the tempest. Although Cartwright is careful to emphasize an honorable peace acceptable to the crown, royal partisanship plays little part in his wishes. The wreath of joys woven from the New Year's wishes to fit equally the country as well as the unnamed individual is designed to crown the triumphant moment when the fears that divide the nation's hearts are conquered.

In common with the commemorative pieces to the royal family, this and the other poetic New Year's gifts celebrate the promise of new beginnings. All these poems of joy and expectation seek the model of peaceful prosperity in the rhythm or cycle of nature. The birth of a child and the return of the year occasion the resolutions and wishes that traditionally mark these moments of change, but for Cartwright natural continuity assumes the dimensions of Caroline myth. When the realities of the late 1630s and 1640s challenge the Stuart aura of unbounded love and peace, his poems avoid the temptation to indulge in nostalgia. He repudiates the blind self-interests of the masses and embraces outstanding individuals of uprightness and compassion, those set apart from all who lack the inner strength Cartwright most commonly praises as "Mind." The ultimate source of the nation's future, the nobility of these worthies is further celebrated in the other poems Cartwright wrote honoring those at the centers of influence. Again virtue and service rather than birth and position are the dominant concerns.

Appropriately, the lengthy panegyric that heads the 1651 volume effusively praises a woman whose charms and powers dominated the Caroline court. At the time Humphrey Moseley gathered the poems together for publication, Lucy Hay, countess of Carlisle, was in the custody of the state for her part in the earl of Holland's ill-fated royalist uprising, and Moseley may have chosen to honor her loyalty to the king by placing her praises first. When Cartwright wrote the poem in the late 1630s, the countess of Carlisle was, in any case, foremost among the women who vied for the queen's attentions and court influence. Cartwright probably joined the many Caroline poets who sang her praises because she was also the patroness of Brian Duppa, but he alone turns exaggerated praise of her outer beauty into greater commendation of her inner splendor. Challenging Jonson in his ability to reincarnate ancient myth in modern figures,[24] Cartwright offers rites to a goddess whose "Limbs leave tracks of Light" as she dispenses "Brightness, and force, Splendor, and Influence." This hyperbolic play on the name Lucy both figuratively and literally acknowledges the splendid and powerful figure who, in the words of a contemporary, "will be respected and observed by her Superiors, be feared by those that will make themselves her Equals, and will not suffer herself to be beloved but of those that are her Servants."[25] Others support the poem's contention that no one can ignore a woman who seems to "appear a Court, and are no less / Than a whole Presence, or throng'd glorious Press" (p. 443). The poem, however, addresses the countess primarily in moral terms as a peerless individual who upholds virtue "by daring to be good at Court." She "beyond all Pretenders" is "So much a friend to't, that with it y'are One" (p. 442). Lucy is, in truth, "your Owne, / Your self sufficing to your self alone"; and Cartwright wittily and earnestly transforms this self-sufficiency into a formal panegyric extolling her capacious mind and "proportion'd Soul." She emanates the nobility Cartwright reserves for those "Who thus rule others, but your self far more," and her presence gives new dimension to his emphasis on the centered self:

> Hence in your great Endowments Church and Court
> Find what t'admire; All wishes thus resort
> To you as to their Center, and are then
> Sent back, as Centers send back lines agen.

(p. 443)

The conceit gracefully defines a relationship that compromises neither the countess' independence nor the poet's high moral seriousness. Cartwright chooses to see in the aloof figure he knew from afar, if at all, his own desire for a responsible, rejuvenated society bound together by like-minded individuals; and for the woman who is "your own Glass and Object," he provides another mirror in which she can view herself aright.

The images he reflects and the light he honors in the countess of Carlisle are again unmistakable in his address to Philip, earl of Pembroke, on his election to the chancellorship of Oxford in July 1641. Pembroke stands forth in a Jonsonian sense as a morally upright individual who gives foundation and new shape to the endangered university. At this time the split between a university loyal to the king and a town sympathetic to the monarch's critics has widened,[26] but the growing political tensions are not the primary source of the poem's defensiveness. Cartwright reacts to the anti-intellectualism of a suspicious and "untaught Towne" that scorns the traditions of knowledge as "uselesse Peeces" and attacks the "now hated Arts." When he welcomes the new chancellor as both a patron and a founder who will infuse new soul into the university, the poet pointedly disclaims scholastic quiddities in favor of the humanist values that form a bastion of civilization in these "times of hazard." Cartwright looks to Pembroke as a defender whose "even life" and courageous nature will protect the institution against unsympathetic laws and will nurture the university's future growth. "Wee give a Title," the last line proclaims, "but receive a Man," a man who Cartwright believes gives in turn the guidance and freedom to "fashion manners to the best" and to "make that freedome live" (p. 542).

Other fashioners of manners and independence are similarly lauded in an important group of poems commending Caroline writers. Two of these commendatory verses, praises written for William Stokes's *The Vaulting Master* and Francis Kynaston's Latin translation of Chaucer's *Troilus and Criseyde,* decorously sustain light praise and graceful compliments; four other poems, however, develop long and substantial commentaries on Jonson, Killigrew, and Fletcher. Although the 1641 publication of plays by Thomas Killigrew was not an auspicious occasion, the important gatherings of poetic tributes for the other two writers encouraged opportunities to express common bonds of social as well as aesthetic values. Those who contributed to the 1638 memorial edition *Jonsonus Virbius* were honoring a major force in the development of Caroline literary and moral vision, while the contributors to the 1647 Beaumont and Fletcher folio were part of a Humphrey Moseley venture described as "a morale-boosting gesture of defiance, a propagandist reassertion of the Stuart ethic at a crucial moment in the fortunes of the Court."[27] Both poems to Fletcher were apparently written in the late 1630s, when Moseley first proposed an edition of these dramatists,[28] and neither contains any of the references to the troubled times found in the many poems published with the 1647 folio. Common to all of Cartwright's contributions, however, is an insistence upon integrity that rises above narrow partisanship and obligatory courtesy. Killigrew gives freely of himself because he remains true to himself, and he emerges as an individual worthy of the praise

Cartwright accords those who refuse to compromise their sense of moral or artistic worth. Fletcher too stands apart from servile imitators eager to please fickle and untrustworthy tastes: "where / Art, Language, Wit, sit ruling in one Spheare" (p. 518), the completeness of the circle reflects the fullness of the "free Author" who leaves his impress on all he creates. Appropriately, Cartwright's most thoughtful and impressive statement of this integrity occurs in his piece "In the memory of the most Worthy *Beniamin Iohnson*."

Although the poem written for *Jonsonus Virbius* remains technically an elegy, lament has little place in this tribute to the "*Father* of *Poets*" and source of illumination. Jonson lives in Cartwright's poem as a writer without equal, and the surging movement heavy with anaphora and contrast catalogues the dead poet's greatness with weighty appropriateness. As the master of custom, language, propriety, order, and wit, Jonson appears to fulfill his own most cherished strictures; indeed the poem reflects the classical values Jonson adapted to his own aesthetic pronouncements and practice. Foremost among these is the Horatian ideal given memorable expression in Jonson's praise of Shakespeare:

> *Thy Muse* tooke harder *metalls, purg'd* and *boild,*
> *Labour'd* and *try'd, heated,* and *beate* and *toyld,*
> *Sifted* the *drosse,* fil'd *roughnes,* then gave *dresse,*
> Vexing rude *subjects* into *comlinesse.*
>
> (pp. 512–13)

The image of the forge conveys more than the primacy placed on careful, even laborious craftsmanship; Cartwright minimizes simple imitation and stresses the poet's individuality. Jonson's "Starre," he insists, "was *judgement* onely, and right *sense,* / *Thy selfe* being to *thy selfe* an *influence*" (p. 513).

Cartwright's conception of this self dominates the second half of the tribute. Aggressively and at times defensively, the poem dismisses charges about Jonson's slavish adherence to the ancients and his waning capabilities. Where lesser poets "cannot stand," Cartwright insists Jonson remains unsurpassed: he alone "put'st true passions on," and he alone "Improv'd farre more" the ancient virtues in his poetry. Though the poem does not make the Jonsonian distinction between imitation and plagiarism, or kidnapping,[29] it too recognizes that great writers transform rather than appropriate traditions into their own creations. Unlike the lesser lights they rise above narrow, selfish interests and encompass the world beyond themselves. Cartwright distinguishes Jonson from others who "transcribe *themselves,* and not the *age*"; and he stresses that "Things *common* . . . stampt by *thee* grow thence *thine owne.*" Where others pandered their base talents, the poem's triumphant conclusion asserts, Jonson aspired to greater heights of virtuous nobility:

> Secure then of *thy* merit, thou didst hate
> That servile base dependance upon *fate*:

> Successe thou ne'r thoughtst *vertue,* nor that fit,
> Which *chance,* and th'*ages* fashion did make hit.
>
> (p. 515)

Jonson stands undaunted in this world, like the noble creators of his society both he and Cartwright praise, because he too is his own ruler: "*Thy* thoughts were their owne Lawrell, and did win / That best applause of being crown'd within" (p. 515). But in likening the aged and infirm poet to an ancient and bare oak, the final image and its traditional symbol of monarchy also become for Cartwright a source of nurture as well as an object of veneration. In the end this nourishment and not solely the strength determines Cartwright's salute to his weathered though unbeaten friend:

> When we shall feed on *refuse offalls,* when
> We shall from *corne* to *akornes* turne agen;
> Then shall we see that these two *names* are one,
> JOHNSON and *Poetry,* which now are gone.
>
> (p. 516)

Recalling Jonson's "Ode to Himself," the final lines appropriately culminate the poem's detailed recreation of the uncompromising virtue Jonson embodies in his poetry. At one with himself, like Killigrew and Fletcher, he epitomizes in his life and work Cartwright's belief that inner and outer worth are inseparable.

A final series of poems, the elegies, often manifests this inseparability in the extreme. The most numerous among the commemorative poems, their adaptations of a well-established form and its predictable pattern of tribute dominate the last part of the 1651 edition. In addition to the nobles honored in the three memorial volumes Oxford issued, the poems often elegize little-known men, women, and children whose deaths may have claimed Cartwright's atttention once he entered holy orders. Beyond the commonplace consolation a minister might address to his congregation of mourners, these poems memorialize individuals whose lives exemplify a laudable completeness unusual even in this conventional form of licensed exaggeration. The elegies commemorating the deaths of women, in particular, strain hyperbole in their attempts to capture the "Ample Vertues" they most commonly associate with "Mind." Paradoxically, those whose actions have left little impression on the world around them embody in the most rarefied form the oneness Cartwright idealizes.

On earth women possessed with minds "So undefil'd, so Beautious, so Refin'd" become generalized embodiments of mankind's original potential. Although several of Jonson's elegies in *Underwood* also stress the perfection of noble ladies' minds, none approaches Cartwright's recognition "that the Mind / Like the first Paradise may unrefind / Boast Native Glories" (p. 543).

Set against conventional images and perfect in their physical beauty, obscure women such as Abigail Long, Lady Newburgh, and Mrs. Ashford are seen to manifest inwardly "All, all the Vertue that on Earth did dwell" (p. 545). Attempts to list their achievements, however, fall short of Donne's soaring celebration of Elizabeth Drury, and Cartwright resorts to the elegist's ploy of inexpressiblity. The "Something" that escapes "Lame Expression" places these virtuous women above mortal corruption and intimates their celestial attributes. Actions can be minimized or ignored in the poems because they are synonymous with being. "Goodness her Soul, not Action, was," the elegy to the unknown Mrs. Ashford contends,

> and She
> Found it the same to do well and to be;
> So perfect that her speculation might
> Have made her self the bound of her own sight;
> And her Mind thus her Mind contemplating
> In brief at once have been the Eye and thing.
>
> (p. 552)

An extreme expression of the gathered self, this bounded being moves the community of mourners to admiration and even inspiration. Great promise also determines the responses in the elegies to men, although here the deaths of even minor lords and forgotten commoners move Cartwright to reassert the need for active virtue.

The death of young Lord Henry Stafford occasions a eulogy that defines the essential nature of this noble behavior. The poem written for a memorial volume requested by the undistinguished lord's family understandably accentuates the honor of the Stafford name, but the consoling sentiments about hereditary worth reveal a characteristic insistence that lineage must be synonymous with virtue. The Stafford line thrives less through money and power than through "rule, & discipline,"

> Whose Vertues were as Bookes before him set,
> So that they did instruct, who did beget,
> Taught thence not to be powerfull, but know,
> Shewing he was their blood by living so.
>
> (p. 538)

A laudatory catalogue of the nobility Lord Henry would have realized fully in later life celebrates this ideal at length. Its contrasting portrait of grasping, callous noblemen draws an unusually vivid impression of the wretched fate suffered by the hapless many dependent upon the whims and vanities of the powerful few. The indictment of noblemen who feed upon the misery of their unfortunate tenants with the impunity of privilege or the pretense of national welfare is not merely a response to the social conditions preceding civil disruption. Cartwright shares the humanists' moral concern about the responsibility entailed by nobility, and he shows no reluctance to remind his social superiors of their obligations. The truly noble, in the poem's view, do not hide behind the trappings of wealth or the security of birth; because they are willing to stand scrutiny, noblemen such as Lord Henry stand foremost in the living memorial of the family lineages their virtues help to perpetuate. Instead of statues, where he might "stand Brasen," Stafford will also live on in the memories of those who understand nobility:

> Our mindes retaine this Royalty of Kings,
> Not to be bound to time, but judge of things,
> And worship, as they merit: there we doe
> Place him at height, and he stands golden too.
>
> (p. 539)

While the events of the troubling times demand praiseworthy nobles, Cartwright understands that self-possession in the unassuming is also to be valued as much as in the aristocratic. The Jonsonian echo in the description of Lord Paul Bayning, "Great unto all: / But Great by no mans Ruine" (p. 532), invites favorable comparison of his estate with Penshurst; and the tribute to his "round and solid mind" testifies to the merit of a lord who ruled others equally as well as himself. In maintaining the distinction between the self-centered and the centered self, a short, measured "Epitaph on Mr. *Poultney*" decorously and simply acknowledges the passing of a friend, master, and husband who lived his quiet life "True to himself and Others."[30] Along with the Baynings and the Staffords, Poultney merits recognition as an undesigning man "Who made these words grow useless *Mine* and *Thine*" (p. 547). Each in his everyday life approaches Cicero's ideal as he strives "to contribute to the general good by an interchange of acts of kindness, by giving and receiving, and thus by our skill, our industry, and our talents to cement human society more closely together."[31] With his country at the threshold of civil unrest, Cartwright includes among these noble individuals the antiquarian Sir Henry Spelman, a man whose steadying influence and uncompromising principles shaped a life of research and writing selflessly devoted to public good: "Nor Hope, Nor Faction, bought thy Mind to side, / Conscience depos'd all Parts, and was sole Guide" (p. 550). When the outbreak of civil war divided the nation and frustrated peaceful pursuits, like-minded individuals had fewer opportunities "for things that are morally right and that conduce to a good and happy life, or to the pursuits of science and learning."[32] The times then demanded the ideal of valorous devotion impressively recognized in "Vpon the death of the Right valiant Sir *Bevill Grenvill* Knight," Cartwright's triumphant celebration of the courageous soul indifferent to circumstances and committed to deeds "not only great and in the highest degree useful, but extremely arduous and laborious and fraught with danger."[33]

One of the last poems he wrote, Cartwright's addition to the verses published by Oxford in 1643 is also one of his finest. His elegy to the Oxford graduate who fought against the Scots in the Bishops' Wars, upheld the royalist position in the parliamentary conflicts, and died a hero's death at Lansdown praises Grenville's exploits with unmistakable conviction and grandeur. A note of embattled partisanship deepens in fervor, and a scornful edge tempers the poem's exaltant strain. In his certainty that a "Diviner Fury" inspired Grenville to lead his troops in the face of death, Cartwright joins the other Oxford poets in their contempt for the rebels who could not destroy this valiant spirit. His insistence that they "cannot Conquer, cause ye dare not Dye" is made in the belief that selfless courage transcends time. At the head of his stand of pikes, Sir Bevil Grenville presents a striking contrast to the men of peace so often praised, yet he embodies in his stand the ideals underlying all of Cartwright's commendatory verse.

The poem's initial contrasts leave no doubt about their nature. The anaphora, balance, and point in the opening verse paragraph reveal Cartwright at his best:

> Not to be wrought by Malice, Gaine, or Pride,
> To a Compliance with the Thriving Side;
> Not to take Armes for love of Change, or Spight,
> But only to maintaine Afflicted Right;
> Not to dye vainely in pursuit of Fame,
> Perversely seeking after Voyce and Name;
> Is to Resolve, Fight, Dye, as Martyrs doe:
> And thus did He, Souldier, and Martyr too.
>
> (p. 555)

Against this image of temperate and unselfish resolution, the poem opposes then dismisses the circumspect men of policy. Less rigidly patterned verse emphasizes the need for "well-weighd Reason" and active engagement when the laws and rights of state and church are subject to the ambitions of rebel fury. Grenville's commitment, "Whole and Free," fulfills with a particularly satisfying and emphatic note the pattern of virtue familiar in Cartwright's poetry. A long sentence depicting the considered and courageous motives that prompted this "Generous Heart" to undertake a selfless and perilous cause ends appropriately: "The Building still was suited to the Ground, / Whence every Action issu'd Full and Round" (p. 556). And once in action Grenville's firmness appears unmistakable in still another of Cartwright's fundamental ideals:

> When now th' Incensed Rebell proudly came
> Downe, like a Torrent without Bank, or Damm;
> When Undeserv'd Successe urg'd on their force,
> That Thunder must come downe to stop their Course,

> Or Grenville must step in; Then Grenville stood,
> And with Himselfe oppos'd, and checkt the Flood.
>
> (p. 556)

He stands the foundation upon which enduring values are built, and when he falls, the man who "offred All" to the church and state continues in death to give.

Grenville inspires all good men who see and hear his exploits. On the battlefield the "Devoted Stand" in the place of their fallen leader, "And the Dead conquer'd, whiles the Living slew." Cartwright scornfully contrasts their steadfastness with the wavering parliamentarian forces. Unlike the noble Grenville, the opposing leader's stature depends solely upon the course of the battle, for without the inner constancy Cartwright admires, such stature is vulnerable to shifting fortunes. With considerable emotional intensity Cartwright insists that in the end Grenville's death must prove a fortunate fall. Because his was a life of nobility and not merely of renown, he stands and lives again among the exalted in Cartwright's poetry, a hero who embodies "Glory for People, Substance for the Wise."

Civil war has in effect changed the context of the praise and not its essential values, a transformation equally apparent in the other fine tribute written in the final months of Cartwright's life, "On the *Queen's* Return from the Low Countries." Cartwright avoids the comparisons to Venus, Astraea, and Christ common in the poems gathered at Oxford to celebrate the queen's return in February 1643 from her search for royalist support; and he concentrates instead on her luminous and "gather'd Mind." Henrietta Maria no longer appears solely as the loving wife and bountiful mother; she is the conquering heroine:

> Courage was cast about Her like a Dresse
>     Of solemne Comelinesse;
> A gather'd Mind, and an untroubled Face
>     Did give Her dangers grace.
> Thus arm'd with Innocence, secure they move,
> Whose Highest Treason is but Highest Love.
>
> (p. 554)

This depiction of the queen's fearless, unwavering commitment to the nation's duty has considerable historical basis, for she did heroically face both an unusually stormy North Sea and shelling by parliamentary ships,[34] but her devoted service gains meaning as well as glorification in Cartwright's poem. In the welcoming verse the queen, whose devoted love had inspired so many tributes, becomes a star joined in movement with another celestial body: "Such was Her mind to th' Kings, in all was done; / The Agents Diverse, but the Action One" (p. 554). This singular love shines undiminished by the "Godly Lyes" and "Holy Perjuries" Cartwright excoriates in a contrasting image of rebel greed and hypocrisy censored in the 1651 edition. Their base motivations give additional luster to the queen's behavior, which appears to radiate a "double Beame." Her splendor emanates from the mind and conscience Cartwright has abstractly honored in his elegies to women and now praises in the specific actions of the queen. "Much shining by Her selfe, but more by Them," Henrietta Maria gives new meaning to the creative force of love; enshrined in Cartwright's poem "Her presence is our Guard, our Strength, our Store; / The cold snatch some flames thence, the valiant more" (p. 555).

The inspiring examples of Henrietta Maria and Grenville epitomize the vision in Cartwright's poetry. Despite a later tendency toward strident denunciation of all who challenge church and crown, the poems avoid the negative partisanship increasingly apparent among some royalists. Cartwright shares their fears of ignorant, greedy faction, and he is attuned to the martial fervor of the ensuing war, but he never allows denigration to displace celebration. Nothing in the events prior to his death in November 1643 seriously undermines his belief in the enduring values of England's traditional institutions. Cartwright actively supports the continuity and order embodied in the university and the episcopacy as well as the monarchy, and he lauds still more their capacity for nurturing the nation. Throughout his poetry Cartwright consistently praises men and women of conscience and compassion who have the potential to affect those around them. An emphasis on the rounded or gathered self underscores the indebtedness to Jonson and his classical heritage, but the self-sufficiency Cartwright admires has none of the withdrawal sometimes mistakenly associated with the earlier poet. Nor, surprisingly, does the poetry offer a religious consolation. In the poems divine providence gives no assurance that the royalist cause will triumph; and aside from conventional elegiac resolve, appeals to religious faith are conspicuously absent. Cartwright instead expresses a humanist faith in the willingness and ability of individuals to nurture national well-being. Henrietta Maria and Grenville are striking but not unique illustrations of the nobility that reaches beyond class. Theirs is a circle of giving scribed largely by the unselfishness Cartwright echoes in his own poetic acts.

During the 1630s and early 1640s, when England slipped from the decade of peace into civil war, the royalty, nobility, and commoners who formed this circle of celebration offered the Caroline world a consistent and serious vision. In praising them Cartwright did more than flatter the powerful or support prevailing policy; overcoming the pitfalls inherent in occasional poetry, he found enduring value in firm, principled contemporaries. Read in their own right and not with mistaken preconceptions of an era seemingly caught up in the fulsome praise of elaborate masques and cynical courtiers, the poems reveal considerable artistic integrity. A "son" of Jonson, Cart-wright assimilates the older poet's moral and aesthetic legacy without losing his own individuality. In the best traditions of Renaissance imitation and panegyric, Cartwright reasserts humanistic ideals in a forceful public poetry that does not sacrifice the uncompromising self-sufficiency it values so highly.

# 3

# George Daniel and the "Onlie True Content"

WHILE the Oxford University poets drew together, first to celebrate the monarchy and then to welcome the king into their midst, England gradually became divided by a war that no one expected and none thought would last long. Once Charles raised his standard at Nottingham and then centered his support at Oxford, the nation seemed to split along a north-west diagonal into royalist and parliamentarian camps, but the loyalties on both sides were often not clearly apparent or always wholehearted. Among the king's supporters in the divided county of Yorkshire, an obscure gentryman from the insignificant town of Beswick voiced at length both the hopes and misgivings of a generation that saw the high expectations of the Caroline reign end in the defeat and execution of the king. Before the course of war forced many of his countrymen to flee the court for the country or at the least to yearn for a Horatian rural solitude, George Daniel had found his own modest Sabine contentment on the banks of the river Devia. From the relative seclusion of his Yorkshire manor, Daniel explored the role of the poet and the value of poetry in a period of monumental upheaval. His often candid and sometimes tortuous reactions to the troubled decades reveal a royalist allegiance, but his partisanship does not distort the perspective of a writer who remains sensitive to the limitations as well as the values of the king's cause.

Throughout the long folio manuscript he gathered together but never published, Daniel struggles to define an active virtue suited to the 1640s. Unlike Cartwright, who died before the royalist fortunes began to decline, Daniel discovered in the years of military and political defeat the wisdom of withdrawal. Caught between the desire to serve and the need to retire, he explores at length the conflict Seneca addresses in the *Moral Essays*. Daniel appreciates both sides of the argument that the wise man "will engage in public affairs unless something prevents him" and that "we ought indeed to withdraw from the forum and public life."[1] He never abandons a humanist commitment to the state, but increasingly his poems tend toward the Senecan resolve, "Nature intended me to do both—to be active and to have leisure for contemplation. And really I do both, since even the contemplative life is not devoid of action."[2] The Stoic belief in the possibility of both retirement and service ultimately leads Daniel, as it had Thomas and Harry Coningsby, toward the liberty Boethius and Lipsius also earlier found in Seneca's contention, "We have been born under a monarchy; to obey God is freedom."[3] George Daniel's uneven and at times contradictory poems record the perplexities and hopes of his troubled search.

The distinctive poetic and political loyalties of Daniel's works are obvious. "A Vindication of Poesie" and "An Essay; Endevouring to ennoble our English Poesie" pay lip service to the classical poets and dismiss Chaucer in favor of late sixteenth- and early seventeenth-century writers. Shakespeare receives passing attention; but Sidney, Spenser, and Jonson, "These justly wee may call / Fathers."[4] Among the many "Sons" are the playwrights and poets who gathered at Falkland's Great Tew or moved in Charles's court; in fact Daniel's list duplicates most of the contenders for the crown of bays in Suckling's "The Wits."[5] His unreserved admiration for "The reverent Donne" also reflects the vogue Donne enjoyed among the first generation to have access to his published works, and he also praises other authors celebrated in important contemporary commemoratives. His poems written in memory of Jonson and on the occasion of the Beaumont-Fletcher edition as well as an attack against the parliamentarian poet Wither and the tributes to Herbert, Browne, and Ogilby are probably not the result of membership in a literary circle or of personal acquaintanceships. Though his father's name appears among those who matriculated at Cambridge's Caius College, no records exist of Daniel's formal education or of his association with the patrons and publishers who shaped the royalist coteries.[6] A self-portrait dated 1649 shows the author at his writing desk against a background of books, and this library may have been his major link with the Caroline literary milieu. Another crudely executed oil painting and a series of apparently early poems about poetry further illuminate a writer who appears bookish, even reclusive, and yet like other country gentry, unusually aware of the world beyond his Yorkshire estate.[7]

The image of Daniel attired in Roman costume and seated with his writing materials in a rural setting evokes a classical tradition that his poems affirm. The contentment that "A Pastorall Ode" finds in rural simplicity far removed from urban strife recalls quite specifically the freedom Horace values in his epistles on the country life.[8] The unrestrained pursuit of virtue that Horace tells Quinctius and Maecenas he finds only in a life removed from the tyranny of both materialistic and popular success remains among Daniel's paramount themes. His "freeborne Muse" will not, "An Epode" declares, become subservient to the dictates of either the powerful or the multitudes:

> To noe Collossus, could I ever bend;
> Or at the Court attend

With my owne Sin, and Follie in a Sheet;
  To prostrate, at the feet
Of painted greatnes.

(p. 27)

The next poem in the manuscript's ordering lauds this uncompromising commitment to truth in the "Father of the Age" and "our Great Lord of witt," Ben Jonson, but another poem also dated 1638 recognizes how easily the London life of literary fame can lead to compromise and servitude. In counterbalancing the recognition and inspiration London offers the poet with the innocence and peace found in the country, Daniel's eclogue does not, however, unduly weight the dialogue in favor of Yorkshire. The pastoral speaker Strephon concedes in his arguments on behalf of a rural happiness, "'Tis true, there is noe ioy but to the Mind; / You, yours in Citties; I, mine here doe find" (2:143). Although Strephon admits that complete happiness may elude mankind, he opts for the contentment and freedom of "A mind and bodie sound, in safe retire":

> I rather here with Silvia chuse to sitt,
> And Sing of harmles Love and Sober witt;
> Of Innocence, of Truth, of Peace, or what
> Calme fancie moves; then chatter to the rate
> Of my Lord's bountie.

(2:143)

The poem's epigraph from "Eclogue VI" recalls Virgil's defense of his early sylvan muse, and later Strephon likens himself to Virgil when he confesses his fond hope,

> perchance,
> Poor Devia, fameles now, may yet Advance
> Something to memorie, and create some new
> Glorie vnto her Current; knowne by fewe.

(2:141)

Without the fiction of the eclogue, Daniel voices the same aspiration in "To Time and Honour." Daniel would join Sidney, Spenser, Jonson, and a host of lesser contemporary poets in their celebration of England's greatness, but he disavows the glory that may reward them:

> Suffice it I may sing upon thy flood,
> Neglected Humber; or my Muse (less proud)
> Sport in the Sedges, of my neighbouring Streame,
> Poore as my verse, neither deserving name;
> And may the village where I had my birth
> Enclose as Due, my Bodie in her Earth.

(p. 16)

In retiring modesty he seeks the example if not the success of Horace and Virgil. Where he can "Center my Joyes, in a poore Countrie Life," George Daniel at first narrowly limits his world.

He also draws inspiration from the wisdom literature of the Bible. A paraphrase of Ecclesiasticus dated 11 January 1639 conveys in quite effective couplets the epigrammatic observations of the unknown Jesus or Ben-Sira, the son of Sirach.[9] In his induction to the paraphrase, Daniel considers the Hebrew teacher another Solomon "For teaching vertue & Instruction," and he admits his attraction to the "darke sayings" embodied in this apocryphal book. Modestly his prefatory comments express the belief "that verse may Comprehend / Fullnes of Matter" (2:212) when the lines are illuminated by divine light. A pilgrim in a shadowy land, Daniel longs for the inward illumination that will guide him toward the cherished Sion. Though Daniel acknowledges his own literary accomplishments in a summary of the poems he has written, he denies in this paraphrase any poetic ambitions. The glory and the honor are God's; the wisdom of this biblical book, however, becomes part of Daniel's lifetime preoccupation.

For him Ecclesiasticus holds together in proverbial form an often Stoic wisdom that informs the lives of both private and public fulfillment. An Old Testament wisdom rooted in the fear of the Lord fosters a reverence for antiquity and authority particularly appealing to a young royalist confronted with the threatening Bishops' Wars. Ecclesiasticus exhorts its readers, "With all thy Soule fear God, & venerate / His owne anointed, & his Consecrate" (2:235); and it assures them that rulers who curb their pride and bow to a just fear of the divine will flourish. Not surprisingly, constancy and patience are also emphasized among the tenets of this wisdom, and the wise man praised in this work values the Stoic assumption that souls "are more free while they are engaged in contemplation of the divine mind, and less free when they are joined to bodies, and still less free when they are bound by earthly fetters."[10] Ecclesiasticus insists,

> He, only he, is wise, who can neglect
> The Sordid end of Mortalls, and direct
> His purgéd Soule to the clear Region
> Of holy things, by Contemplation;
> Labours for Knowledge, & revolves the writt
> Of profound ancients, till he compass it.
>
> (3:82)

For him this wisdom is the source of greatest joy, but its bounds are evident. The glories of God elude even those who contemplate their splendors, for as Daniel would also come to realize, "His worke is perfect All, but Man is Weake / To Apprehend the height, much less, to Speake" (3:95). The celebration of glory, however, also encompasses the illustrious men who ruled wisely, and the last part of Ecclesiasticus recalls their fame at length. The justly famous announcement "Now let's the Praise of famous Men rehearse" initiates a survey of Israel's rulers that sweeps across the centuries. An epigraph from Virgil on the title page of his paraphrase suggests that Daniel appreciated especially a history with epic breadth, but an afterword stresses the greater magnificence of the "glorious Light" and "Divine fire" he longs to celebrate.

The first of the manuscript poems underscores his desire in "An Addresse: by the Author: Not Impertinent to the Following Poems." This lengthy and diffuse rumination may actually have been written later than the biblical paraphrase, at a time when "The Drum beats loud, to fright our Villages" (p. 4) and swords have displaced pens. Faced with this hostile and indeed incomprehensible world, Daniel turns inward. The "Freedome, and love of Truth," which for him are "all I boast," lead him away from what he considers to be his country's hypocritical pursuit of religion. In humble anonymity Daniel longs to find the sphere of wisdom the Roman Stoic Aurelius created within his mind. But Daniel's avowed intention "To laugh at fortune, and the world despise" does not presuppose an indifference to his nation's plight. Although the poem commends the solace and mirth of wine and contemplation, it shares too Seneca's reluctance to condone an Epicurean disengagement from public affairs. Despite its *contemptus mundi* strain, "An Addresse: by the Author" expresses Daniel's instinctive faith in the service luminous individuals can give to their country. Like Cartwright and Carew he is inspired specifically by the wonder of the monarchy, for "Something, under what Name, I doe not know," Daniel admits, "Strikes me, in Majestie" (p. 7). When he beholds "Our Royall Master, in Afflictions old; / But vig'orous, in vertue" (p. 7), the sight of Charles fills Daniel with hope as well as awe, and he cannot turn his back on the benighted times. Tacitly, this royalist allegiance also seems to assume, as Seneca argues, that "wherever he secretes his leisure" an individual "should be willing to benefit the individual man and mankind by his intellect, his voice, and his counsel."[11] The volumes of poetry Daniel composed in rural solitude reveal in any case his not entirely successful struggle to write the truth and to celebrate a light increasingly obscured in the chaos of Charles I's final years.

This direction is apparent in his first ambitious poem, "The Genius of this Great and glorious Ile." Described in the manuscript as an "imperfect" work written in 1637, the long poem develops the conventional Caroline view of England's peace and prosperity. The Genius of England who appears to the poet traces the country's "happines and peace" down to the Tudor period. A seventeenth-century audience would not have objected to the unsympathetic dismissal of Henry VIII as "A Profane, Profuse, Proud Polygamist,"[12] and it would have agreed that the idyllic vision of abundance had its birth in the reign of "blest Eliza." By the middle decades of the seventeenth century, memories of the troubled last years of Tudor rule had faded, and many shared Daniel's nostalgia for that golden era of creativity.[13] Similarly, praise for the reigning Stuart, the new "Charlemaine," and celebration of the nation's tranquillity are, it has been seen, common hyperbole in the many university and court panegyrics. Daniel's summary of the past and his praise of the present, however, go beyond chauvinism or flattery; his emphasis upon the prosperity and creativity associated with peace accentuates an abhorrence of war.

The narrative adds its voice to the Virgilian irony other contemporaries have begun to stress. Before the poem commends the peaceful rule of Elizabeth and her successors, a passage in its brief survey of the internecine War of the Roses exclaims, "O Dulce Bellum! but they doe not know / The fears and Dangers which on it attend, / Who vtter thus" (1:169). With the reign of Charles I, the poem again returns to the folly of war. England's Genius exhorts her children to contrast their present happiness with the carnage of the past, and she urges them to compare their state to that of Germany ravaged by the Thirty Years' War. Daniel, who admired Carew, might conceivably have read a copy of his elegy on Gustavus Adolphus, and he would have encountered praise of England's bountiful peace in *Coelum Britannicum,* the other Caroline masques, and the university commemoratives; but his poem gives special emphasis to the belief, "how sweet is warre / To giddie Faction! and all Change how deare" (1:184). Unlike the poem's sometimes artificial praise of England's earlier glory, a new stridency in the verse communicates the immediacy of the poet's concern. Anticipating Clarendon's famous description of the halcyon pre-civil war period, Daniel encourages his country to "Turne in your Squinted Eyes, and Seriouslie / Learne how to prize the blessing you enioye" (1:185). Though the prospect of actual war with Scotland or any other nation is remote in 1637, the poem cannot conceal its dismay with shortsighted countrymen who refuse to see in Charles's reign "What Happines, noe Nation ever knew" (1:185).

Daniel believes England owes its extraordinary prosperity to the king's guidance, and he insists upon unquestioning loyalty to him. Later poems declare that the institution of the monarchy possesses an aura that Daniel can neither analyze nor resist; here England's Genius asserts without reservation,

> what
> I am, or can be, I must pay the King;
> Hee is my Gvide: Why should I derogate
> From my owne right? 'Tis noe Discoursive thing,
>     High Maiestie, but vnder heaven doth bring
> An awe, and more; a distant Reverence,
> Beyond dispute claiming obedience.

(1:182)

Daniel demonstrates no better than the other Caroline panegyrists how the king's reign ensures the nation's prosperity, and he does not explain majesty's hold upon the people. The reverential awe he accords the monarch along with perhaps his fear of disruption leads him to insist that kings are above scrutiny. Although the onset of war later modifies Daniel's unquestioned loyalty, at this point he pleads, "Oh, Touch him not, nor looke vpon / The Royall throne, but with Devotion" (1:183).

Poets, he would agree with Carew and Cartwright, have a particular obligation to uphold the monarchy. Within the poem's vision of history, the association the earlier Caroline writers also made between peace and creativity implies a mutual dependence that becomes explicit by the end of the poem. Elizabeth and her Stuart successors have created an atmosphere in which literature has flourished, and in turn writers both confirm and perpetuate this era through their own creativity. Monarch and poet best meet their mutual needs when the source of peace and fruitfulness, the king, also becomes the inspiration of praise and celebration. The poetry England's Genius promotes seems natural and effortless:

> Know all perfection, in your gracious King.
> Leave far-fet fiction, and in truth display
> > A vertue; 'bove what Fancie e're could say.
> Goe here, beyond your selves; let Poesie here
> Bove Fiction, in a higher Truth appeare.
>
> > > > (1:187)

More strongly than Carew, Daniel encourages the celebration possible only in this "happie Ile," or Hesperides, where peace and poetry together flourish. With an earnestness and conviction not equally apparent in the sophisticated court masques and in the sometimes perfunctory university poems, he envisions in the present Stuarts the epitome of past glory and the hope of future splendor. With Carew and Cartwright he shares the belief that all who would celebrate greatness will find it in Charles and Henrietta Maria, for they inspire even the simple country poet to sing the glories of their names.

Celebration also preoccupies Daniel in his other early historical poem, a narrative written in 1639 of Warwick's role in the War of the Roses. The Latin quotation from Horace on the title page of *Vervicensis* emphasizes the obscurity of many unsung heroes, and the ghost who appears in search of a poet to record the fame that will then allow Warwick's shade to pass with Charon into the underworld also acknowledges the power of poetry. An aside on the greatness of Henry V is unequivocal in its belief that virtuous actions will live in "Truth's bright Annals" when the transitory memorials of brass and marble have long vanished. Daniel has no illusions about time's remorselessness, but in this work he does not raise the fear present in later poems that poetry itself may be an illusory triumph over "greedie Time, and merceles Decay." Warwick appears briefly in the previous poem a worthy figure of "Courage and high Spirit," and *Vervicensis* now holds out the hope that his name may be saved from oblivion.

Daniel is circumspect, however, about the significance Warwick gains in time. Throughout his poetry Daniel adheres to the view that time repeats itself, and he seems constrained in *Vervicensis* to reconcile the narrative about the famous kingmaker Warwick with the rebellion brewing in 1639. An "Argument and Apologie" assures the reader that the poem "Is not to move pretences, how / Designes may be revivéd now" (1:127); instead Warwick's fate should be seen "More clearlie" as a warning to those who misinterpret the leniency a monarch displays and attempt to "worke theire Ends." Discreet parallels between the weak rulers of Warwick's era and the present king are, in any case, unclear in the narrative's account of the dangers facing government. Daniel accepts the medieval and Renaissance view that all men in power stand vulnerable to fate, and he reveals the common mistrust of "giddie-headed Popularitie." Throughout its chronicle of Warwick's shifting allegiances, *Vervicensis* recognizes how easily men of policy can shape the loyalties of nobility and commoners alike, yet the poem also understands how the crown contributes to its own undoing. Without stressing the tacit reproof of his own king, Daniel emphasizes the danger of rebellion when a ruler like Henry VI does not assert himself in a forceful, consistent policy.

He has only praise for Charles I when he first considers England's immediate crisis. The poem itself on the "Royall Expedition against the Scotts" is lost, but two addresses prefacing and concluding the missing work suggest that Daniel envisioned national honor and glory in the king's "great Designe." Both poems also express at much greater length the poet's own prospects of royal service. Conscious of the subordinate role the muse now assumes in a world at arms, Daniel offers the king a commemoration that may withstand the ages. His tribute to the power of poetry becomes, moreover, a graceful compliment to the king's ability to inspire writers as well as soldiers. Poems, Daniel concludes, may outlive the annals of history and the memorials of stone through the enduring nature of their subject, the king. Created and creator reverse roles in Daniel's belief that even the modest poet gains a name for himself when he sings the glories of a great and just ruler.

The failure of the king's Scottish campaign and the threat of further conflict frustrate the poet. At first, in "A Strange Maye," Daniel seems optimistic about the imminent renewal of the halcyon climate envisioned earlier. Although the poem avoids specific reference to England's difficulties, its description of an extraordinarily fruitful May blighted by the frost accompanying a northern wind alludes quite probably to the outbreak of the Second Bishops' War in May 1640. Daniel's hope that the period of seemingly miraculous productivity will soon recur with the ascendence of

"The Sun, in June" holds out the promise of the manuscript's first poem that Charles's "illustrous Beams" will restore the nation's unparalleled prosperity. Another poem entitled "After a storme, going a hawking" does not, however, fully envision the tranquillity lost in the unexpected disturbance. Rather than join the others in their country sport now that the intemperate times have been relieved, Daniel seeks the quiet of his study only to realize in this meditative poem the elusiveness of his own figurative hawking. Where Lovelace will later find in the struggle between the falcon and heron a complex emblem of the civil war, Daniel compares the hunt to a solitary recreation in which "bright reason" soars into the realm of truth. But the mood that likens poetry to the noble flight of the falcon easily slides into that of the poem "Vanitie." Daniel sees that the figurative falcon may escape control, and he laments the fall from original perfection. While "After a storme, going a hawking" is not as bleak as "Vanitie," its emphasis on man's limited and false perception tempers the poem's initially positive response to the gentle relief. Daniel's disquiet reflects, in part, the uncertainties of the nation's future, and when the northern storm brings the "Cloud of Calamitie" again, he openly admits his misgivings.

The rest of the title dates this poem in the period after the calamity "had somewhile overspread vs, and the whole Kingdome plunged in warre. 1.6.4.1.," a time when poetry can no longer flourish. Even though civil war did not break out until the next year, Daniel recognizes that "Composed fancies" have no place in a disruptive world whose "stormie daies" demand "vnpolite fformes." Much of the poem nostalgically recalls the freedom and repose of an untroubled study, where sense and fancy soar with the muse toward the essential verities. Daniel wants to believe that this ideal can be attained, a desire that may produce the sometimes unconvincing and naive affirmations of earlier poems; but the immediate realities frustrate this search. Threatened with the country's growing instability and denied a sympathetic audience, he realizes that the sensitive poet's only hope lies in the future. With peace now a distant prospect, Daniel seeks solace in the anticipation of a time when the return of Astraea will restore the nation's golden era. Although he admits this restoration now appears remote, he ingenuously looks toward his own poetic triumph. Then he hopes to rise on the wings of his muse beyond the most honored classical and contemporary poets: "Then, my dear muses, wee may meet and Sing / In Peace Secure, the fears, which wee now bring" (1:95).

Now he turns increasingly inward. Following the series of poems on the growing storm, a piece simply titled "Freedome" reconsiders less ambitious expressions of country retirement. Daniel's contentment with rural pleasure and his reservations about a demanding public life recall Jonson's "To Sir Robert Wroth" and its Horatian tradition. Daniel's commitment to the simpler world lacks, however, Jonson's satiric edge, and his preference for unvexed hours of playful musing concedes that this freedom is possible only "if the rigour of the times allow." Daniel refuses to sentimentalize the realities of the 1640s, and in the end his conviction falters. He wants to believe that freedom can exist in patience if not in cherished serenity:

> if the rigour of the times allow,
> I am content; if they will not, I know
> A pleasure 'bove their Malice; and the close
> Barr's of a prison, cannot hinder those,
> My owne free thoughts; where I sometime may have
> A visit from the Muses, which shall save
> My Name from Envie, and oblivion.
>
> (p. 45)

But Daniel's assertion lacks the lyric forcefulness apparent later in Lovelace's similar defiance, and he strikes at best a posture of heroic bravado. He is more convincing when he considers the Stoic contentment possible in the privacy of the countryside. This freedom thrives in the "wholsome withdrawing place" Lipsius praises, where "the mind lifteth vp and advanceth it self."[14] The recreation Lipsius's treatise *Of Constancie* describes as the "exercise of wisedom" aptly characterizes the contemplative retirement that Daniel pursues in a central group of poems, *Scattered Fancies*. "Here I either plie my selfe with diligent and earnest reading," Lipsius anticipates Daniel, "or els sowe in my heart some seed of good cogitations, and thereby lay vp some wholsome lessons in my minde, as it were weapons in an armorie, which are alwayes ready with me at hand against the force and mutabilitie of Fortune. So soone as I put my foote within that place, I bid all vile and seruile cares abandon me, and lifting vp my head as vpright as I may, I contemne the delights of the prophane people, & the great vanitie of humane affaires."[15]

Forty-nine odes gathered together in 1645 represent the "scattered fancies" of a poet who continues to record his troubled though not, he claims, depressed responses to "this long winter of generall Calamitie." On several occasions he also says that these musing and effusive poems represent "Noe proper Treatise"; they are a form of solitary recreation intended to replace the substantial poetry no longer possible in a tumultuous era. Restrained by fears of censorship and unwilling to heed the dictates of critics and the demands of flattery, Daniel develops the themes of freedom and contentment in the various moods that "privilie expresse / The summe of all my Thoughts" (p. 128). With a candor and earnestness befitting the intimacy of his ruminations, he admits these are the "Simple Thought" of an unassuming poet: they are

> Slender Odes, to the varietie
> Of Chance, and Time.
> With these, I please my selfe; and sing away

> My weight of Cares, to linger out the Day
> In Liricke Rhime.
>
> (p. 150)

In these odes solace and reaffirmation depend upon a necesary detachment from the folly, passion, and madness endemic in the nation. Daniel wishes the "Sad Infants, of a groneing Time" could emulate Pliny's infant at Saguntum and "shrinke Nameles" back into their mothers' wombs, but those already caught up in the civil strife can seek comfort in the knowledge that theirs is a "Common Lot." The most specific commentary on the revolution, "Ode VII," accepts the present evil as part of a timeless conflict between tyranny and justice destined to continue until the end of the world. Though its opening stanzas contend "Who this Should be, the Judging Reader knowes" (p. 80), the poem's image of a tyrannical leader surrounded by an ignorant multitude probably does not represent Pym, Cromwell, or any other specific revolutionary leader.[16] The monstrous figure is one more manifestation of the evil in the epic struggles of both David and Hercules; it is, more generally, the satanic force that has been foiled "A thousand, thousand Times." Seen in this context, the present parliamentary tyranny loses some of its immediate horror, while the assurance of order within the apparent chaos affords further comfort. Daniel also bolsters his own spirit with the cryptic belief,

> There is an Art taught, where true Arts are taught;
> (For tis not strength alone
> Prevailes against his bone)
> Will foyle him soone, and bring his strength to naught.
>
> (p. 82)

The poem never suggests where this school exists; however, its final stanzas seem to place it somewhere in the solitary communion with the muses:

> Then muster up Collossus, to affright
> Stupid, and retchles Men;
> Who know, nor how, nor when,
> Nor why, they yeild; their exercise, thy might;
>
> And I will Sing away my Common Cares,
> With everie Sand of Time;
> Where Rapture shall Sublime
> My new-borne Soule, in an immortall verse.
>
> (p. 82)

In this and the other odes the potential for re-creation as well as recreation seems contingent upon the perspective of time. Without it the survey of the present in "Ode XXXII" is oppressively pessimistic:

> See all the world unfram'd,
> Strangelie disjoynted, lamed;
> And Common Men, (who have noe project, to
> Advance their Fortunes) run a madding too;
> Sneake in their Follies; pyre
> At madnes, Misterie;
> and we may See
> The infection spread to All, in some degree.
>
> (p. 126)

But Daniel derives some solace from the knowledge that Lucian had seen a similar self-destructive vanity "And tis but now the same." Reluctant to laugh with Lucian at folly or to decry suffering that providence may have ordained, Daniel accepts his fate as part of a historical rhythm. Though this knowledge offers little hope that the poet can influence the factions and discords he abhors, it leads to the contentment and freedom Daniel cultivates.

His ideal of "Selfe Content" scorns and even defies the times it cannot hope to change. "Ode XXIII" especially and effectively pictures this ideal in the example of a lonely redbreast "Bidding defiance, to the bitter Ayre; / Upon a wither'd Spray." Perhaps the song of this solitary singer provides in the barren winter setting the singing school where Daniel earlier said true art is taught; at least it inspires the poet "To sing away, the Times uncertaintie, / Safe in my Selfe" (p. 114). Other odes specifically describe a sober, humble recreation born out of contemplation of an ineffable "Pleasure, beyond Times controule," and these poems propose to unfold the vast pages of nature's book and to sing the magnificence of its creator. On the wings of his fancy, Daniel asserts that he can "more securely ride / All winds and weathers, with a Constant Joye" (p. 90), safe from the buffets of the "Angrie Heavens." Though the odes offer no songs in this mode, they variously reaffirm Daniel's faith in a freedom that resides somewhere within the range of his muse. Certain that this ideal cannot be discovered in the worldly pursuits of power, honor, and wealth, "Ode V" contends that contentment may ultimately lie in "Innocence." There the poet's muse may be schooled in the rapture that leads beyond conventional values,

> And in the Sober heights of vertue, Clime
> To goodlie ravishment;
> Untouch't by Envie, un-impaired by Time;
> For to be free, with a heart Innocent,
> Is onlie true Content.
>
> (p. 79)

Ultimately freedom and innocence exist beyond the immediate reach of the poet, but the odes try to show that they can be approached by withdrawing inward. Daniel acknowledges in "Ode VIII" that the "wished Port of rest" eludes his wearied search, and he longs for the moment of perfect repose:

> There Centred, Rest in all her Joyes doth Rest;
> Full in her Peace, with Joy and Glorie Blest;
> Still may wee travell out our Age, in Feare,
> To find that upon Earth, which is noe where,
>> But onlie there.

(p. 84)

The next ode envisions a fulfillment imprecisely located somewhere outside the ravages of time. Like the description of tyrannical evil in "Ode VII," the vision of perfection stresses an archetypal completion not unlike the Caroline view of monarchy or the Christian anticipation of heaven:

> Here, never Ending Love
>> Runns in a liveing Streame;
>> Peace sitts under the Beame
> Of Glorie; all that move
>> Is holie, here;
>> Pale Doubt, and Feare,
> Exiled are, and Envie comes not neare.

(p. 86)

Daniel longs for a peace obviously remote from the troubled present, a tranquillity other odes seek in "the better Arts of Innocence." "Ode LVII" in particular proclaims the inward security possible even in a humble or "meane" position: "Safe in the brazen tower / Of my owne brest; let Fortune laugh or loure, / I cannot fall" (p. 164). Although other odes include traditional Stoic assurances that their author will not compromise his integrity or indulge in servile flattery, the patient endurance of Stoicism is still not Daniel's primary interest. He seeks instead by turning away from the cares of the world the "greater Libertie" that resides both within and beyond the self. "To gaine that freedome," the ode concludes, "I will loose Each part / Of man, to see my Selfe, in my owne Heart" (p. 164). The heart freed from the tyranny of misguided senses and dissociated from conventional values is "free to Truth" (p. 75). Other odes also value virtue and divinity as the ends of freedom, "Where the true pleasure lives, without controule / Of Doubt, or Feare" (p. 74); but the goal remains rapturous contemplation and praise. One of his simplest expressions of this ideal, "Ode XXII," defines such rapture as the essence of his poetry:

> Such be my Poesie: that number may
> In Clear expressions, all my Thoughts display;
>> Such Rapture fill my Thought,

> As I may utter nought,
> Beneath the dignitie, of a free Muse;
> And guided, by my Genius, Chuse
>     Objects sublime; adoreing God, the high
>     Author of Truth: such be my Poesie.

(pp. 112–13)

Daniel recognizes, however, the limits of his poetic freedom. Odes that would emulate the lark, nightingale, and falcon in song and flight ultimately realize how earthbound the muse remains. Occasionally the poems lapse into self-effacement, apologizing for "Muddled and lame" attempts to add a feeble voice to nature's hymn of praise; but the fault is not always with the poet. Daniel laments his inability to escape the fetters of mankind's dust and sins. He longs for a liberty that he at times admits his cherished innocence cannot provide:

>     how would I skip!
> In my new Robes, of Innocence and veiwe
> Things in their Causes, absolute and true.
>
>     Then, in a scornfull heat,
> And brave Disdaine, enfranchis'd would I flye,
>     To kisse that Skye,
> Wee now admire; and find a fixed Seat
>     Above the lower Region, where
>     Th' attractive Earth, I need not feare;
> But move without my Load, and at one Step
> As eas'ly mount the orbe, as downward leape.

(pp. 130–31)

Though he clings to the belief that even imperfect nature and flawed sense can glimpse if not capture the original purity of truth, the fallen state of man frustrates the contemplation of perfection, and moments of meditative musing end in sudden darkness or "Emptie Shadowes." In his moods of doubt he further questions whether the individual can ever begin to understand himself, much less attain more than a fleeting glance of the unchanging light. At these skeptical moments Daniel even reconsiders the traditional faith in Stoic self-containment. "Fortified in my Reason," he confesses in "Ode XXXIX," "once I thought / (But nought / Availes our owne Surmises) that the power / Of fortune could not Storme me. Ah, noe more" (p. 135). Yet this mood, like the others, does not dispel the general optimism of the odes. *Scattered Fancies* reflects both the faith and the doubts of a candid, musing poet who responds freely to the emotions of a troubled time. They are, Daniel adds in a postscript dated 17 July 1647, "Fragments; which were intended, not to the publike Eye, but his owne retired Fancies, to make Light that burthen which some grone under" (p. 168).

Throughout the odes he also assures himself that his poetry will express truth more substantially when peace returns. Then the constrained muse will no longer limit herself to the "soft Liricke" and "Slender Odes" designed to please rather than inspire. Once the hostile audience of critics and censors has lost its power and the stable world of peace has been reestablished, Daniel hopes to transform the ideals of the odes into an exultant "Heroicke Number." Meanwhile he consoles himself,

> I doe not yet despaire
> When silver-winged Peace againe shall Shine,
> To raise a Poesie, in everie Line,
> As high, as full, as faire.
>
> (p. 128)

The nature of this poesie remains undefined, but it is clear that security and ease are necessary. With the return of the peaceful days idealized by the earlier Caroline writers, Daniel implies, the undistracted poet can approach absolute truth with refined sensitivity, and he can communicate his perceptions to an audience unafraid to recognize merit. Although they are vague in their assertions, the odes nevertheless insist that poetry will once again "high things teach" when virtue finds true expression in a time of peace.

For the poet caught in a decade of civil strife, the pastoral eclogue meanwhile less ambitiously supplements the odes. The date 1648 on the eclogues' title page and the political allusions in the last two of them suggest that Daniel wrote four of these five dialogues during and after the completion of *Scattered Fancies*. Unlike the often personal odes, the eclogues are characterized by the detachment Francis Quarles similarly creates through conventional personae.[17] In probing, well-handled dialogue, suitably named rural figures bring together the doubts and hopes Daniel raises in his other poems. Neither speaker in any of the eclogues becomes merely a straw figure, and although Daniel's biases do not remain suppressed, the formal exchanges reveal his own conflicts in a verse unencumbered by vague musing.

With a focus and an economy missing in the odes, Daniel pursues their concern about the difficulties of seeking truth. Thus the speakers Maelibeus and Dorilus agree that the world has become stormy and contentious, but they differ over the extent to which knowledge can be found and communicated in such circumstances. Although each decries the proud wits whose persistent skepticism threatens the peace and religion of the commonwealth, neither is certain how to attain the truth—"A firme and setled Being [that] doth not move / Or floate with humane fancies, as they rove" (2:155). Once again Daniel insists flesh and words both obscure the "ray" of original perfection the soul possesses and frustrate attempts to regain the forfeited illumination. Dorilus optimistically argues that people would not differ if individuals could "make full-form'd Conceptions appeare / To others in the

Light to vs they Stand" (2:160); but despite the poem's praise of an unnamed writer, probably Sir Thomas Browne, Daniel seems to recognize that even reason's "brightest Notions" suffer when they assume the imperfect "forme of words." Apparently any sense of the absolute must remain imperfectly formed within the "Shades" of the imagination. At the end of the dialogue, the eclogue finds some consolation in the shepherds' song:

> But high and Contemplative Soules
> Can find a light beneath the Poles;
> And with firme feathers rise to see
> That Light which makes the Sun to bee.
>
> (2:162)

Contemplation and communication, it would seem, still exist at odds.

Inspiration also remains debatable. Although both speakers in the next eclogue propose to liberate the fancy and enhance its expression, Halon and Eudoemon disagree about the value of a traditional poetic recourse. Halon wholeheartedly upholds the time-honored loyalty to Bacchus: "'Tis wine, the Ioy of life, the Strength of witt, / The fire of fancie, Edge of all Conceipt" (2:173). With equal conviction Eudoemon argues "how happie are the fires / Which Sober Fancie kindles in ye Mind" (2:168). While Daniel does not celebrate the conviviality and friendship commonplace in the contemporary Cavalier songs of wine, he recognizes in this poem the loyalty other poets such as Lovelace and Brome pledge with each brimmer. The pleasures of drinking that Halon professes extend beyond welcome escape; those who refuse to join him in toasts to "our bright Hopes, the riseing Shepheard's Starre," he contends, show their "want of Loyaltie" (2:169). Without clarifying the vague allusion, the poem acknowledges the gesture of royalist support implicit in drinking toasts to the king and his cause. Eudoemon's, and perhaps Daniel's, tendency is to withdraw into "A free and quiet mind," certain that "Only retiréd thoughts may See / The rayes of such felicitie" (2:178). Halon, however, finds equal brightness in the god of wine: "The Light of Ioy, the Life of witt / And all true flame infuses" (2:179). Neither argument prevails in the overly long exchange, which ends inconclusively in the shepherds' separate songs to light.

When the subject has obvious political significance, the difficulties of expressing the truth increase. Damon and Amintas's topical eclogue lamenting the rise of Parliament stresses the quandary of loyal shepherds who must "retract, what we have sung before" and "Celebrate the Glories, of a late / Usurped Power" (p. 179). In this thinly veiled denunciation of London's betrayal of the king, Daniel examines the plight of the royalists and the prospect of war. His loyalist leanings are apparent in the poem's recollection of the bounteous years of peace enjoyed under "this Great Shepherd" Charles and in its portrayal of the giddy multitudes swept up in the threatening storms from the southeast, but he does not resort to mindless adulation of the king's cause. The poem, on the contrary, is unusually candid in its belief that Charles became "remisse" when he surrendered some of his authority to Parliament. Daniel refuses to compromise his long-held belief that majesty cannot admit a rival, and he does not conceal his dismay at the king's behavior:

> Hee, all the while remisse, is well content
> To see how she can manage Government;
> Lulled by her Sugred Sayings, and the oft
> Repeated vowes, which (ah) She never thought.
> Hee, from his owne Hand, gives his Ivorie hooke,
> Which even His Father and Himselfe had tooke
> Of Pan, with Solemne vow.
>
> (p. 174)

Allusions to the execution of Strafford, the abortive attempt to arrest the five members of Parliament, and the royalist repudiation at Hull trace the king's plight in explicit detail. By the late summer of 1642, apparently when the poem was written, Daniel could see little hope for Charles and his supporters. Although the king did, in fact, rally considerable support once the war began that autumn, Amintas and Damon recognize but cannot explain the parliamentary hold over the country; and they view his journey into the Midlands as "his last Refuge, a wan hope, to bring / Himselfe, to former Glories of a Kinge" (p. 177). Disheartened by the further spectacle of the tyranny sweeping the streets of London, they can only plaintively lament, "What may wee doe?"

For them and for the aspiring royalist poet, the prospects are bleak. Bound in loyalty to a man whose fate touches all in the kingdom, they share together the inexpressible "Horror" and "darke Extasie" that overwhelm Damon at the end. Under the new tyranny that censors writing as well as removes the inspiration for poetry, they cannot freely sing their thoughts; and even if they could, "what is left, to Sing? our Glorie's gon, / Our Loves are Lost, or not worth thinking on" (p. 179). The dilemma has no easy resolution. While Damon tries to console his companion, "Yet in our Loves, wee're free," Amintas ends the dialogue unable to accept a grief that has silenced his pipe and left a "worne and wearied Quill." Their final song to Apollo offers a wreath appropriately woven mainly of brambles, nettles, and woodbine, "For Joy is Dead, and Glorie faint; / Witt, banished our feilds" (p. 180).

The sorrow and frustration deepen in the last eclogue. Written during 1646, the year Charles fled Oxford for Newark and the Scots, this dialogue between Hilas and Strephon is Daniel's most extensive discussion of the difficulties confronting the royalist poet:

> Let rather Silence seize all Tongves, then bring
> One Accent not to gratulate the King.
> The Lord of All wee are; whose Equall Rule
> Made muses pleasant to the noble Soule;
> And did inspire Each brest, informe each braine,
> With flame, in wonders of his happie Raigne;
> But now, the time is Come All wee can Say,
> Sounds like the Horrors of Departed Day.
>
>                  (2:193)

Hilas and Strephon recognize that truth cannot guide a "cleare Pen" where passion, self-interest, and partisanship tempt poets to distort the issues. They also regret the inability to find the style "deep enough to Sing / Royall Distresses and lament a King" (2:195). Although Strephon invokes the examples of Suckling and Jonson in a glowing tribute to their poetry, the eclogue voices little hope that they will inspire others. They wrote with a power and insight no longer attainable, "A measur'd Idiome, to make cleare and plaine / What here, in confus'd Notions, wee descrye, / By iarring Accents" (2:196). Despite the wistful belief that perhaps Cleveland or "Our late-made Laureate" may rise to former heights of expression, Daniel seems to fall back once again upon the faith in future success. All poets, Strephon concludes, should admit the limitation of their powers as well as their circumstances; for his own part, and presumably also for Daniel, "Me, peace-surrounded, mirtles may secure; / But thistles now my burning Browes immure" (2:198).

The source of this anguish, the plight of the king, dominates the eclogue's quite remarkable second half. Daniel's criticism of treasonous rebels who disguise their selfish motives behind pleas of loyalty is a familiar charge among royalist supporters, but his concerns about the king's actions reveal a growing sense of Charles's doom. Without equivocation, Strephon fears that the monarch who had apparently consolidated his power in Oxford and then bargained his position away with the parliamentarians "Not may, but must, / Inevitably fall, to their vniust / Tirrannous wills" (2:201). The apprehension is consistent with Daniel's belief that monarchy can never compromise its authority, although this pessimism sounds a new note of despondency not completely mitigated by Hilas's suggestion that all rulers are subject to a preordained fate. The poem also expresses grave doubts about the wisdom of the king's flight from Oxford, and once again Hilas's speculation that Charles must have some reason for trusting the Scots lacks conviction. Daniel does not share the hope of Cleveland and Vaughan in their responses to Charles's desperate gamble,[18] and in the end he can only refuse to second-guess the king. The faith of the confirmed monarchist does not, however, dispel the doubts of the political realist, for the poem concludes with the shepherds' final song of sorrow and their vow to abandon all verse.

When Daniel speaks again in his own voice, "The Author" confronts his worst fears. The Latin epigraph of this 1647 poem invokes the Horatian desire for the "sacred grove" or "forest" of "shadowy peace" and "shadowy places,"[19] and it also provides a context for Daniel's reconsideration of the plight of the poet caught in the nation's conflict. While the poem does not achieve Horace's urbane humor, it too is a personal justification for a life of poetry removed from politics. Daniel's initial survey of three other famous "Grove-frequenters"—Orpheus, Virgil, and Spenser—does not sentimentalize the often harsh fates of writers torn apart by frenzied Thracians or completely ignored by contemporaries, but the poem still professes a faith in the enduring nature of their poetry. From the anonymity of his "owne Shades content," Daniel admires their flights of fancy, believing that "vertue cannot Dye" and "true Complexion" cannot alter. Although the theme is now commonplace among his poems, Daniel faces the depredations of war with renewed hope and conviction,

> Vertue is ever Safe; and wee may See
> Loyaltie prized, and depress'd majestie
> Enthroned, as glorious as wee whilome have.
> These wee may see; if not, the well-met grave
> Will shew us more. Hee, who considers that
> A Losse, is ignorant to value Fate.
>
> (p. 171)

Other defeated royalists also gradually begin to renew their faith in some future restoration,[20] though not all are equally willing to embrace the Christian consolation of eternal glory. In any case, Daniel's hopeful resignation cannot conceal his bitter reaction to the inescapable realities of parliamentarian power:

> triumph in the overthrow
> Of Truth and Justice. You the seamles Coat
> Have torne; and dipt the Fleece without a Spott
> In Cisternes of Profanesse. Ring the Bells!
> Y' have done, y' have done the worke.
>
> (p. 171)

Now that the established, Episcopal church has been abolished and the king has lost much of his freedom and authority, withdrawal becomes more than ever the most attractive and dignified response to the royalist calamity. Although Daniel cannot achieve the equanimity Horace expresses at the end of his epistle, he too resolves to distance himself from the chaos of his age.

Images of flight and freedom characterize a series of occasional poems written during this period to honor writers whose commitments to virtue are inspiring examples to the hostile times. A 1648 ode written in response to

Herbert's *The Temple* longs to emulate this "Glorious Larke" and "flye! / Up to the Region, of thy Glories where / Onlie true formes appeare" (p. 66). The earth-bound poet, weighed down by "Selfe-borne-Cares," reluctantly admits, however, that he can only admire a writer who soars with the voice of Horace and the wings of Casimire. The "freeborne mind" of Thomas Browne also informs two poems occasioned by *Religio Medici* and *Pseudodoxia Epidemica*. In these 1646 and 1648 pieces, Daniel praises the rare individual who has managed to capture the light obscured in the mist and clouds. His is the rigorous scrutiny of "a mind, soe free, soe full" that all who read his lucid and unaffected books join with Browne in similar liberation: "Each may move within his proper Sphere / And bee with Him, as free, as Hee is here / With all the world" (p. 63). The first of a pair of poems to John Ogilby acknowledges as well the role the translator plays in restoring the "abundant Ray" of genius. Daniel maintains that Ogilby has not merely translated Virgil into English; he has freed the Roman writer from the vagaries of time and enabled others to share Virgil's original radiance. Arms are not, he pointedly concludes, the only means of power. Despite the daunting future that royalists confronted in July 1647, when presumably this poem was written, Daniel can still aver, however tentatively, "Mean-while, iust Admirations may raise / Merit, on Earth; to give desert, a place / Beyond ye mouth of Envie" (1:25). It is an optimism fundamental to these and Daniel's other poems.

When he wrote his next major work, *Trinarchodia*, the worsening political realities further challenged this optimism. The date *"Septimo die Novembris"* 1649 and the dedication to liberty suggest that this long, three-part poem on the reigns of Richard II, Henry IV and Henry V may have been written at least in part after Charles's defeat and death. The deposition of Richard and the Lancastrian succession had already been, of course, the subject of Shakespeare's *Henriad* and Samuel Daniel's *The Civil Wars*, but the events leading to the War of the Roses had greater immediacy now for a nation in civil war. Pamphlets supporting each side of the conflict between Parliament and monarch during this time turned particularly to Richard's troubled monarchy,[21] and it is not surprising that a poet earlier attracted to that century of conflict would find in that struggle inspiration for his "warr-taught / Numbers." For him and for his contemporaries, the revolt led by Wat Tyler, the challenges of restive nobles, and the demands of recalcitrant parliaments raise fundamental questions about the limits of government; and the temptation to find both historical precedents and parallels is quite natural. Although he never considers *Trinarchodia* the epic poem he had earlier envisioned, its densely figurative and allusive blend of history and philosophy remains Daniel's most ambitious commentary on his personal and national crisis.

The reality of Charles's defeat and the prospects of future kingship are never far from the center of Daniel's study of their historical counterparts, the decline of Richard II and the rise of Henry V. Specific parallels, such as the comparison between the peasant revolt against Richard II and the Leveller movement, together with implicit suggestions, such as the invitation "If wee looke better, wee may see it nigher," create immediacy. Asides sometimes draw the obvious inference "wee perhaps haue seene / Outrages Equall to the worst they did" (3:148), and often the historical relevancy is unmistakable in the intensity of the narrative's criticism. Daniel's continued scorn for the self-serving Scots and meddlesome priests implies, for example, seventeenth-century parallels; and his undisguised hostility toward the London citizenry obviously reflects a royalist's frustrations, fears, and doubts. Parliaments not surprisingly emerge as "ever curbe-Kings," religious zealots are a constant source of trouble, and the multitude reconfirms its unstable nature. Legislators, zealots, and commoners all appear in Daniel's indictment as venal figures familiar in the satire royalists developed during the civil war; but this outpouring of animosity does not merely enable Daniel to accept his own fears about a threatening present that he tries to distance in the narrative. From the outset in this chronicle of a parallel time, Daniel attempts to understand the pattern of contemporary events within the larger movements of history.

As he begins his narrative, Daniel is ambivalent about whether "necessary fate" preordains the events of history. Willing to let more penetrating minds resolve the issue, he recognizes the natural inclination to invoke fate when it suits the occasion:

> Our Iudgements span to bring in Providence;
> Fancy assists to the discouerie;
>     And something a farre off, wee wonder at:
>     Like Spectrums in a Dreame, wee know not what.
>
> (3:137)

His belief that nature follows a "regular" and "smooth" order underlies an assumption that events progress with a "fixt Determination," yet his narrative allows considerable latitude for individual responsibility. When Daniel insists, for example, that "some fate / Of great disaster" always follows the kind of dissipation Richard displays, he argues for a causality and responsibility quite distinct from his contention that Richard cannot be blamed for the folly of youth since "Fate had determin'd" he must assume the crown before he had matured. Difficulties arise when Daniel seems to contradict the poem's belief that an individual can be the "Pilot in his owne Designe." He appears to believe that rulers bring about their own success: "Weake Princes still haue beene vnfortunate; / A wise one cannot, for Hee makes his owne, / And sitts beyond the Scourge they tremble at" (3:186). But unless he assumes fortune is always linked with strength, Daniel moves into troubled waters when he later admits,

> But noe Harbour's Safe
> Vnto a Prince that is vnfortunate.
> Turne how you will, Fate has a firme decree:
> There is a wracke at Land aswell as Sea.
>
> (3:217)

Unwilling to accept a random universe, he seems to tangle the motivation in the thread of fate the narrative consciously weaves.

While the poem's images of spinning, sailing, music, and astronomy and its allusions to fate and fortune create a sense of inevitability, its vision of monarchy suggests that the wise ruler helps to shape his destiny. Despite their initial tentativeness about the notion of a preordained fate, the opening stanzas of *Trinarchodia* insist upon majesty's need to be forceful. Daniel undercuts the temptation to speculate about the course history might have taken if Richard's father had lived longer, and he refuses to lessen the young ruler's responsibility for his own behavior. Earlier historians readily attribute much of Richard's difficulty to evil counselors, but Daniel scorns the rationalization also used so readily in the 1640s by Clarendon and others to excuse their king's unwise decisions. Though the poem admits the contingencies of time and place, it further denies any pervasive sense of fortune. Aloof from the common view, the monarch must rely upon the awe and mystery Daniel believes are inherent in the institution of the monarchy; once the king loses this wonder, however, and becomes liable to the judgments of his subjects' narrow interests, he encourages factions. And "When Scepters totter once, they fall to ground" (3:175). This fate, which in the last of the eclogues Charles I seems destined to fulfill, determines the downfall of his earlier counterpart, Richard II. At first Daniel appears reluctant to criticize the king for not exercising his entrusted power, but the narrative of Richard's struggles with parliaments and nobility soon admits the king's responsibility for the ill-fated reign. Even within the uncertain limits that fate and destiny have imposed, Richard remains too complacent about appearances and too preoccupied with himself; more important, he misuses opportunities to assert his authority and, in the poem's central images, to guide his vessel of state and to strike the proper harmony. Although occasionally regal, as in his defiance of the rebel Wat Tyler, Richard more often commits the "Unkingly Act" of heeding his subjects' demands. The sight of this eagle yielding finally to the assault of ravens, gulls, and magpies prompts the anguished cry, "that Kings should be soe Tame!"

Without insisting that Charles I is remiss to the same degree or in the same way as Richard II, the poem shifts the burden for revolution away from the monarchy itself and onto the individuals who fail to shoulder the responsibilities of the times. Quite understandably, Daniel tries to redirect his troubled thoughts from painful reality by attacking the self-interest that leads some to distort justice and transforms others into ravenous beasts, but a heavy-handed account of London's capitulation to the rebels and several sarcastic asides about a timeless parliamentarian avarice do not justify the king's inactivity. *Trinarchodia* places the monarch firmly in a traditional universe:

> Kings, like the Sun, move, Lights vnto the Rest.
> The Earth is fixt; that is, the People are
> Dull clods, & only by his Rayes refresh't;
> Whose motion glads it round.
>
> (3:195)

Hereditary right at best creates the monarch's central position; it cannot guarantee the revolutionary motion. "Weake Kings," in the poem's view, "are standing suns" who find their axes cracked and themselves displaced by the earth. Within the elaborate pattern of astronomical imagery "The Zodiacke of Honour whirles vpon / Th' Imaginarie Poles of Right and Power" (3:196), and prudence guides the spheres. The ideal source of light and life that Daniel envisions must therefore be "A Sober, Prudent, yet an Active Spirit" (3:182) who brings to his office the strength of will and vigor Richard obviously lacks. The poem does not unfold in detail how the king might have maintained his radiance, for Daniel is not an analytical poet, but the narrative has no sympathy for the ruler who displays unkingly passivity. Events of the last decade have made all too clear the ineffectuality of right without accompanying power, and Daniel cannot ignore the inescapable consequences of imprudent compromise. He thus unmistakably implies his own monarch's failure to fulfill a position that commands a nobility it cannot ensure.

With the promise that "euery scæne affords / Something Allusive" (4:23), the account of Henry's accession emphasizes the political uncertainty Daniel believes now characterizes a nation also deprived of its "well-framed Monarchye" and subject to tyranny. The new tenor is apparent in the narrator's opening recognition,

> Tis in mee now doubly Distempered;
> A Stormy Day and an vnquiet Age;
> Vsurping Clouds, the Sun,—my head—
> Involv's; but more than both, th' vnguided Rage
>     Of an Insultinge Conquerour, who shreds
>     Maiesty like the mounting Poppie-Heads.
>
> (4:2)

Again the fickle multitude and ambitious office seekers receive considerable attention, but Daniel is now less vehement in his denunciation of the opportunists who first turn against Richard and then desert Henry IV. The second part of *Trinarchodia* accepts more philosophically the realities of power politics and the folly of change. Without the sanction and aura of the established monarchy, Henry IV must rely, in Daniel's view, upon an expediency that neither placates the people nor achieves an easy rule. Until the death of Richard removes the rival king, Henry remains a usurper and a tyrant who struggles against rebellion to consolidate a reign begun in rebellion. Although the poem eventually and grudgingly admires Henry's ability to straddle his shifting bases of power and to stand firm, in the end its account of the physically weakened and prematurely old ruler underscores the irony of his efforts:

> Not Richard now (whose Resignation
> His weaknes was, his merit soe his Crime;)
> Appear'd more abiect; Harrie bleeds Compassion
> Vpon that Dust; so knead 'em; & but Time
>> The Accident of Life, decides how much
>> Richard was weake & Harrie was not Such.

(4:97)

Though Richard II receives much less attention in the poem's second part, he indeed already overshadows Henry IV. Daniel limits the vanquished king's role to a short account of his death at Pomfret, and surprisingly he develops no parallels between the regicide of Richard II and the execution of Charles I. But in the "Royall Sorrows," he commemorates a dignity later ages would highly honor. The Richard of his narrative accepts his fate with the equanimity many seventeenth-century loyalists saw in the Stuart king's Stoic fortitude: "All accidents are Equall in the Rate, / Of Minds subdu'd; The Glories he had knowne, / The Greifes he dwelt in, now appeare but One" (4:29). The king, quite simply, has had the opportunity to "know Himselfe," a knowledge Daniel deems the essence of "true Philosophye," and this wisdom enables him to transform ignominy into triumph. "Hee who Contemnes the Power / Of Tyrannye," the narrative proclaims, "is more then Conquerour" (4:30); he is also in his moment of greatness uncircumscribable. While he ruled, Richard often let the splendor of monarchy diminish; now from the narrow confines of Pomfret his majesty shines to the astonishment of an admiring world. Here the king has found the liberty Daniel has espoused in his poetry, "for this Restraint / Enlarg'd his Soule to all the freedome which / May be in flesh" (4:30). Within his self-possessed, unconquerable mind, Richard escapes his earthly confines and achieves the liberation possible in so many of the poems for the musing soul that would fly toward the essential truth somewhere beyond "The Iayle of flesh." Daniel somberly admits that the ultimate freedom lies in the death Richard meets at Pomfret, an end the poem tersely labels "a Martyrdome," but the narrative does not glorify the monarch in a heroic account of his death. Richard, moreover, does not loom through the "mist of Murder'd Maiestie" the way the martyred Charles I would dominate the imaginations of royalists resigned to Cromwellian rule. Rather than offer a poetic parallel to the king's *Eikon Basilike,* Daniel concedes that the death of Richard and the subsequent reign of Henry IV are part of a larger pattern designed "to adde more Glory to Another" (4:33). Henry V completes the redemption of monarchy begun, however fleetingly, in the final days of Richard's life.

In the midst of desolation, where darkness prevails and poetry has lost its voice, the third part of *Trinarchodia* reasserts Daniel's belief that strong monarchy will reemerge. Though he "cannot Speak it," he invites his readers to "Pull by the Curtaine" and see in the reign of Henry V "by what means 't may be" (4:104). Without any mention of his own monarch's failure, Daniel praises in Henry V the triumph possible when a ruler recognizes the "iust extent" of his office. The poem is realistic about the use and effectiveness of power, and it insists great achievements await kings who are not reluctant to assert themselves. Unlike the indecisive and indulgent Richard, the king shows the resolution and determination Daniel longs for in a kingdom similarly "rent & mangled, gapeing wide / In wounds of Faction" (4:108). Henry unites his fragmented nation as Charles never could because Henry also understands the inspiring glory of "true Maiestie" and "Great hopes." In this idealized portrait of monarchy and its "Life-giveing Light," a "Strange Destinie" favors the ruler who knows himself and his course of action. Henry appears to be an instrument of heaven, which blesses the English with spectacular victories, but in the fields of France and against seemingly insuperable odds, it is the king himself who shapes the chains of fate into his own crown of state. "His Prowesse," the poem testifies, "Span'd / Fate; to make Glorie only worth his hand" (4:195), and his example remains for Daniel a testimony to the possibilities of royal grandeur.

The subsequent decline of England's fortunes during the weak reign of Henry's son, who "makes way for fate," confirms the evanescence of greatness as well as the danger of irresolution; the accomplishments of Henry V, however, remain a glimpse of the light Daniel hopes may shine once again. A short piece following the conclusion of *Trinarchodia* almost as an envoy voices the tacit hope of the poem's third part. "Crastini Animarum. 1650" describes the darkness surrounding an Interregnum world of considerable despondency:

> The Sun (whose heat gives Life & Light makes bold
> Earth, & from Earth, the Creatures manifold)
> Is shrunke into the Socket; & we now
> (Lost to his flame) can scarce hope when, or how
> He from the Dismall Tropicke, shall repasse,
> That we may live, in Light, as once it was.
>
> (4:202)

Where truth now appears treasonable and loyalty infirm, poetry has no expression and glory no form; Daniel, however, still maintains his faith in the reascendence of the sun/son and the resurgency of verse. Within the year, Charles II's ill-fated Worcester campaign would dampen these hopes, but the royalist ideal would endure to inspire the Restoration expectations. During a period of national crisis, when traditional monarchist forms and values had lost their force, this hope is surely also realized in the kingship restored by Henry V in *Trinarchodia*.

Although Daniel himself recognizes that he has at best "meanly pourtraied" Henry V, the account of the decline and rise of the three Plantagenets offers, then, more than chronicle turned lame verse. Despite the ambiguities of its language and its poorly punctuated, often elliptical text, *Trinarchodia* conveys in immediate terms the struggle to find meaning in civil upheaval. Elaborate figurative language and vague philosophical ruminations sometimes impede good dialogue and action, but they capture the perplexities of a writer trying to reconcile his faith in monarchy with the realities of its destruction. At heart a royalist and an idealist, Daniel nevertheless does not ignore realpolitik or overlook the shortcomings of individuals. Like earlier Renaissance writers drawn to the same period of history, he senses some larger pattern in the flux of time, even though its parts seem somewhat blurred. Viewed from the perspective of his other long poem, *Idyllia*, the cyclical design appears to possess direction.

This survey of mankind's quest for freedom offers "Thrumbs of Discontents: / From the large Webbe of Care" (4:235) that suggest the vanity of human wishes. Throughout their contemplation of the voyages that history repeatedly undertakes, five "Idylls" and "L'Envoy" hold together loosely and unevenly the hopes and doubts basic to Daniel's vision. *Idyllia* again criticizes the self-interests that lead to betrayal, and it denounces disruptive religious critics and zealots. In reaction to the tyranny the poem finds possible in all forms of government, Daniel also unabashedly confesses his loyalty to monarchy. Now more than ever, nostalgia characterizes his desire,

> Were Maiestie as Calme as we have knowne
> It in one Starre, through the whole Horizon;
> Vnstain'd as our Ideas; or the Hand
> More Spotles, who late rul'd ye Land;
> Who if a place be Lawfull to assigne
> In heaven, for Soules departed, there doth raigne.
>
> (4:219)

But once again Daniel insists that kings undermine their authority and the nation suffers when monarchs concede their prerogatives. Most impressive in this difficult, often cryptic poem is the detachment with which its author attempts to give coherent shape to the self-destructive course his country and its inhabitants have charted.

Instead of the specific parallels suggested in *Trinarchodia,* Daniel views the current search for freedom within the larger rhythms of time. Mankind's efforts to grasp liberty are seen in *Idyllia* as attempts to regain a prelapsarian life: always the image of "former Freedome" beckons just beyond human embrace. The biblical, classical, and contemporary figures surveyed in the poem confirm the ease and regularity with which the prospect of liberty disappears and tyranny emerges. The pessimistic pattern varies only in the particulars envisioned by Cato or Agrippa:

> Wee Fancy at a distance, & contrive
> Beatitude in future, but still live
> Distracted to the End our Selves propose.
> Thus to our selves, our selves still interpose;
> Wee are our owne deceivers.
>
> (4:210)

Accordingly England's efforts to sail by the "Faire Sister-starres" freedom and religion cannot succeed when the interests and ambitions of the individual hinder the journey. Their new Eden only a mirage, the voyagers at best will return to the "new originall" foreseen by Daniel: "the world is All / One Phoenix" (4:225).

And yet freedom from this relentless cycle is possible. At the end of the first idyll, Daniel reasserts his growing belief in the importance of an "inward mind Secure." Without this sense of Stoic self-containment, an undefined ability to ignore both the clamors of the multitude and the forces of tyranny, individuals are doomed to emulate the fate of Sisyphus; for the possessed and fearless minds, however, the endless repetition ceases:

> And this is Libertie; this we may find,
> This we may keep; thus happie in our mind
> All Government is easie; and may be
> Made one, or Any, Equall Libertie.
>
> (4:212)

The freedom possible for those who know themselves does not imply total withdrawal from the affairs of state, although the remaining idylls seem less concerned than the eclogues and *Trinarchodia* with successful government. The progress they trace follows a deceptive and destructive quest for liberty that promises little more than temporary stability. Ultimately time will both terminate and complete this journey. The weary pilgrim of Daniel's Ecclesiasticus and the musing searcher of *Idyllia* will finally enjoy liberty outside of temporality in the Salem the poem envisions at the journey's end. Cleansed by the waters of forgetfulness and moved beyond the folly of the search, the fortunate will escape the ceaseless rhythms of history and enjoy the freedom and repose Christian Stoics like Lipsius locate in heaven, "our true and rightfull countrey, whether let vs aduance all our cogitations."[22] "Where only Truth / Is Center'd," the poem recasts the odes' temporal retreats into biblical terms, "Peace, can be"; all else is vanity.

Seen in the context of both the poem and the canon, the resolution has a satisfying inevitability. Throughout the poetic record of his reaction to the breakdown of traditional monarchist society, Daniel holds on to his faith in an ineffable order and to his desire for peace; the immediate threat of chaos only deepens his awareness of their fragility. Rather than turn away from intense engagement and remain silent, Daniel tries to find purpose first in a celebration of an England at peace, then in the value of an inner tranquillity, and finally in the prospect of a Christian afterlife. Although his muse never climbs to the heights he envisions and his ideas sometimes are labored and obscure, his four volumes of poetry struggle to contain the threat of revolutionary change in a characteristically seventeenth-century manner. As his world comes apart and the future looms ominously, George Daniel draws toward an inner life increasingly Stoic in the freedom it asserts yet firm in the traditional Christian understanding of human progress. In this teleological view of history, the traumatic events of the 1640s become part of a larger movement, a tragic drama that ends in comedy for those who are patient.

# 4

# Richard Lovelace and the "Gallant Thorough-made Resolve"

NOT all the king's supporters viewed the unfolding tragedy of the 1640s from the relative safety and anonymity that George Daniel found in his Yorkshire estate. Some, like the poet Mildmay Fane, earl of West-moreland, were forced to compound for their sequestered property before they could return to their country houses and a rural retirement. Others followed the king's standard from Nottingham into the campaigns of the Midlands and toward eventual defeat at Naseby. In the popular literary view that they themselves often helped to create, these followers include the Cavaliers, the proud and undaunted men of action who "Saile against Rocks, and split them too; / I! and a world of Pikes passe through."[1] Among the poets who rallied to the king's support during the years of civil war, Richard Lovelace has long been considered the unrivaled embodiment of the Cavalier spirit.

Though his earliest datable poems link him with Oxford and with the university panegyrics, his best-known lines seem to many inextricably con-nected with aristocratic ideals of chivalry and honor.[2] "The most amiable and beautiful person that ever eye beheld," the graceful, witty gentleman of Anthony à Wood's biography willingly offered both his patrimony and his talents "to keep up the credit and reputation of the king's cause." Much remains unknown about Colonel Richard Lovelace's activities during the civil war, when he may have spent most of the time on the continent as an officer in General Goring's regiment, but two events are indisputable. In 1642 this heir of an established family was, in Wood's account, "made choice of by the whole body of the county of Kent at an assize, to deliver the Kentish petition to the house of commons, for the restoring the king to his rights and for setling the government, &c. For which piece of service he was committed to the Gatehouse at Westminster." Six years later Lovelace was implicated in the abortive royalist uprisings of 1648 and imprisoned in October for six months at Peterhouse, where Wood alleges "he fram'd his poems for the press." The man whose hand Marvell playfully says "so rudely grasps the steely brand" and "so gently melts the Ladies hand" appeared to his contem-

97

poraries a paragon of "Valour, Vertue, Love, and Loyalty" who dared "in a time distracted so to sing," diverting sorrow, raising spirits, and "Making us quite forget our seven yeers paines."[3] Modern criticism has begun to challenge this traditional view of an undaunted royalism, but the poems that inspired Lovelace's countrymen resist the recent attempts to find in them disillusionment, distrust, or paranoia.[4] Throughout the years of struggle and defeat, these varied, often Stoic poems confirm his friend Charles Cotton's belief that Richard Lovelace's "stable brest could no disturbance know. / In Fortune humble, constant in mischance" (p. 223).

Cotton's characterization praises a self-sufficiency developed in Lovelace's increasingly troubled responses to the royalist fortunes. Although the chronological sequence of his reactions to the personal and national calamity cannot be traced with any certainty, the licensing of *Lucasta* in the Stationers' Register on 4 February 1648 suggests that the volume of poems published around June 1649 was completed before Lovelace's imprisonment in October and the King's execution in January 1649.[5] Their tone and structure further suggest that the poems Lovelace saw through the press while in prison are "fram'd" or arranged to reflect some sense of Lovelace's changing attitude. Though the poems in *Lucasta* cannot be dated for the most part, tonally and thematically they are at times significantly different from those issued in the posthumous 1660 edition. Together the dominant concerns in both volumes reveal their author's search for the "stability of mind" and the "well-being of the soul" Seneca says the Greeks define as *euthymia* and his essays call tranquillity.[6] When the splendor of the Caroline years diminishes and the light of the beloved Lucasta becomes remote, Lovelace tends toward greater self-containment. Unlike Daniel, who withdraws into a solitary, contemplative life at Beswick, Lovelace seeks the freedom possible among good friends and with fine wines. Bound in a spirit of loyalty and inspired by the heroic resolve of the king, he asserts in *Lucasta* the invulnerability of the "stable brest." But the years of defeat temper his defiance and strengthen his Stoic indifference. By the time he completes *Lucasta. Posthume Poems*, Richard Lovelace accepts the royalist loss within the larger rhythms of fortune; he also understands that "Success comes to the common man, and even to commonplace ability; but to triumph over the calamities and terrors of mortal life is the part of a great man only."[7]

The search for fulfillment begins with the poet's separation from the unknown lady named in the titles of both works. The valedictory poems "*To Lucasta,* Going beyond the Seas" and "*To Lucasta,* Going to the Warres" open the 1649 volume, and "Calling *Lucasta* from her Retirement" concludes the original collection with the desire for reunion. Another poem added after the line "The end of LUCASTA Odes, &c." completes the edition with the very long tribute to Lucasta, "Aramantha. A Pastorall." None of these four poems about separation and reunion compromises its seriousness in the fashionable poses Lovelace assumes in other verses to his Amaranthas, Chloes, and Gratianas. While many of those verses adopt urbane and witty variations of Petrarchan adulation, these celebrate the illumination radiant in Lucasta. A symbol of the love and honor that inspire nobility, Lucasta becomes in the course of the first volume an embodiment of the royalist ideals once celebrated in the Caroline masques and now lost in the civil war.

The opening poems of parting leave no doubt about the poet's faith in the transcendent principles Lucasta inspires. The valediction ostensibly written to Lucasta on the occasion of the author's "Going beyond the Seas," perhaps to Holland or France,[8] reflects the possible influence of Donne, but this bid for faith and trust has none of the earlier poet's reservations. Confronted with the reality of angry seas and an uncertain voyage, the speaker insists

> Though Seas and Land betwixt us both,
>     Our Faith and Troth,
>   Like separated soules,
>   All time and space controules:
> Above the highest sphere wee meet
> Unseene, unknowne, and greet as Angels greet.
>
> (p. 17)

Whatever affinities this declaration may have with fashionable Platonic theories,[9] the lines provide a striking entrance into a group of poems preoccupied with constancy, change, confinement, and release. In later poems separation and turbulence assume more threatening dimensions, and sailing gains a Stoic significance; the initial desire to transcend if not control time and space does not, however, disappear. Lovelace exalts the "unconfin'd" oneness of love, and in the second song *"To Lucasta,* Going to the Warres" he links this love with honor. Its argument for inconstancy resolves the rival claims of lady and sword with the famous declaration, "I could not love thee (Deare) so much, / Lov'd I not Honour more" (p. 18). Despite its context of swords, horses, and shields, the word *honor* evokes more than the traditional chivalric association of *honos* or reputation.[10] The poem's faith in the values and principles upheld by the sword supports the same idealism expressed in their love; mutual trust is possible when both lovers are committed to *honestum,* the morally just or honorable.[11] By the end of *Lucasta,* the poems recognize the futility of war and abandon any desire to leave "the Nunnerie" of Lucasta's "chaste breast, and quiet minde." Apart from her, the speaker turns his search for honor inward, ultimately withdrawing into the safety of the "stable brest" and "quiet minde."

Not all these subsequent poems to Lucasta are distinguished from the obligatory and at times conventional compliment characteristic of Caroline poetry. The Lucasta celebrated in "The Rose" appears the quintessence of this flower; in an "Ode *Lyrick*" her "marble heart" becomes a monument; and in *"Lucasta's Fanne,* With a Looking glasse in it" her eyes surpass the most opulent mirror. The hyperbole in *"Lucasta* Weeping,"* on the other hand, gracefully turns the traditional conceit of eclipsing the sun into an effective play on the light her name suggests. This radiance at the center of *"Lucasta's* World" revitalizes the Petrarchan notion of icy fire, and the presence of *"Lucasta,* taking the waters at Tunbridge" transforms the "happy floods" fortunate enough to come into contact with her *"Vertue, Honour, Love* and *Blisse."* The love and honor mentioned perfunctorily in this poem's last lines regain the substance of the opening lyrics when midway in the volume and then at the end political realities displace poetic artifice.

*"To Lucasta.* From Prison" celebrates her radiance in an ever more bleak and threatening decade. Unlike the conventional compliments to Lucasta in the other poems, this epode abandons studied praise and returns to the more serious theme of separation. The speaker's desire to escape the "Shackels" of Lucasta and to "fancy all the world beside" leads to a troubled consideration of the figurative mistresses of reformation pursued by the nation during the 1640s. At the time he wrote this poem, Lovelace may actually have been in prison, although the situation he surveys cannot be precisely dated. Lovelace's most recent editor contends that "This poem was obviously written in 1649," when Lovelace remained in Peterhouse Prison, "since it alludes to the King's beheading (30 January)."[12] In fact the Parliament, not the king, is "th' fairest body that's beheaded," or without the monarch's leadership; and what are possibly allusions to the Kentish Petition and the parliamentary actions of 1642 may well date the poem as written during the period from April to June 1642, a time that Lovelace spent in the Gatehouse after delivering the Petition of Kent.[13] The more probable dating, or one at least earlier than the book's licensing in February 1648, seems in keeping with the poem's tone. The search for a new love has none of the blind loyalites and vengeful horror of an embittered, disillusioned royalist. Like Clarendon and some of the moderate thinkers who ultimately sided with the monarch, the speaker concedes the need for reform:

> A *Reformation* I would have,
> > As for our griefes a *Sov'raigne* salve;
> That is, a cleansing of each wheele
> > Of State, that yet some rust doth feele.
>
> > > > > (p. 50)

The play on *"Sov'raigne* salve" grants the king the authority for any reform, and the next stanza recognizes that reformation demands skillful men who will not overthrow all. Parliament has its role "As a maine Prop from Heav'n sent," but Lovelace shares Daniel's misgivings about a body cut off from its head. The poem further stresses the growing recognition in the numerous pamphlets and ballads that the rallying cry of religion, liberty, property, and public faith is a call only to greater bondage.[14] Deprived of the values traditionally upheld by responsible government, Lovelace turns to the origins of light and life:

> He who being the whole Ball
>   Of Day on Earth, lends it to all;
> When seeking to ecclipse his right,
>   Blinded, we stand in our owne light.
>
> And now an universall mist
>   Of Error is spread or'e each breast,
> With such a fury edg'd, as is
>   Not found in th' inwards of th' Abysse.
>
> (p. 51)

The apocalyptic overtones in the ominous image of blind fury and ignorance describe a universe in chaos, but the darkness is not absolute. However tentative and ambiguous the next stanza may be, it ends the poem with prayerful hope:

> Oh from thy glorious Starry Waine
>   Dispense on me one sacred Beame
> To light me where I soone may see
>   How to serve you, and you trust me.
>
> (p. 51)

The "sacred Beame" and "Starry Waine" would seem to extend the metaphoric image of the king with an allusion to Charles's Wain, the northern constellation Ursa Major. Comparisons between the king and both the sun and Charles's Wain occur regularly in Caroline literature, and Lovelace's adaptation suits a conventional loyalism. But the lady addressed in the poem's title and in the first stanza also appears throughout *Lucasta* as a metaphor for light—in a later poem she is, in fact, "*Lucasta* that bright Northerne star" (p. 102). In its reassertion of constancy and faith, the conclusion in effect merges the identities of Charles I and Lucasta: the final lines both return to the "thy" of the opening stanza and refer to the king of the previous stanzas. The elusive nature of their light leaves ambiguous the desire "How to serve you, and you trust me." Since the speaker includes himself among the "we" who have eclipsed the king's light, he may ultimately express the nation's quandary: most Englishmen at least in the early years of the revolution proclaimed their desire to serve the king, and many recognized they could not do so without their monarch's trust. But the speaker may also intend simply a personal plea to Lucasta. By deliberately diffusing the figurative light, Lovelace tactfully achieves both praise and criticism; at the same time the merging of Lucasta and Charles accentuates their mutual symbolic importance. They are for Lovelace synonymous with the complex of unstated values a royalist in the 1640s identified with love and honor. In the enveloping darkness of these years, both Lucasta and Charles emanate the light that gives inspiration and guidance.

Lucasta's radiance shines even more triumphantly in the poem originally intended to complete the edition, "Calling *Lucasta* from her Retirement." Its yearning for reunion develops the concern with separation absent in all but the last of the Lucasta poems scattered throughout the volume's second half. In the penultimate poem of the series, the dialogue *"Amyntor* from beyond the Sea to *Alexis,"* an Alexis reluctant to part from his Lucasta is urged to come with her away "From thy tempestuous Earth / Where blood and dearth / Raignes 'stead of Kings" (p. 102). In the final ode the speaker implores "Sacred *Lucasta"* to dispel the darkness and destruction of a war-ravaged nation. With an extravagance reminiscent of the Caroline masques, he envisions the emergence and ascendance of a now almost totally abstract figure. Seated in the triumphant chariot that the poem imagines, Lucasta fulfills all that Charles and Henrietta Maria symbolized in the Whitehall festivities. Simultaneously sunlike and martial, Lucasta embodies both Venus and Mars, the lady and the sword, as she appears to bring in her regal progress a source of life and the return to a golden age. But the promise of this new Astraea remains in the end only a hope:

> See! She obeys! by all obeyed thus;
> No storms, heats, Colds, no soules contentious,
> Nor Civill War is found—I meane, to us.
>
> (p. 106)

Though the speaker attempts to recall from her retirement the means to an idyllic life, he recognizes that the light symbolized in Lucasta shines at best only in the narrow world of lovers. And even this radiance diminishes:

> Lovers and Angels, though in Heav'n they show
> And see the Woes and Discords here below,
> What they not feele, must not be said to know.
>
> (p. 106)

Their celestial love lacks finally the buoyant faith so unmistakable in the edition's first two poems. Lovelace wants to believe that the suffering of civil war can be transcended even if it cannot be transformed, but the poem admits a willful blindness: the lovers "must not be said to know" the pain they seem to have left behind.

The pastoral "Aramantha" added to the completed volume confronts "the Woes and Discords here below." Separated from her beloved Alexis and disguised as the figure Aramantha, Lucasta has lost much of her human identity as she moves freely through her Elysium of natural beauty. The queen of the flowers, who turn to her instead of to the sun, this generating force of nature fittingly has a royal residence in the "stately grove." Among the flowers and particularly at the "Court oth' Royall Oake," Lovelace recreates the ordered, bountiful world of monarchy no longer possible in England. An obscure account of Lucasta's separation from her beloved and a long description of a white heifer destined to be ritually slaughtered imply in their rhythm of sacrifice and restoration some hope for the nation's future,[15] but the symbolic "Virgin-star" Lucasta leaves little doubt about the country's present plight. Lucasta is another Astraea:

> chac'd by *Hydraphil*, and tract,
> The num'rous foe to *Philanact,*
> Who whilst they for the same things fight,
> As *Bards* Decrees, and *Druids* rite,
> For safeguard of their proper joyes,
> And Shepheards freedome, each destroyes
> The glory of this Sicilie.
>
> (p. 117)

Neither partisanship nor illusion clouds Lovelace's recognition that both warring factions have destroyed a golden age. The veiled allusion to England's fate criticizes the pride and folly of a people who have lost sight of the good in their stubborn resolve "to stand or fall, / And win a little or lose all." Confronted with the discovery of his long-lost Lucasta, Alexis reacts with understandable decisiveness:

> His armes hung up and his Sword broke,
> His Ensignes folded, he betook
> Himself unto the humble Crook:
> And for a full reward of all,
> She now doth him her shepheard call,
> And in a *See* of flow'rs install.
>
> (p. 118)

The sword no longer serves any purpose and the seas now present a welcome calm for lovers "Fast pinion'd" only "in each others armes."

Despite the obvious ways in which the resolution answers the initial lyrics to Lucasta, the development from separation to reunion does not fully encompass the complexity of the collected poems. The readiness to abandon war and to embrace a pastoral life, a decision Carew and Daniel in their own ways also make, seems in the 1640s the only possible course for many royalists. Lovelace, however, sees both the temptations and limitations of this retirement. Lucasta appears most attractive when in the last two poems her world is most artificial, and there the ideals are most accessible through the imagination. What she embodies has little place in darkened England, and in their praise of her the poems approach the extreme and by now remote idealization of the Caroline masques. Yet their almost wistful escapism does not undercut the attractiveness of all that Lucasta symbolizes. Although the martial heroism of dashing men on horseback, the traditional image of the Cavalier, has proven of little worth, the private commitments to love and honor have continuing value. England has lost the peace a decade of writers has associated with the Caroline monarchy, but Lovelace has not foresaken the imagination and idealism so strikingly apparent in the court productions and in the last poems to Lucasta. He knows that the Stoic answer to the question "What is the happy life?" is simply "peace of mind, and lasting tranquillity. This will be yours if you possess greatness of soul; it will be yours if you possess the steadfastness that resolutely clings to a good judgment."[16] In the self-containment characteristic of other poems in the 1649 publication, Lovelace seeks to regain freedom and tranquillity. His sense of Stoic happiness encourages the idealism and the imagination apparent in two of the volume's most famous poems, "To Althea, From Prison" and "The Grasse-hopper."

In praising the Cavalier trinity of love, wine, and loyalty, "To Althea, From Prison" defies the restriction of prison gates with a graceful verve and witty seriousness that enhance an essential Stoicism. Unlike Roger L'Estrange's contemporary version of the same theme, the poem has neither the woodenness nor the verbosity of the stilted sermon, "Contentment cannot smart. Stoicks (we see) / Make torments easy to their Apathy."[17] The emphatic belief that "Stone Walls" and "I'ron bars" cannot contain "Mindes innocent and quiet" reexpresses in convincing albeit traditional terms the Stoic ideal of tranquillity. Lovelace obviously understands the inspiring appeal of love and patriotism, and he does not need Seneca's essay "On Tranquillity of Mind" to remind him that Bacchus "the inventor of wine is not called the Releaser [Liber] on account of the licence it gives to the tongue, but because it frees the mind from bondage to cares and emancipates it and gives it new life."[18] The poem sings of liberation with an unfettered fancy that creates in the enthrallment of Althea and the bondage of Bacchus a paradoxical freedom that defies the proverbial wisdom, "bondage bringes, the freest man in awe."[19] Lovelace's inventive lyrical inversions of the prison conceit do not, however, ignore the realities outside. The songs about the king's "sweetnes, Mercy, Majesty, / And glories" are sung "With shriller throat," as if the singer must urgently assert these truths; and a loud voice will sing "How Good / He is, how Great should be" (p. 79). No attempt is made to conceal the king's diminished state; in fact, the tentative "should" rather than the positive "shall" may reflect the contemporary dismay with a ruler who has not been as decisively regal as he should have been. The realism and tacit criticism ballast the soaring idealism that proclaims the invulnerability of the mind and soul.

Although the inspiration and expression are Lovelace's, the vision remains deeply rooted in the Stoic beliefs that "It is the power of the mind to be unconquerable" and that "the highest good is harmony of the soul."[20]

A similar Stoicism shapes the volume's other famous poem of Cavalier freedom, "The Grasse-hopper." Lovelace's address to his friend Charles Cotton develops its Stoic resolve from a complex understanding of a traditional emblem. The carefree insect who sings away the summer's sun and sports in "The Joyes of Earth and Ayre" only to prove a "Poore verdant foole! and now green Ice!" would seem to illustrate the familiar Aesopian moral. Seventeenth-century fables of the ant and grasshopper relish the ant's scornful dismissal of the irresponsible singer and warn against the fate of "carelesse Epicureans."[21] Lovelace shares their recognition of transient joys, but he is less sternly moralistic and more Anacreontic in his conclusion that the grasshopper's fate should "Bid us lay in 'gainst Winter, Raine, and poize / Their flouds, with an o'reflowing glasse" (p. 39). The "Genuine Summer" he and Cotton will create in defiance of their "frosen Fate" resembles the fulfillment enjoyed by the "Happy Insect" in Abraham Cowley's imitation of Anacreon's "The Grasshopper." This "Epicuræan Animal" reigns with its full cup "Happier then the happiest *King*," and the friends too with their song and wine will be "richer then untempted Kings."[22] The grasshopper in Cowley's poem, however, "retir'est to endless *Rest*" without experiencing either age or winter; Lovelace and Cotton must survive hostile times that turn the green of summer into ice. They can endure and even find "everlasting Day" when Cowley's grasshopper is no more because they understand the original meaning of Anacreon's poem.

"The Grasse-hopper" avoids Cowley's Epicurean embellishments and develops the essential classical note apparent in Thomas Stanley's version of "The Grassehopper." "All," in his contemporary translation of Anacreon,

> Thee the Springs sweet Prophet call;
> By the Muses thou admir'd,
> By *Apollo* art inspir'd,
> Agelesse, ever singing, good,
> Without passion, flesh or blood.[23]

In the original Greek the oxymoron of passionless singing is clearer: the passage defines the grasshopper in terms of the wise man or sage of Stoic literature.[24] Stanley recognizes this association explicitly in his prose commentary on the ode included in *Excitations Vpon Anacreon*. "The whole Ode is excellently paraphras'd and explain'd," he observes, "in the life of *Apollonius Tyanæus*, lib. 7. cap. 5 [sic]."[25] Stanley recounts the meeting between Demetrius and Apollonius at what was formerly Cicero's villa, where the two men seated under a plane tree hear across the summer's air the sounds of the grasshoppers. For two thinkers who must live through Domitian's suppression of philosophers, the music is poignantly relevant: "O happy and truly wise; You sing the song the Muses taught you, subject to no censure or misconstruction; by them freed from the slavishnesse of hunger and humane envies: and dwelling in these bushy tenements (which they provided for you) celebrate their happinessse and your own."[26] Lovelace could not have read this commentary before he wrote "The Grasse-hopper" because *Excitations Vpon Anacreon* was not published until 1651, but he knew Thomas Stanley well, and he may have seen or at least discussed the translations much earlier. Certainly the rest of the account Stanley includes would have been even more germane for him:

> *Apollonius,* though he knew well whereto these words tended, gently reprov'd him, as more cautious then the time requir'd; Why, saith he, desiring to praise the Grassehoppers, dost thou not do it freely and openly, but even here seemest to fear, as if there were an Act against it; *Demetrius* replyed, I did not this so much to shew their happinesse, as our own misery, They are allowed to sing, but we not to whisper our thoughts: Wisdome as a crime is laid to our charge.[27]

Without having known Stanley's translation and commentary or having read Philostratus's *The Life of Apollonius of Tyana,* Lovelace would still have appreciated the plight of those similarly oppressed. He would also have known that the grasshopper had long signified the musician, the nobility, the political outcast, and even the talkative companion.[28] More important, he would have understood the lessons of Stoic patience to be learned from the grasshopper.

Anacreon's Stoic grasshopper frequently appears in the emblematic and zoological lore of the seventeenth century. In gathering together much that was traditionally associated with the grasshopper, Thomas Moffett's *The Theater of Insects* particularly stresses the moral implications of the grasshopper's behavior. Besides acting as a portent of happier times and "a spur to provoke men to endure labour," the grasshopper teaches fortitude and reserve. Creatures living in a lowly position near the earth cheerfully "make the lowness of their condition more easie to them. But we men," Moffett chides, "if cast from any high place, we presently despair, and are afraid at every turn of the wheel of Fortune."[29] That "Grasshoppers of all other Insects seem to be without passion" also leads Moffett to moralize, "but the perturbations of our mindes do carry us on so headlong, that upon every slight cause, yea none at all, we wax hot with anger, pine away with grief, burn with envy and jealousie."[30] An emblem of the grasshopper from Joachim Camerarius, *"Expecto Donec Veniat,"* also unmistakably stresses the patience associated with the grasshopper. Lovelace was undoubtedly acquainted with the Dutch writer's work, and the resemblance between his poem and the motto are obvious: "The little grasshopper in hopes of spring patiently endures the cold: / The sound mind even in distress hopes for aid."[31] Besides citing the behavior of Job and the Italian proverb *"Di qvesto me contento, et meglio spero* (I am content with this, and I hope for better)" to exemplify the faith in divine assistance and heavenly reward all should have, Camerarius also emphasizes that a "prudent man, bearing for an immoderately long time and patiently the attacks of adverse fortune, awaits with a resolute spirit a better fate." The Stoical nature of this conduct is underscored in the emblem's final proof, the lines from *De Rerum Natura:* "Wherefore, if anyone would govern his life with true reason, / A man's real wealth is to live sparingly, / With an even temper."

This Stoicism also protects the friends in Lovelace's poem against the north winds that bring the storms of political disruption.[32] Though the "thou" addressed in the two halves of "The Grasse-hopper" deliberately blurs together the grasshopper and Cotton, Lovelace assures his friend that theirs need not be the fate of Aesop's grasshopper. The "sacred harthes" and the "show'rs of old Greeke" are not the escapism of royalists who have retreated solely to the warmth of country estates and the solace of wine and songs. Fires in the hearths will consume themselves, but sacred hearts may "burne eternally," and in the rebirth suggested by the showers, royalism may reign anew:

> Dropping *December* shall come weeping in,
>   Bewayle th' usurping of his Raigne;
> But when in show'rs of old Greeke we beginne,
>   Shall crie, he hath his Crowne againe!
>
> (p. 40)

In their congeniality Lovelace and Cotton will recreate the "Raigne" of Christmas festivities forbidden in 1647 by parliamentary action, and in their hearts as well as by their hearths they can also anticipate the restoration of the church and monarchy.[33] Although the poem does not assert the religious faith implicit in Camerarius's emblem, the friendship in Lovelace's poem presumes as essential Stoic patience:

> Thus richer then untempted Kings are we,
>   That asking nothing, nothing need:
> Though Lord of all what Seas imbrace; yet he
>   That wants himselfe, is poore indeed.
>
> (p. 40)

Together Lovelace and his friend will reign with a sovereignty greater than any monarch simply because they understand the self-possession Anacreon and others idealize in the grasshopper.

As Lovelace recognizes at greater length in "Amyntor's Grove," wine and song alone cannot stave off the realities of a hostile world. The temptation to withdraw into the country house and to abandon all to a sensual gratification has an undeniable attraction that the poem ultimately qualifies. More so than in Carew's celebration of Wrest Park, this tribute to the aristocratic life enjoyed perhaps at Endymion Porter's Aston-sub-Edge envisions an Epicurean retreat.[34] Surrounded by paintings that seem to transform the walls into "one continued Tapistrie," Amyntor, Chloris, and their children enjoy an enclosed and artificial paradise of sensuous pleasure. Here exotic scents and rare art delight the senses of those invited to bind their "loose hayre with the Vine, / The Poppy, and the Eglantine." Freed by a bacchanalian reverie found nowhere else in Lovelace, the imagination and the senses experience a liberation close to stupor:

> So drencht we our oppressing cares,
> And choakt the wide Jawes of our feares,
> Whilst ravisht thus we did devise,
> If this were not a Paradice
> In all, except these harmelesse sins.

(p. 73)

The imaginative and sensual ravishment reflects in its violence the urgent, even desperate attempt to flee from reality into a world Lovelace knows after all cannot be another paradise. With the entrance of the two children and the concluding prayers for the future, the blessings of this miniature masque can only desire and not ensure a time in which "No Serpent lurke," "No sharpe frost cut," and "no North-winde teare." However inviting the seductive and self-indulgent retreat of Amyntor's Grove may be, Lovelace realizes that the children as well as the poet must inevitably confront the cares and fears outside. There they may understand and appreciate the Stoic contention that pleasure "is a matter of the understanding, and we assign it to the mind," and not as the Epicureans argue "a matter of the senses."[35]

Appropriately this sovereignty of the intellect appears most strikingly in the ideals of noble patience and heroic fortitude Lovelace sees in the double portrait of Charles and his son James painted by Peter Lely at Hampton Court late in 1647. Though some art scholars express reservations about the execution of a painting they find more characteristic of Dobson and Fuller than of Lely, Lovelace praises in its bold and harsh strokes a depth not usually associated with Lely's work.[36] His declaration that "None but my *Lilly* ever drew a *Minde*" in fact describes the subtlety of his friend's portraiture in terms traditionally reserved for the poet. Where later art critics find a stern, tempest-marked countenance,[37] Lovelace sees with the poet's eye the "sweet" scorn and the "sacred" contempt of *"happy misery."* Separated from the queen and the Prince of Wales, who had left England when royalist fortunes fell, the father and son of Lely's painting show none of the grandeur and intimacy of Mytens's and Van Dyck's earlier family portraits; yet to Lovelace the bleakness of their situation appears to draw the two even closer to each other in a "griefe triumphant." The king's *"clouded Majesty"* presents to other monarchs the "shaded booke" in which they may find "their proudest, richest looke," but to the son the "quick luster" shining gloriously through the mist "enlightens his owne eyes." In the isolation and defeat the war had brought by 1647, father and son steadfastly stand an inspiration to each other:

> He cares his cares, his burthen feeles, then streight
> Joyes that so lightly he can beare such weight;
> Whilst either eithers passion doth borrow,
> And both doe grieve the same victorious sorrow.
>
> (p. 57)

The moment of greatness captured in the poem's response to the painting epitomizes for Lovelace the heroic bond that inspires all royalists who draw together in their own kingly patience and heroic suffering.

None of the other poems in *Lucasta* asserts so triumphantly the paradoxes of the unconquerable mind. The fate of the "Royal Captive" in Lovelace's extravagant compliment to "The Lady *A. L.*" anticipates, however, the next volume's greater preoccupation with the theme of victory in defeat. Although its involved, even tortuous comparison between the speaker and a condemned prince probably intends no explicit allusions to the immediate political situation,[38] the courage the "great Soule" displays in the face of certain death reflects Lovelace's growing attraction to the Stoic resolve: "I prefer to conquer rather than to be captured."[39] The undefinable "something there" within the prince that "Fate cannot overcome" moves his conqueror to give him both his freedom and his own crown, but in the poem's paradoxical view of heroism, traditional victory becomes defeat. The reprieved and triumphant captive "ne're 'til now thinks himself slave and poor; / For though nought else, he had himselfe before" (p. 62). Charles's troubles may well give poignancy to the prince's reaction to the burdensome crown, and the royalist temptation to withdraw from the affairs of state may also be present, but the dominant sense is the desire for the self-possession and tranquillity denied the prince "Who first had lost his Body, now his Minde." As Lovelace further explains in the song "A Guiltlesse Lady imprisoned; after penanced," joy can be found in grief and triumph in ignominy as long as the soul and mind remain free.

The paradoxical victory over defeat, imprisonment, and imminent death extends finally in *Lucasta* to death itself. The Christian resolution traditional to seventeenth-century elegies encourages the paradoxes Lovelace develops in the poem written on the death of Charles Cotton's sister, but in the face of grief he does not dwell on the consolation of eternal reward. Though he assures Cassandra Cotton's mourners that death brings birth, his poem encourages them at much greater length to assert themselves and to triumph over their grief. In decidedly Stoic terms the poem "To his Deare Brother Colonel *F. L.* immoderately mourning my Brothers untimely Death At *Carmarthen*" offers a similar resolve. William Lovelace was killed while fighting with the king's forces his brother Francis commanded, yet the poem forgoes the obvious opportunities to extol William's noble sacrifice for the royalist cause and to proclaim his enshrinement among the unforgettable heroes of the war. Instead Lovelace's poem about the futility of grief encourages Francis to meet the "I'ron decrees of Destinie" with "thy firme selfe." In a military metaphor befitting William's death, the poem defines the heroism that ensures victory:

> But this way you may gaine the field,
> Oppose but sorrow and 'twill yield;
> One gallant thorough-made Resolve
> Doth *Starry Influence* dissolve.

(p. 86)

The complete collapse of the royalist position and the execution of the king would force Lovelace in later poems to reconsider the terms of the victory over destiny, but even the poems published in 1649 suggest a conception of honor more complex than that traditionally found in his poetry. Though Colonel Richard Lovelace fought on the battlefields of the 1640s, war and martial heroism assume little importance in comparison to the honor that gains Francis Lovelace the field. Even when the poet toasts the man who led his regiment in the Scottish campaign, his drinking song "To Generall *Goring,* after the pacification at *Berwicke*" has trouble putting the best face on a peace won "at the Foes rate," or on their terms. Particularly in his poems to Lucasta, Lovelace sees the futility of a war that separates both the poet and the nation from the ideals they seek, and certainly in the collection's last poems he turns away from the nation's conflict. At other times wine, poetry, and friendship are means through which he confronts rather than escapes the tempestuous times. His inspiration on these stormy seas is the distinctly Stoic philosophy that "it takes a brave and resolute spirit not to be disconcerted in times of difficulty . . . but to keep one's presence of mind and one's self-possession and not to swerve from the path of reason."[40] Though his flights of imagination at times seek in an elaborate pastoral world and through masque-like symbolism the sense of completion George Daniel also longs to realize, in *Lucasta* Lovelace remains paradoxically a less solitary and a more self-contained Stoic than this Yorkshire loyalist. Like Cartwright, moreover, he retains a greater awareness of the community that binds the self-possessed.

The poems recorded on 14 November 1659 in the Stationers' Register and published together with *Elegies Sacred To The Memory of the Author* in 1660 reaffirm the importance of an inspiring symbolic fulfillment as they both challenge and reconfirm a Stoic faith in the unassailability of the human soul and mind. Little is known about Lovelace's life after his release from prison in 1649, when according to Wood and Aubrey he lapsed into greater melancholy, became dependent upon the charity of others, and died in the squalor of Gunpowder Alley. Lovelace's considerable literary activity during the last years of his life and the impressions of him left by his friends in their elegies tend to dispute this version of misfortune,[41] although uncertainty surrounds the poetry that appeared in *Lucasta. Posthume Poems*. Lovelace had died two years before his brother Dudley Posthumous Lovelace and his friend Eldred Revett saw this collection through the press, and there is no way of knowing whether he had arranged the poems before his death or, for that matter, whether they were all written after the completion of his first volume. Except for the series of datable occasional poems at the conclusion, the second volume resists chronological analysis. Significant changes in tone and focus, however, differentiate many of its poems from those published in 1649. The poems to Lucasta, which are all grouped together at the opening, set the tone of Lovelace's increasingly detached and indirect response to the years of revolutionary change.

Lucasta is the subject in ten of the opening twelve poems, none of which contains the pointed political commentary of the earlier Lucasta poems. The expected play on her name reemphasizes a radiance that rivals the sun as a source of life as well as light, and poems about her sable muff and black patches continue to display deft and witty compliment. The poems' adulation conforms for the most part to the traditional Petrarchan mode, except for the uncertainty sometimes present in the conventional hyperbole. This ambiguity becomes apparent in the initial poems, "Her Reserved looks" and "Lucasta laughing." The first saves the tired poetic notion of living or dying by the lady's smile with a comparison to an anamorphic painting that presents in different perspectives an angel or a devil. When the smile becomes in the next poem a laugh, it is less easy to interpret. Lucasta laughs while the world has "put on its shroud"; she laughs until she cries "At our ridiculous pain; / And at our merry misery" (p. 122). She may be laughing at lovers caught up in the throes of unrequited love, or she may be mocking a nation consumed with self-destruction. The poem's answer leaves both possibilities open, although it implies a political dimension to the Petrarchan situation:

> That which still makes her mirth to flow,
>  Is our sinister-handed woe,
> Which downwards on its head doth go;
>  And ere that it is sown, doth grow.
>   This makes her spleen contract,
>    And her just pleasure feast;

> For the unjustest act
> Is still the pleasant'st jest.
>
> (p. 123)

From a political perspective the two oxymorons "ridiculous pain" and "merry misery" appear bitterly ironic, and the aloof lady seems cruelly callous in her response to "sinister-handed woe." But from Lucasta's transcendent position, grief that grows before it is sown may appear "ridiculous" woe and suffering a source of merriment. The poem does not deny the injustice of the situation; it suggests that laughter may be the only defense in circumstances that cannot be altered.

Lovelace's desire in this and the next Lucasta poem is to distance himself from events beyond his control. "Night. To *Lucasta*" can be read as a conventional Petrarchan compliment not unlike some Lovelace had published earlier, but an oppressiveness characterizes the opening apostrophe to the "loathed Jaylor" night that

> dost arise our living Hell,
> With thee grones, terrors, furies dwell,
> Untill *Lucasta* doth awake,
> And with her Beams these heavy chains off shake.
>
> (p. 126)

Though the speaker never clarifies the nature of his captivity, the chains are not borne with the spirited lightness of the prison poems in the 1649 edition of *Lucasta*. This "Bondslave" finds both night and day equally dreary, giving urgency to the hope that Lucasta will rejuvenate the world. Together the entrapment and detachment in "Night. To *Lucasta*" and "Lucasta laughing" imply a new degree of alienation finally explicit in the last of the Lucasta poems, "The Ant."

"The Ant" develops conventional praise of Lucasta in an unexpected and troubling direction. Like its counterpart, "The Grasse-hopper," this emblematic poem begins with a traditional image. The ant whimsically portrayed in the opening stanzas as "great good Husband" and "large example of wise thrift" inevitably evokes classical and Christian associations. Besides the obvious relationship to Aesop, the opening image of the ant bent under its single grain recalls the "excellent and thrifty housekeepers" described by Aelian and Pliny; the wisdom of its ceaseless labor, moreover, echoes the biblical injunction to "Go to the ant," that independent and provident laborer, "and be wise."[42] But Lovelace may also intend a contemporary allusion in the parenthetical line "(For thy example is become our Law)." Although its political overtones are as elusive as those in "The Grasse-hopper," the poem probably alludes to the Puritan penchant for seriousness and the laws passed to curb festivities. In chiding the ant for its dour, consuming industry, the first half of the poem playfully exaggerates the threat posed by this "almighty foe," confident of the redemption that Lucasta's radiance brings. In her presence ants indeed "art worse than prodigal," for she restores the green world and invites "all to play and sport." This witty subversion of the ant's traditional emblematic significance becomes unsettling, however, when the poem's second half undercuts the conventional moral.

Those who refuse to heed Lucasta's light and law are doomed. Abruptly changing its tone, the poem loses its amused tolerance and attacks the *"Austere* and *Cynick"* ant that continues to "drive on sacred Festivals, thy Plow; / Tearing high-ways with thy ore charged Wain" (p. 135). The mirthless creature who cannot share the grasshopper's pleasures now bears resemblance to the zealous reformers bent upon remorseless destruction. Now a "miserable Ant," it is destined to fall prey to "fatal foes." Lovelace ignores traditional assurances about the rewards of frugal, industrious, and prudent conduct; in popular fable the ant may have jeered at the grasshopper's winter plight, but in the poem's macabre wit, Margaret Pie and John Daw have the last laugh: "Thy Self and Storehouse now they do store up, / And thy whole Harvest too within their Crop" (p. 135).

The conclusion leaves no room for sentiment. The ant, the pie, and the daw are all part of an inescapable rhythm:

> Thus we unthrifty thrive within Earths Tomb,
>   For some more rav'nous and ambitious Jaw:
> The *Grain* in th' *Ants,* the *Ants* in the *Pies* womb,
>   The *Pie* in th' *Hawks,* the *Hawks* ith' *Eagles* maw:
> So scattering to hord 'gainst a long Day,
> Thinking to save all, we cast all away.
>
>                                                     (p. 135)

Defeated royalists might find some consolation in the conviction that their oppressors will in turn be destroyed, but beyond this, the stark moral offers little solace. Predatory jaws and imprisoning tombs indiscriminately consume grasshoppers as well as ants, and only those who seize the moment and reach out for the light Lucasta brings can hope to stay the final darkness. Without dwelling as he does in "The Grasse-hopper" on the joys of mirth, Lovelace again inverts the proverbial wisdom of the familiar fables and emblems of the ant; this time, however, his reaction to the overly serious ant is bleak. Lucasta's light becomes lost in the gloom, and events lose their purpose in the ravenous maw of time. Without her purposeful and joyous presence, indifference and libertine abandon are tempting alternatives Lovelace confronts in the poems that follow.

He responds to this temptation most directly in the bacchanalian song of wine and love, "A loose Saraband." The liberation extolled in earlier poems of love, camaraderie, and loyalty loses its power of inspiration as Lovelace catches the tone of disillusionment and cynicism increasingly heard in the drinking songs of the Interregnum.[43] The stately court dance Lucasta had inspired in another poem, when a touch of her hand transformed "Grief, Despair, and Fear" into a saraband (p. 131), becomes in her absence the disordered whirl of "Mad Love" and "wilde Canary." The dance responds to the rhythm of the times:

> See all the World how't staggers,
> More ugly drunk then we,
> As if far gone in daggers,
> And blood it seem'd to be.
>
> (p. 140)

In the nightmare of violence that surrounds him, the reveler in "A loose Saraband" asks, "Lord! what is Man and Sober?" Reason, responsibility, and restraint appear to have no role in the abandonment and intoxication of "Still Drinking and still Kissing." Contemptuous of fool's honor, the reveler never rises above immediate sensual gratification:

> Let others Glory follow,
> In their false riches wallow,
> And with their grief be merry;
> Leave me but Love and Sherry.
>
> (p. 141)

None of the grasshopper's mirth and spirit is found in the rollicking abandon; its disavowal of honor does not, however, endorse complete nihilism.

"A loose Saraband" stops short of the abandon Lovelace satirizes in "A Mock-Song." The revelers in this ironic poem embrace the predatory times they have created and now exploit. With the monarchy and the established church destroyed and their "brave *Oliver-Brutus*" supreme, the rebellious forces have nothing to restrain their excessive appetite:

> Now the *Sun* is unarm'd,
> And the *Moon* by us charm'd,
> All the *Stars* dissolv'd to a Jelly;
> Now the *Thighs* of the Crown,
> And the *Arms* are lopp'd down,
> And the *Body* is all but a Belly:
> Let the *Commons* go on,
> The Town is our own,
> We'l rule alone.
>
> (p. 155)

The heraldic allusions suggest the fate of Charles, Henrietta Maria, and their supporters,[44] but the passage also recognizes the far-reaching implications of history's revolutionary course. Lovelace shares the common royalist belief that avarice motivates reform, and he is not alone in perceiving the ironic parody of the creation in the reformers' overweening pride. Though he appreciates the disillusionment and frustration that prompt the speaker in "A loose Saraband" to scorn the pursuit of honor, Lovelace has no doubt about the result. The revelers' last boast, "For our Dragon hath vanquish'd the St. *George*," underscores the apocalyptic chaos in store for the nation. The tripping rhythm and the blatant irony of "A Mock-Song" disarm, however, some of the threat; and neither poem supports the assertion that "Lovelace's libertinism lacks balance and suggests a total disillusionment with experience."[45] Even without the symbolic light of Lucasta, the other poems in the posthumous collection resist the understandable but dangerous disregard for honor. Many of the most significant propose alternatives to "The Ant" that develop emblematically the Stoic resolve with which Lovelace triumphs in defeat.

The poem on the snail that follows "The Ant" may well be, in fact, a deliberately designed companion piece. As the "Wise Emblem of our Politick World," the snail counters the ant's "large example of wise thrift"; as the "great stay'd Husband," the snail also invites comparison with the "great good Husband, little Ant." A creature who lives "Strickt, and lock'd up" in a shell both its cloister and its tomb, the snail has come to terms with the constricting and threatening forces that loom so ominously in "The Ant." Lovelace's playful, learned depiction of its self-sufficiency captures in miniature various arcane notions, but the essential significance of "The Snayl" is established in the first verse paragraph:

> Wise Emblem of our Politick World,
> Sage Snayl, within thine own self curl'd;
> Instruct me softly to make hast,
> Whilst these my Feet go slowly fast.

> (p. 136)

The snail conveys meaning for a "Politick World" because "much it may teach us, for our caution, to have a care of our enemies, who do privily lay snares for us when we do not see them."[46] Emblems of a snail pinned to the ground by an arrow attest to the wisdom of cautious vigilance, and the prudence of proceeding "slowly fast" is another emblematic commonplace. Lovelace may well have had in mind the emblem of the snail that counsels *"Lente sed Attente"*—"When thou a *Dangerous-Way* dost goe, / Walke *surely*, though thy pace be *slowe*."[47] Its advice is well-suited to the "Sage Snayle," which avoids the industrious ant's fate by emulating the sage or wise man of Stoic literature.

The poem celebrates the contemplative but disciplined life of responsible withdrawal. Lovelace's "analys'd King" is the "great stay'd Husband" who rules "still within":

> Thou, thee, that's thine dost Discipline;
> And when thou art to progress bent,
> Thou mov'st thy self and tenement.
>
> (p. 137)

Although the passage may glance obliquely at the ill-fated Charles I,[48] its immediate contrast is with the ant's husbandry. The *"domiporta"* or house-carrying snail exemplifies in emblem literature the Ovidian maxim "Who lies well hid lives well," but as Camerarius suggests with the help of Seneca and Persius, the better gloss "Live with yourself" does not endorse any retreat undertaken without concern for reason, judgment, and public good.[49] With none of the ant's destructive consequences, the snail's progress resembles the laboring movement of the snail in another Camerarius emblem that exhorts "learn from me labor and true virtue, / If you desire to be 'decorated' with the honor of true praise."[50] Curled within itself in an emblem of self-sufficiency, Lovelace's snail has both the detachment and the time to contemplate or "tast" the "sweets of Nature" that the ant ignores in its frantic energy, and though it too must yield to nature's rhythm, it dissolves into the rarefied air with none of the violence and ignominy that mark the ant's demise. The snail's end befits the fate of the Stoic wise man, who dies without reluctance because he "lives as one who has been lent to himself."[51]

In living and dying well, the snail provides the defeated royalists with an inspiration all the more obvious at the end of the next poem, "Another." This lighter piece concludes its mock heroic depiction of the snail's doubleness with sudden and pointed seriousness:

> But banisht, I admire his fate
> Since neither Ostracisme of State,
> Nor a perpetual exile,
> Can force this Virtue change his Soyl;
> For wheresoever he doth go,
> He wanders with his Country too.
>
> (p. 138)

Again emblem literature underscores the Stoic belief that "to the wise man every place is his country."[52] The snail in Camerarius's erudite interpretation exemplifies the virtuous individual of Stoic tradition who triumphs over misfortune through virtue and truth.[53] Camerarius's learned commentary and Lovelace's fanciful application recall in less exalted terms Seneca's response to his own exile: "And so the mind can never suffer exile, since it is free, kindred to the gods, and at home in every world and every age; for its thought ranges over all heaven and projects itself into all past and future time. This poor body, the prison and fetter of the soul, is tossed hither and thither. . . . But the soul itself is sacred and eternal, and upon it no hand can be laid."[54] The poem's ambiguous collocation "banisht, I admire" merges the poet and the snail to give poignancy to Lovelace's own plight. He and the other loyalists forced to live in various degrees of exile might quite naturally see in the snail's solitary journey a "Wise Emblem of our Politick World." They might also see in the mortal struggle narrated in "The Falcon" another emblem of the triumph over fortune.

The soaring falcon who rules the skies as the heir to Jove's imperial eagle and the cousin german of the sun enjoys the unrestrained freedom for which Lovelace's poems often yearn. When this "Free beauteous Slave" perches on her mistress' wrist, the falcon also becomes a gracious compliment reminiscent of "A Lady with a Falcon on her fist." Her devoted service to the lady's commands and her dazzling flights—which falconers consider "the most noblest and stately flight that is"[55]—suggest the chivalric ideals synonymous with the term Cavalier, but the poem invites no specific symbolic dimension until its tenor suddenly shifts in an abrupt consideration of the falcon's "lofty fate." Lovelace's detailed narrative of her combat with the heron ends with a funeral procession of mourning birds that implies a momentous but elusive import. While the struggle and fall of a bird traditionally linked with royalty encourage a parallel with Charles I's fate, the poem does not sustain a specific historical reading. It develops less explicitly than "The Ant" and "The Snayl" emblematic associations with particular relevance to the 1650s.

An emblem from the collection of Joachim Camerarius once again illuminates the ways in which Lovelace views the falcon's death. Camerarius's emblem of the heron in its foe's grips depicts a strategy found in contemporary discussions of falconry: "The Custom of the Hearn when she sees the Hawk, stooping at her, and no way of escape, is to turn her Long Bill upwards, upon which the Hawk not being able to stop, runs itself through, and so both often drop down dead together."[56] Or as Lovelace describes the encounter,

> Swift as the Thunderbolt he strikes,
> Too sure upon the stand of Pikes,
> There she his naked breast doth hit
> And on the case of Rapiers's split.

(p. 144)

The motto under the emblem headed *"Exitvs In Dvbio Est"* seems equally relevant to Lovelace's poem: "Doubtful is the outcome and uncertain the battles of Mars: / Not unusually he who just now appears the victor is conquered."[57] Since Lovelace had already drawn upon Camerarius in "The Snayl," Lovelace probably knew the following passage as well: "Who is there who would judge it to be possible for the uncertain and false outcomes of wars to be better represented than by this obvious similitude?" From the battle between the falcon and the heron Camerarius moralizes at length about the uncertainty of fortune, citing among other classical illustrations Seneca's reaction to Sextus Pompey's and Lepidus's defeats, "which made clear to the world how rapid a fall could be from the highest to the lowest, and by how different a road fortune could destroy a great power." Virgil's account of war in *The Aeneid* also prompts Camerarius to note further, "The saying may also be read 'There is no salvation in War: we all beg thee for peace.'" The uncertainties and destruction of war so obvious to Camerarius in the emblem of the falcon are also unmistakable in Lovelace's response to the death of this magnificent bird. But like his other emblematic poems, "The Falcon" complicates traditional associations.

Although Lovelace shares Camerarius's awareness that the heron would not ordinarily prove a match for the falcon, he is less willing to attribute the falcon's death to fortune. The "bold Gen'ral" who commands the air with all the authority and guile of a masterful tactician forces her "desp'rate" quarry into a suicidal reaction:

> Noble he is resolv'd to fall
> His, and his En'mies funerall,
> And (to be rid of her) to dy
> A publick Martyr of the Sky.
>
> (p. 144)

"Wild" at the "affront" she takes in having missed him with her first charge, "The raging foe impatient" strikes again, "Wrack'd with revenge, and fury rent." Both destroy and are destroyed. Without assigning blame "The Falcon" regrets the mutual misfortune and finds a consolation that is missing in the emblem:

> But ev'n in her expiring pangs
> The *Heron's* pounc'd within her Phangs,
> And So above she stoops to rise
> A Trophee and a Sacrifice;
> Whilst her own Bells in the sad fall
> Ring out the double Funerall.
>
> (p. 144)

The falcon's valiant attempt to rise with its prey challenges the emblem's motto by turning defeat into triumph. The victory, however, is bittersweet:

> Ah Victory, unhap'ly wonne!
> Weeping and Red is set the Sun,
> Whilst the whole Field floats in one tear,
> And all the Air doth mourning wear.
>
> (p. 145)

The solace remains the elegiac promise that the falcon's "eternal name shall live."

The falcon will live in the memories of royalists who share Lovelace's understanding of the civil war. Supporters of the monarchy who had good reason to believe that the king would emerge victorious from battle might understandably appreciate the poem's rueful rationalization. Confronted with a zealous foe bent upon destroying its enemy at all costs, they had learned that their boldness, gallantry, and pride could be as fatal as the falcon hurtling to its unexpected death. They might also see the same self-destructive valor in the embodiment of the Cavalier spirit, Charles I. Like the falcon of emblem and poem, the king unexpectedly fell, driven by his regal inability to compromise. And in death, as the nation learned, "*He* nothing common did nor mean / Upon that memorable Scene."[58] On the platform outside Whitehall, the king's inspiring death upheld the royalist ideals once celebrated in the Banqueting Hall within. Charles I's death also expresssed in the most memorable fashion the dignity, grace, and fortitude that Lovelace saw in the Lely portrait and that he admired in the Stoic sage. They are the inspiring values of that royal bird the falcon triumphant in death.

But the poem never forgets that it is a "Victory, unhap'ly wonne." The falcon's heroic efforts to rise with the heron sound the "sad fall" of a "double Funerall." Although "The Falcon" does not explicitly moralize, like Camerarius's emblem it conveys a Virgilian recognition of war's cost. The falcon and the heron are forces of opposition swept up in an inexorable movement analogous to the course of history. With neither the bleakness nor the grim humor that characterizes "The Ant," their destinies reveal the loss inevitable in the uncertain struggles of time. From this emblem of mortal conflict, Lovelace understands with considerable sympathy and remarkable detachment the elegiac lesson of civil war. Transcending a narrow, partisan view of history, Lovelace's poem resists the pessimism of "The Ant" or the indifference of "A loose Saraband" and embraces the optimism of "The Snayl." Amid the sorrow of the nation's suffering, Lovelace saw that in emblem literature the falcon can also illustrate "The virtuous mind, and truely noble spright."[59]

His next emblematic poem asserts with greater irony that victory and destruction are often, moreover, inextricably one. "A Fly caught in a Cobweb" exemplifies a "Small type of great ones, that do hum, / Within this whole World's narrow Room" (p. 155). The fly that catches at the people's breath before being caught in the spider's "airy net" obviously and ironically illustrates the courtier's fate. Lovelace refers to the "Court Fly" in the poem on Lucasta's black patch, and the fly appears commonly at court in Aesop's fables. John Ogilby, for example, typically contrasts the parasitic fly with the industrious ant when he warns:

> But when a Tempest comes, and *Fortune's* Frown
> Tumbles thy King, as other Princes, down,
> Then in vast Circles may the Hungry *Fly*
> Round empty Halls, and keep his parch'd Trunck dry;
> There shall the spider subtile Meshes spread,
> And having seiz'd thee, feast upon thy Head.[60]

Lovelace may well have the political implications of Ogilby's fable in mind, but he does not draw the usual morals about idleness, vainglory, and uncertainty. Instead he inverts another commonplace about the fly to give further historical immediacy to its plight: "Was it not better once to play / I' th' light of a Majestick Ray?" Emblem writers like Robert Farley would answer, of course, in the negative, for they saw in the fly drawn to the candle's flame the fates of Icarus and Phaeton, and they were certain that "many times glory doth fooles undoe."[61] Lovelace, on the other hand, ignores the warnings about pride and prefers the glorious striving of Phaeton:

> Yet hadst thou faln like him, whose Coil
> Made Fishes in the Sea to broyl;
> When now th' ast scap'd the noble Flame,
> Trapp'd basely in a slimy frame;
> And free of Air, thou art become
> Slave to the spawn of Mud and Lome.
>
> (p. 156)

Defeat with the "Majestick Ray" or king, the poem implies, is nobler than the fate of those doomed to roam as aliens searching for sustenance. When they are caught, as Ogilby suggests flies inevitably are, they are both consumed and they consume. The spider who gradually sucks away the fly's life and then turns the fly into a web to catch others becomes an apt emblem of the 1650s:

> Strange witty Death, and cruel ill,
> That killing thee, thou thine dost kill!
> Like Pies in whose intombed ark,
> All Fowl crowd downward to a Lark;
> Thou art thine En'mies Sepulcher,
> And in thee buriest too thine heir.
>
> (p. 156)

The macabre wit twists the biblical story of the ark into an ironic parody of Noah's saving efforts: the fly will bury its own kind in a coffin or pie it has helped to make.[62] But the fly will consume more than its heirs, for the "Strange" and "witty" death contains a further poetic justice.

Like the heron's death the fly's destruction involves its enemy's death. To catch the fly's heirs the spider must spin its deadly web from its own viscera and, in the poem's final irony, thereby consume itself. In the end the fates give the victory to the fly:

> As the *Rhinoceros* doth dy
> Under its Castle-Enemy,
> As through the *Cranes* trunk Throat doth speed,
> The *Aspe* doth on its feeder feed;
> Fall yet triumphant in thy woe,
> Bound with the entrails of thy foe.
>
> (p. 156)

The epic death evoked in the final image of the fly caught in the entrails of its enemy[63] is summarized in the comparison to the rhinoceros pinned in death under the elephant. Both Aelian and Pliny note that the overmatched rhinoceros gets under the elephant's belly, eviscerates the defenseless foe, and then often dies under the weight of its mortal enemy.[64] In Renaissance emblems the rhinoceros illustrates the motto *"Non invicta recedo,"* a phrase indebted to Martial.[65] Under Camerarius's emblem of a rhinoceros sharpening its horn, the moral is unmistakable: "To conquer—for to fall down in death is beautiful praise, / But it is a disgrace to retreat from battle with trembling step."[66] Camerarius cites among his illustrations the duke of Florence's resolve to defend Charles V at all costs, and Lovelace could have supplied similar examples from the English civil war, but the poem characteristically avoids specific historical parallels as it seeks consolation in the midst of defeat. In the 1650s triumph over woe ultimately demands the quiet courage implicit in the poem's final emblem and evident to Lovelace's contemporaries:

> So you that must encounter Want, and Care,
> To overcome your hard, and crabbed skill,
> Take courage, and treade vnder foote dispaire,
> For better hap, attendes the vent'rous still:
>    And sooner leaue, your bodie in the place,
>    Then back returne, vnletter'd with disgrace.[67]

Against despair solace may be found in the heroic virtues of fortitude and perseverence.

The consolation is less forthcoming in Lovelace's final poem in this vein, "The *Toad* and *Spyder*." The duel between these natural enemies describes at great length and in precise detail a miniature military campaign; unlike "The Falcon," however, the poem singles out neither creature as a type or emblem. Against a foe reputed among contemporaries as "most venomous and remarkable for courage and strength," the spider demonstrates why her most enthusiastic admirers marvel "that in so small, or in a manner no body at all

. . . there could be so great force, such incredible audacity and courage, such sharp and hard bitings, and invincible fury."[68] But Lovelace does not capitalize upon their belief that "The *Toad* might be very fitly compared to all *envious, cruel, malicious,* and *tyrannical* men."[69] Horrid though he may be with his foaming mouth and speckled skin, the "Pol'tick *Toad*" emerges from his den a "glorious Combatant" and a "glorious General" who dies in "glorious Despair." The victorious spider, on the other hand, "gluttons her self full" on her enemy, as rats gnaw on the heads of heretics enclosed with them in baskets, "Vomiting her *Stygian* Seeds, / Her poyson, on his poyson, feeds" (p. 164). And when the spider renders her victim passive, she vents her "ingenious Rage" in protracted torture:

> one Eye wittily spar'd, that he
> Might but behold his miserie;
> She on each spot a wound doth print,
> And each speck hath a sting within't;
> Till he but one new Blister is,
> And swells his own Periphrasis.

(p. 166)

Lovelace's equally obvious wit distances but does not diminish the violent nightmare perplexingly dismissed in the spider's inevitable victory. The web Arachne spins at the end into a stately pavilion in honor of Pallas Athene, the goddess whose help she has had in defeating the toad, becomes another enclosure safe from the surrounding violence. But Lovelace never explains why Athene would aid the woman Ovid claims she turned into a spider after Arachne had defeated her in a weaving contest, and he avoids any comment on the triumph of Arachne and Athene. The narrative does not approach the political allegory of John Ogilby's "The Battel of the Frog and Mouse," nor does its tone suggest the bitterness of a defeated loyalist who identifies with the spider's witty conquest.

"The *Toad* and *Spyder*" illustrates clearly Lovelace's tendency to be suggestive rather than explicit. To a greater extent than Daniel's symbolic narratives, the emblem poems in this series often establish contexts that invite biographical and political readings yet avoid the direct parallels expected in allegorical narrative. Poems that evoke an immediate historical reference often distance themselves from the situation through a fanciful and whimsical wit. The natural world may indeed allow Lovelace to impose an order impossible in the realities of revolutionary upheaval, and it certainly allows him to understand and even accept his nation's crisis. By transposing the suffering and chaos of civil war into the neutral arena of nature, the poems gain detachment and perspective: events seem less monumental and their outcomes less uncertain when seen in the larger rhythm of nature's law. Lovelace does not conceal his disgust and horror at this self-destructive world, but from this vantage point he also sees beyond the bitter partisanship of war a tragic struggle in which both sides at times elicit sympathy. And in actions as diverse as those of the snail, the falcon, and the fly, Lovelace often finds the inspiration for meaningful conduct.

The values he admires are explicitly praised in the group of occasional poems that follow "The *Toad* and *Spyder*" and conclude *Lucasta. Posthume Poems*. The diverse relationships they commemorate and the principles they uphold suggest that near the end of his life Lovelace was neither the isolated nor the despondent figure Wood and Aubrey imagine. Written the year before he died, a poem for the marriage of the younger Charles Cotton continues the preoccupation with confinement and darkness. "The *Triumphs* of PHILAMORE and AMORET" cherishes in Cotton the radiant vitality that "'spite of Fate and War creates a Court" where friends forsake their benighted world for "an universal cheerfulnesse." In the panegyric to Lely, art provides the refuge against "all devouring time" and friendship overcomes "barbarous Neglect." Those who understand these values have the self-possession Lovelace stresses in his concluding invitation, "Now my best *Lilly* let's walk hand in hand, / And smile at this un-understanding land" (p. 183). Another friend, Eldred Revett, soars in his divine poems above Parnassus and "us small *Ants* there dabling in its dew" (p. 186); while in a translation of Hierocles published the same year, the "Posthume Victorie" of John Hall rivals that of Samson: "in thy fall / Thou pull'st the house of Learning on us all" (p. 191). All of these commemorative pieces celebrate the triumphant spirit Lovelace defines most explicitly in his central occasional poem, "Advice to my best Brother. Coll: *Francis Lovelace*."

The poem occasioned by one of the three ocean voyages Francis took in the 1650s never loses Lovelace's distinctive voice, though it closely imitates Horace's Book II, Ode X.[70] The deep waters and dangerous coasts Horace warns Licinius to avoid loom much more ominously in the argument for the golden mean that Lovelace presses upon his brother. The ocean cradle lulls the unwary into dream upon dream "untill / Horrour awake your sense, and you now find / Your self a bubled pastime for the Wind" (p. 175); and the "palsie Earth" is no more stable in its inconstancy. The "giddy earth," like the wheel of Ixion, "ne'r whirling leaves to reel / Till all things are inverted, till they are / Turn'd to that Antick confus'd state they were" (p. 175). The disorientation and betrayal described by Lovelace are also more threatening than the extremes Horace portrays in the humble and proud abodes. Lovelace translates Horace's ramshackle or run-down building into a "cobwebb'd Cot" with "wrongs entail'd upon't," and the Roman mansion of envy becomes a "Pallace for to breed / Vipers and Moths, that on their feeder feed" (p. 175). To these oppressive images, both of which recall the world of the fly and spider, Lovelace adds a criticism of pretense not found in Horace. His most significant change, however, occurs in the paradoxical advice to his

brother to raise a dwelling beyond the reach of envy by building low.
Horace's analogy to the "giant pine" and "lofty towers" becomes in Lovelace's interpretation,

> The blust'ring winds invisible rough stroak,
> More often shakes the stubborn'st, prop'rest Oak,
> And in proud Turrets we behold withal,
> 'Tis the Imperial top declines to fall.

> (p. 176)

Lovelace alone among the seventeenth-century adaptors of Horace changes
"*pinus*" or pine to oak. This important alteration recalls the fable of the oak
and reed, which for Ogilby exemplifies the wisdom of the political tem-
porizer who yields "till Time shall later Acts repeal";[71] but the oak also
alludes more immediately to the king. Lovelace develops this common symbol for royalty in "Aramantha," and the complementary phrase "Imperial
top" makes a similar allusion to Charles probable in the poem to his brother.
By substituting this description for Horace's lofty or tallest towers, Lovelace
suggests that a stubborn monarch unduly concerned with propriety brought
about his own destruction because he would not bend or compromise. The
curious verb in the line "'Tis the Imperial top declines to fall" implies,
however, still another twist to the meaning of "Imperial." Although the
passage in its Horatian context contends that the highest objects are the most
vulnerable or inclined to destruction, in Lovelace's version the line also states
that the highest-minded refuse or decline to fall. Because of their position,
Lovelace warns his brother, kings often suffer, but the kingly or noble remain
unbroken. As he counsels Francis in the next lines, "A breast of proof defies
all Shocks of Fate, / Fears in the best, hopes in the worser state" (p. 176). The
advice contains a defiance lacking in Horace's similar counsel to fear and
hope. Lovelace's adaptation of Horace's reminder that gentle spring inevitably follows harsh winter does not minimize the necessary courage. Acutely
aware of hostility and treachery, he nevertheless avoids pessimism. Despite its
note of caution, the poem ends with a positive admonition not found in
Horace: "In strictest things magnanimous appear, / Greater in hope, howere
thy fate, then fear" (p. 176).

The conclusion reduces to a couplet the understanding Lovelace has
gained in the two decades that radically changed his and the nation's fortunes. Compared with the first poem, "*To Lucasta*, Going beyond the Seas,"
the advice to a brother about to journey beyond the seas is less confident and
more considered. The tempestuous years of civil war have driven many of his
contemporaries to seek a safe haven, and Lovelace at times similarly yearns
for the refuge of withdrawal. Particularly in the bleaker period of royalist
defeat, when buoyant tributes to love and wine become dangerously self-
indulgent and escapist, Lovelace grows increasingly sensitive to a darkness

and a horror that enclose all. Yet his awareness of the rapaciousness that indifferently consumes ant and grasshopper alike never undermines his essentially Stoic belief in the power of the mind and soul. The assurances he gives his brother about a "breast of proof" come from the understanding that no place is safe from the ever-present dangers except within. In the homely example of the snail as well as in the inspiring behavior of the king, Lovelace celebrates anew the ancient faith in the stalwart, unconquerable will. Because he understands equally well the distinction between foolhardy courage and wise conduct, he warns his brother not to forget the Horatian mean, but his emphasis on hope and magnanimity eschews the resignation and negative consolation of some earlier poems. To a brother about to embark on a long sea voyage, Lovelace offers the encouragement Renaissance poets found in the emblem of the sea journey—the heroism of an Aeneas, "The valiant mind, whome nothing can dismay" for "This man hath trauail'd well."[72]

This vision is less clearly present in Lovelace's final work, a satire "On *Sanazar's* being honoured" that stands near the end of the volume apart from the preceding occasional pieces and the concluding translations. This address to an unidentified individual warrants its position because it may have been among the last poems Lovelace wrote and because it summarizes his understanding of the poet's role in the 1640s and 1650s. Lovelace is not by disposition a satirist, and his complaints about the onerous and unappreciated poetic muse are not original. The poem shares, however, with Lovelace's other two satires, "A Mock-Song" and "A Mock Charon," a fundamental scorn for all who have compromised the principles of an ordered society in their self-centered greed. Like the unidentified rebel Charon welcomes to the underworld, the unnamed poets Lovelace attacks in the long final piece have lost their honor. They too have satiated their greed at the expense of civilization's traditional values, and they too have consumed themselves in envious and factious attacks. The ideal they have compromised exists for Lovelace in the golden age of Augustus, where poets and warriors stood equal:

> Who best had written, and who best had fought;
> The Self same fame they equally did feel,
> One's style ador'd as much as th' other's Steel.
>
> (p. 193)

When he specifically invokes the spirit of Sandys, Wenman, and Falkland, Lovelace locates the ideal in the 1630s and the Caroline circle of Great Tew, the gathering of humanist wits Clarendon later celebrates as another university.[73] Above them the poem exhorts, "Arise thou rev'rend shade, great *Johnson* rise!" For Lovelace the "masc'line Spirit" of "Father *Ben*" embodies the classical virtues of the Augustan era his poetry seeks to inherit. Lovelace can lay little claim to the weighty moral seriousness of Jonson, and except for his final poem, he exhibits none of the satirist's anger; his patrimony is

Jonson's decidedly Stoic sense of integrity. Lovelace values an honest, unillusioned awareness of human potential and a constant, disciplined commitment to humanist morality premised upon a faith in the capacity of the good to endure. For him the heroic struggle was not on the battlefield, where he distinguished himself, but within the individual; and this inner struggle rather than the war itself remains the subject of his poetry. There in the celebration of the victory still possible in defeat he fulfilled the Augustan ideal of the poet/warrior.

# 5

# Alexander Brome and "the Safe Estate"

ALTHOUGH Alexander Brome also lived through the collapse of the royalist cause, unlike Richard Lovelace he left no memorable lines of
triumph and defeat. While Lovelace lost his estates and languished in prison,
Brome pursued a successful legal career, taking time to write in varied voices
about his country's crisis. "Eminent in the worst of Times for Law, and
Loyalty, and yet more for Poetry,"[1] he moved from his obscure country
origins in Dorset to a position of some prominence in both the legal and
literary circles of London. By the time the three editions of his *Songs And
other Poems* appeared in the first years of the Restoration, Brome was a well-
established attorney before the King's Bench and at the courts of Westminster and Guildhall; he had also published a comedy, edited collections of
Richard Brome's plays, and contributed poems to major commemorative
volumes.[2] His translations of Horace, issued later, won him further contemporary acclaim, and soon after his death in 1666 the fame of this corpulent,
balding, and prosperous Londoner seemed secure: in the opinion of Edward
Phillips's *Theatrum Poetarum* (1675) "among the Sons of Mirth & *Bacchus*,
to whom his Sack-inspired Songs have been so often Sung to the sprightly
Violin, his name cannot chuse but be immortal."[3] With the turn of the
century, however, Brome's eminence began to diminish; today he is chiefly
remembered as a minor poet who supports with seemingly effortless wit the
royalist cause. While this judgment of his stature is not entirely unwarranted,
the modern tendency to slight Brome's poetry may be unjust.[4] Brome
managed not only to endure but to flourish in the tumultuous years of the
monarchy's decline, destruction, and restoration; and his *Songs And other
Poems* offers a tough-minded, often unique alternative to conventional literary notions of the loyalties and values of war-wearied Englishmen.[5] With
neither Lovelace's defiant idealism nor his tempered Stoicism, Alexander
Brome resolves to go about the business of daily living patiently and pragmatically.

The loyalism of this self-made Londoner, indeed, at times develops a fine
distinction between accommodation and compromise. Distanced from the
ritual invocation of the court entertainments and the common expectations
of the Oxford ceremonial verse, Brome also finds little solace in the enclosed

worlds of the country-house life and the solitary pastoral retreat. On occasion
his poems approach the detached, *contemptus mundi* strain of George Daniel's
ruminations, but more often their satiric and even skeptical scrutiny develops
the unsettling assertiveness of Richard Lovelace's "A loose Saraband" and "A
Mock-Song." In the vanity of a nation violently separated from its traditional
values, Brome confronts the "steady drift into disillusionment" that a recent
history considers "one of the most obvious features of the 1640s and
1650s";[6] and he questions at great length the love, honor, and loyalty others
in this study have accepted. A devil-may-care shrug and an alcohol-induced
reverie are in his poems obvious alternatives to a widening spectacle of
maddening folly, yet neither adequately characterizes Brome's response.
Though his poems flirt with a cynical indifference, Brome never abandons
the loyalist belief in principled individuals as he is drawn inward in search of
an inviolable existence. In pursuit of this safe estate, he ultimately celebrates a
self-possession founded upon a Stoic humanism that links him with William
Cartwright as well as with Richard Lovelace.

Unlike their poetry, however, his political songs, ballads, odes, and epistles
follow the admittedly homely muse he finds appropriate to those "verseless
times." Poems to his fellow poets Richard Lovelace and Charles Cotton
describe a darkened world inimical to "true poesie."[7] Unlike George Daniel,
who had ambitions toward heroic narrative, Brome argues half-seriously that
the fantastical events of the present best suit the ballad: "For a man may be
furnished with so much matter, / That he need not lie, or rail, or flatter"
(1:214). Less ironically, he refers to his poems as "harmelesse lines" uncon-
cerned with the affairs of state and written to amuse himself and selected
friends with "short and sweet delight" (1:244). The tributes of his friends
and associates agree that the wit and wine of his poems flow with the
unrestrained mirth of a "chearfull heart." For some the lively, merry, and
frolicsome songs recall Anacreon's light, untroubling verse—a poetry that
never labors pretentiously for strong lines and "far-fetch't Metaphors." During the bleakest of England's hours, these unstudied and "familiar" poems
provide not only the diversion of a trifling entertainment; they also counter
treason with loyalty. Izaak Walton is not alone in his assertion,

> Here's a Collection in this book
> Of all those chearfull songs, that we
> Have sung so oft and merilie
> As we have march'd to fight the cause
> Of Gods anoynted, and our lawes.
>
> (1:60–61)

Among the common descriptions of his uplifting voice is the gratitude that in
these chaotic decades Alexander Brome shouldered the poet's burden and
"*Atlas*-like thou didst that world sustain."[8]

He does so without the Cavalier commitment so often associated with Lovelace. Missing from the Cavalier trinity of wine, women, and royalism in Brome's poems is an inspiring Lucasta; women in fact have little role in his political songs and ballads. Relegated for the most part to the first section of *Songs And other Poems,* they inspire wit rather than loyalty. The only poems that bring women and war together, in fact, provide pretexts for set pieces exploiting the relationship between sexual and military conquest.[9] When Brome's love poetry most resembles Lovelace's, as it does in "To his Mistress," the conclusion argues for a promiscuity much closer to Suckling's libertine philosophy. Along with specific metaphors and situations, Brome often appropriates Suckling's view of the "wise" lover and advances a similar iconoclasm.[10] The speaker has no reservations about proclaiming "I'm a Schismatick in Love" (1:70), for the poems assume a studied solipsism. The wise lover, in Brome's adaptation of Suckling, knows that the "tempting toy thy beauty lies / Not in thy face, but lovers eyes" (1:108); and he characteristically falls back upon the recognition, "Nor is't men's worth, but wealth, makes Ladies love 'um" (1:78). Where fancy reigns supreme and all becomes relative, a libertine indifference and a pragmatic materialism break the conventional bonds of constancy and undermine traditional assumptions about beauty. The stabilizing hope Lovelace sought in the inspiring image of Lucasta ceases to have value, and freely flowing cups of wine serve on occasion to liberate the jolly heart from any concern with women. The effect is calculated cynicism, an attitude apparent as well in the one political poem that might otherwise be linked with Lovelace, "The Royalist."

At the head of the first section of political poems in all three editions, this drinking song has obvious similarities with Lovelace's "To *Althea,* from Prison." Each celebrates the unvanquished spirit of the loyal subject, likening the prisoner to a bird who though encaged continues to sing, and both poems assert the liberating powers of wine. In the absence of an uplifting Althea, Brome's poem, however, derives its inspiration solely from the king's misfortune. The health it proposes to Charles I seeks consolation in the face of the bitter reality all royalists knew in 1646, the date of this song:

> We do not suffer here alone,
>   Though we are beggar'd, so's the King,
> 'Tis sin t'have wealth, when he has none,
>   Tush! poverty's a Royal thing!
>
>                                              (1:117)

Brome does not express Lovelace's reservations about a ruler who in defeat is now drawn closer to his fellow prisoners, and he does not proclaim the mind's invulnerability. His tough-minded speaker accepts the war's outcome with a scornful shrug and proposes instead to buoy the spirit through a carousing song that promises to imitate the whirling, unstable world. All cares will cease to matter in alcoholic reverie, and in the circling motion of the mind and glass a new order may emerge:

> Me thinks the Travels of the glasse,
>   Are circular like *Plato's* year,
> Where every thing is as it was;
>   Let's tipple round; and so 'tis here.

(1:118)

The resolve empties the circle of the self-possession Lovelace embraces and transforms this traditional symbol of self-containment into one of blatant escapism. The glasses that keep the round inspire a carefree indulgence reminiscent of "A loose Saraband," and the senses seem to have usurped the domain Stoics attribute to the mind. Brome's poem tends toward the libertine indifference that Lovelace's poetry resists, and many of his other pieces develop a similar detachment, but none of them unambiguously voices his own commitment.

Except for the epistles and commemorative pieces, which seem generally written *in propria persona,* Brome's ballads, odes, and songs speak in a range of voices from across the social and political spectrum. At the beginning of *Songs And other Poems,* a prose epistle cautions the reader that the author's beliefs must not be confused with the speakers' attitudes: "those Odes which may seem wild and extravagant, [are] not to be Ideas of my own mind, but characters of divers humours set out in their own persons. And what reflected on the Times, to be but expressions of what was thought and designed by the persons represented; there being no safe way to reprove vices then raging among us, but to lash them smilingly" (1:51). Failure to heed this distinction, in fact, may explain the modern judgment that his poems are "sour little songs . . . eloquent of a bitterness which, in the end, lacks all nobility and degenerates to an ill-tempered sneer."[11] Brome, who earlier had written a successful play, creates another form of drama in this pageant of figures that shows a country in revolution groping for identity. Through critical scrutiny of these characters, Brome often ridicules self-serving hypocrisy, but occasionally the distinction between the author and his personae blurs as Brome himself attempts to come to terms with the national upheaval. The result is a tonal complexity not found in Lovelace's espousal of the Cavalier values; its range and nuance reveal the ironic and ambivalent involvement of an author unable always to distance himself from the follies of the times and "to lash them smilingly."

The earliest of the dated poems, "The Saints Encouragement," offers one touchstone for Brome's avowedly satiric vision. In this ironic response to the parliamentarian actions of late 1642 and early 1643, Brome underscores the absurdity of the zealous reformer who apparently sees no contradiction in his exhortation to preserve the nation by destroying it. The heavy-handed irony of the rebel's zeal exploits a technique common to the royalist satires, and the refrain "The clean contrary way" complements a common contemporary view of the rebellion's madness.[12] Relentlessly the poem's ironic portraiture exposes the ways the kingdom's government, religion, and prosperity have been compromised under the guise of reform. Parliamentarian claims that Charles has been misled by his counsellors and that the war is being fought against the king's body and not the office are ridiculed as sham; boasts about their triumphs on the battlefield and their reforms in the legislature are dismissed as delusions. The poem in effect shares the attitude of the royalist pamphleteer who notes in 1643, "For by this strange division of the King from himself, or of his person from his power, a traitor may kill Charles, and not hurt the King: destroy the man, and save the magistrate; the power of the King in one of his armies may fight against his person in the other army, his own authority may be used to his own destruction, and one may lawfully set upon him, beat, assault and wound him, in order to his preservation."[13] Within the contradictions of the reformers' rhetoric, the poem discloses the irony of their values and the basis of their actions:

> We subjects Liberties preserve
>   By prisonment and plunder,
> And do inrich our selves and state
>   By keeping the wicked under.
>
> (1:208)

The satiric devices of inversion and self-revelation give similar impact to a series of obviously ironic portraits. Another call to arms in "The *Scots* Curanto" shows that the Scots thrive on the English difficulties: the cynical speaker of this 1645 poem gloats that the pretense of reformation will "tickle the minds of the giddy-brain'd rout" and "We'l gain by their loss and folleys" (1:211). The same call taken up three years later in "The Levellers rant" blurs common greed and ideology, but once again the sinister implications of reform are not lost in the speaker's claim,

> 'Tis no lesse then treason,
>   'Gainst freedom and Reason
> For our brethren to be higher then we.
>
> (1:127)

When religious reform becomes a "matter of trade," as it is in "The Holy Pedler," and Parliament proves to be little more than the charlatan of "The New Mountebanck," the country seems hopelessly caught in the grasp of the rapacious. During the course of the civil war the names of the exploiters change with the fortunes of battle; their aims, however, remain constant. As the Saint of 1643 becomes the Independent of 1648 and the prospects for the radicals' victory brighten, "The Independants resolve" flaunts the blatant greed of "The Saints Encouragement":

> Let the King and his Kingdom groan.
> The Crown is our own and so shall continue,
>   We'l Monarchy baffle quite,
> We'l drink off the Kingdomes revenue,
>   And sacrifice all to delight.
>       'Tis power that brings
>       Us all to be Kings
> And we'l be all crown'd by our might.
>
> (1:138–39)

Another of the earliest dated poems, "An Ode. Written in 1643," leaves no doubt about the disaster that will follow now that the lesser stars and planets have pushed the figurative sun from its rightful course and "blind *Phaetons*" have seized control. The poem's thinly veiled commentary on the rebellion of Parliament ignores Charles's misguided attempt to enter Commons and to seize five members, while the ode's traditional imagery and its dire warning of catastrophe suggest the loyalty to the monarchy and a sense of natural order developed explicitly in "A Serious Ballade":

> I love the King and the Parliament,
>   But I love them both together;
> And when they by division asunder are rent,
>   I know 'tis good for neither.
>
> (1:219)

The hope in the poem's refrain that "the King and his Realms agree" values a harmony premised on the assumptions that Parliament remains subordinate, religion unsullied, and law undisturbed. The speaker may well voice the moderation found in 1645 among the proponents of peace, but his allegiance to the principles of mixed monarchy and a unified church would have been shared by the great majority of Englishmen in the 1640s.[14] As the "good subject" concludes in a poem written the year before,

> One God, one King,
> One true Religion still,
>     In every thing
> One Law both should fulfil.
>
> (1:172)

Threats to this unity quite naturally appear to be the forces of ambition and anarchy personified.

While other contemporary ballads and songs also decry a mercenary, lawless age,[15] Brome's poetry is especially sensitive to the period's confusions and frustrations. Even in the early stages of the war, before the royalist cause seemed doomed, Brome was realistic about the conflict's destructiveness. The maddening contradiction of a war ostensibly fought for peace is painfully apparent to the speaker of "The Riddle": "good subjects" cannot win, this 1644 poem contends, whichever side ultimately triumphs. Caught between factions that threaten their lives and property, they can only express anguished perplexity:

> Both say they wish and fight for peace,
>      Yet wars increase.
> So between both, before our wars be gone,
> Our lives and goods are lost, and we're undone.
>
>                                                  (1:172–73)

Later events strengthen the personae's insistence on the social and economic victimization of the country. The long account of misfortune narrated by the rustic in "The Clown" makes much the same point as the equally desperate voice in "The Commoners": the average citizen is subject to the whims of the powerful, and "all are undone for ever" (1:118). The sentiment and even the language of these poems from the years 1645 to 1647 reflect the nation's frustrated longing for peace and the bitterness of a war "devouring like so many Locusts and Caterpillars, all our grass, hay, corn, bread, beer, fuel and provision of all sorts, without giving us one farthing recompense and leaving us . . . to starve and famish."[16]

Throughout the poems of this period, Brome refuses to admit that political and religious principles are anything more than a pretext for ambition. "A Satyre on the Rebellion" composed during this increasingly bleak time of royalist fortunes summarizes the criticism voiced by the various personae. The satire laments the hardships the country must endure when those in power "know no other godliness but gain" and surveys the self-destruction of a nation that has unsettled the body politic, seized the reins of "a glorious *Phoebus*," and preyed upon "loyal Subjects." Its speaker, who can "only weep our misery and ruth," expresses the helplessness of those who share the lament:

> How wretched is that State! how full of wo,
> When those that should preserve, do overthrow!
> When they rule us, and ore them mony raignes,
> Who still cry Give, and alwayes gape for gains!
>
>                                                  (1:284)

The power of money—an inescapable reality for Saint, Independent, and commoner alike—is also a familiar theme among other royalist satirists,[17] but Brome stresses particularly the pervasive acquisitiveness of society. The theme, which occurs quite often even in his love poetry, remains for him the overriding motive of civil disruption.

Brome further contends that the current struggle is merely part of the timeless spectacle of human vanity in which "All the world keeps a round" (1:154). The circular pattern of rising and falling that he sees in "this mad age" is clearly a form of universal mutability. Ambitious upstarts intent upon displacing their betters and turncoat opportunists responsive to changing fortunes confirm for Brome the truism that the times turn around and nothing is constant. Though this philosophy is occasionally offered by the speakers as an excuse for their actions, the poems do not lightly dismiss the recognition that

> In this grand wheel the world we're spokes made all,
> But that it may still keep its round,
>                    Some mount while others fall.
>                                    (1:148)

The political revolution brought about by the years of upheaval strengthens Brome's sense of cyclical rhythm, and from this perspective he will come to conclude that the English civil war in the long run changed little.

Brome's response to the horror of civil war conveys, in essence, the same attitudes developed more fully in two other undated works included in *Songs And other Poems*, a paraphrase of the first chapter of Ecclesiastes and a translation of Lucian's "An Essay of the Contempt of Greatnesse." The biblical vision of pointless, circular existence and the classical attack on the hollowness of status are echoed in Brome's skepticism about the human inclination to gratify "palate, pride, and lust." Ecclesiastes in particular provides Brome, as it did Francis Quarles, with an outlook "Very Seasonable and Vsefull for these Times";[18] and he replicates much of the Old Testament wisdom in his poetry. But as the certainty of the royalist defeat deepens, the poems also turn to Lucian and, in the words of the satirist's cynic, "consider how few things, how small / A wise contented man may live withall" (1:330). Brome does not share Daniel's reluctance to condone Lucian's scrutiny of human folly, and he does not similarly stress the religious consolation of the Bible. Like the Stoic visions of Boethius and Lipsius, the classical translation and the Old Testament paraphrase encourage a sometimes detached and often critical search for the happiness possible day to day. Their recognition that little of lasting value can be found in an uncertain world complements the poems' growing preoccupation with the fulfillment possible in the critical decades that challenge loyalty, integrity, and personal resolve.

From the outset the bulk of Brome's political poems, like "The Royalist," acclaim the revivifying power of the cup and affirm the biblical belief "There is nothing better for a man, than that he should eat and drink." In seeking to bolster loyal spirits through mirthful camaraderie, Brome justifies the contemporary tributes to his wine-inspired muse. Celebrations of the liberating powers of alcohol have, it has been seen, an established classical tradition, and drinking songs flourished as well in seventeenth-century drama and among Cavalier poets, but Brome's poems go beyond convention. During the years of conflict, laws prohibiting the drinking of healths to the monarch gave a political dimension to the social gesture of good fellowship, and by the end of the 1640s, drinking poems became a significant vehicle for social and political commentary.[19] Brome's drinking songs and catches often capture the spirit of the other popular sons of Bacchus, Hugh Crompton, Thomas Jordan, and Henry Bold; however, in their preoccupation with wine, his poems seek a liberation not found to the same extreme either in these writers or in Lovelace.

At their simplest the poems welcome the escape from oppressive reality in the carefree pleasures of drinking. Free-flowing canary and rounds of sack are ready means of solace for speakers who find no profit in the world's cares and who appreciate blithe spirits. Those who form the circle and keep the round disavow burdensome thought; they "hang caring and working" as they lift their goblets and spirits. Others who embrace the fellowship extolled in "The Club" and unite in the circle of turning bowls in "The Painters entertainment" banish all melancholy and measure time solely in terms of mirthful drinking. Liberated by the contents of their cups, the carousers in these poems not only praise the obliteration of an alcoholic stupor; they also celebrate the powerful fancy of a "wit-refining drink." Within the circle of the round, imagination makes them all monarchs, and they rule a golden realm:

> Now in our fancies we will suppose
>   The world in all its glory,
> Imagine all delight that growes,
>   And pleasures that can
> Fill up the vast soul of a man,
> And glut the coy pallat, the eyes, ears and nose,
>   By the fancy presented before you.
>
> (1:134)

The illusion of transforming if not transcending existence continues to hold the poet's attention, and a number of his carousing speakers propose their own kingdoms and universes. None, however, envisions the inspiring loyalties of Lovelace's poems. Wine becomes the newly crowned monarch, drink-flushed faces are stars or heavens, and the circular motion of the round and the tipsy spinning of the head vie with the turning of the times and the movement of the planets. The ingenuity with which Brome explores the analogies is soon exhausted in repetitious variations common to other Cavalier drinking songs,[20] but the tone is more interesting than the wit. The devil-may-care shrug of "The Good-fellow" conveys casual indifference and studied disdain, which appear even more obviously in "The Companion." Its dismissal of conventional philosophy for the wisdom of the bottle tends toward the emptiness of "*Copernicus*," a poem whose world specifically excludes any concern for either the king or women as it deliberately turns away from traditional sources of direction. When "The New-Courtier" attempts to restore the monarchy to the revolutionary world, the resolve seems drained of inspiration:

> Since it must be so,
> Then so let it go,
> Let the Giddy-brain'd times turn round,
> Since we have no King, let the goblet be crown'd,
> Our Monarchy thus we'l recover.
>
> (1:128)

The cup has been emptied of the spirit that uplifted Lovelace, and its alcoholic contents have become an end in themselves. Liberated, the imagination is consumed with escapism and stupefaction.

Among the drinking poems the two imitations of Anacreon illustrate clearly the tendency toward libertine abandon in the section headed by "The Royalist." Both adaptations capture the light, carefree air of Thomas Stanley's seventeenth-century translations of Anacreon, and either poem lends substance to the contemporary comparisons of Brome and the Greek poet. But the exuberant preference for drinking loses its simple, jaunty tone, and the invitation to forget worry assumes a scornful note foreign to Anacreon's mood. Although the first stanza of "Content. Out of *Anacreon*" follows the classical writer's theme of time's remorselessness, a second and decidedly not Anacreontic stanza adds an assertive, even reckless note to the carefree beginning. In the end the decision to ignore the turning of the times and to drown melancholy in rounds of cups follows from pessimism:

> Times keep their round, and destiny
> Observes not where we laugh or cry,
> And Fortune never does bestow,
> A look on what we do below:
> But men with equal swiftness run
> To prey on others, or be prey'd upon.
>
> (1:137)

The poem's certainty that "we can take no course, / To be better or worse" encourages a fatalism that leads in the companion piece to the conclusion, "'Tis better lie drunk then dead." Brome reaches this Anacreontic tag in "Mirth. Out of *Anacreon*" by scorning conventional honor. Where Stanley distances the ivy-entwined drinker from those who "run to martial fights,"[21] Brome's similarly crowned reveler proclaims,

Then Honour we account but a blast of Wind,
  And trample all things in our mind.
    The valiant at arms,
    That are led by fond charms
    Get their honour with harms
  While he that takes up
  A plentiful cup,
    To no danger is brought
    But of paying his groat.

                                            (1:138)


  The temptation to forget the cares of today and the worries of tomorrow grows with the realization that little can be done to alter the nation's destructive course. The invitation "Come let us be merry" in an untitled 1648 poem stems from the conviction that neither side can do the nation anything but harm:


    'Twixt Square-head and Round-head
      The Land is confounded,
    They care not for fight or battle,
    But to plunder our goods and cattle.

                                            (1:210)


The complaint had a good deal of currency in the latter years of the war, when soldiers such as the speaker of "The Trouper" allegedly supported their good cheer by exploiting the land.[22] Those forced to bear the expense of war, the poems argue, must in turn either consume or be consumed. With a logic ironically suited to a world the poems agree is mad, the urgent call for dissipation argues an unexpected liberation. Like the plundering troops, punitive laws fining the king's supporters and sequestering their estates were unavoidable, but those with no concern for money could paradoxically free themselves from the pain of the nation's woes:


    Our money shall never endite us,
      Nor drag us to *Goldsmiths-hall*,
    Nor Pyrates nor storms can affright us,
      We that have no estates,
      Pay no taxes or rates,
      But can sleep with open gates,
    He that lies on the ground cannot fall,
    We laugh at those fools whose endeavours
      Do but fit 'um for prisons or fines,
    While we that spend all are the savers.[23]

                                            (1:136)

At issue in these poems is the fundamental tension between an expedient compromise and a calculated indifference. The conflict is posed most obviously in "The Polititian" and "The Antipolititian."

Both poems clearly see a world where fate, time, and fancy keep the "grand wheel" ever turning; "The Polititian," however, develops a more biting, cynical tone. Its predatory amorality espouses an almost Hobbesian denial of any absolutes beyond the self. Refusing to concede that nature originally created a hierarchy within mankind, this 1649 poem also anticipates the *Leviathan* in stressing pride and greed. No government, it contends, has any inherent value beyond the power wielded by office, and those who rise above the others derive their position merely from the esteem accorded them. The solipsistic bias of the earlier love poems and drinking songs leads in "The Polititian" quite naturally to expedient timeserving. The poem accepts the world on its own terms, satisfied that the "wise man" who "first best loves himself" will survive. Its decision to "act and juggle as others do, / Keep what's our own, get others too" flaunts self-interest and counsels policy; any other course is folly. Traditional honesty and love simply have no value among wise men, "For he that sticks to what his heart calls just, / Becomes a sacrifice and prey / To the prosperous whirlegigs lust" (1:149).

The cynicism of "The Polititian" takes to an extreme the premise that the safest estate lies in self-enjoyment; its companion piece holds out the more optimistic possibility of safety without compromise. The freedom and contentment encouraged in "The Antipolititian" are to be found "Below" the politicians' sphere of envious and ignoble ambition. The poem's speaker concedes that life is uncertain and honor often insubstantial; he shares, however, Lucian's reluctance to be seduced by "grasping superfluities that cloy, / And indispose the mind, and with them bring / Cares and vexations" (1:329). Like him he urges the quiet, simplified life. The desired contentment in Brome's poem, the conditional "If I can safely think and live, / And freely laugh or sing," depends upon the convivial circle formed by friends. "Good Company and good wine" are essential to a supportive fellowship closer to the ideal of Lovelace's "The Grasse-hopper" than to the aim of Brome's carousing drinking songs. "The Antipolititian," in effect, moves away from abandonment toward a self-possession central to both Brome and the other royalist supporters in this study.

Convinced that flattery, position, and wealth play central roles in an "idle, empty pageant," the speakers in other poems of the same period weigh the value of politic expediency against the contentment of a detached estate. "The Leveller" and "The Royalists Answer" represent extremes in the political positions of the late 1640s, but their speakers' common agreement about the importance of honest, good fellowship confirms Brome's apparent preference for the attitudes of "The Antipolititian." Although the Leveller endorses the myth of egalitarianism voiced in "The Polititian" and repeats that poem's skepticism about the inherent worth of honor, he backs away from the policy implicit in his recognition of the natural desire for self-advancement. Despite deep-seated reservations about the ways of the world, the Leveller appreciates the nation's need for meritorious leaders; his own inclination, however, is to detach himself from the concerns of national well-being:

> For my part let me
> Be but quiet and free,
> I'le drink sack and obey,
> And let great ones sway,
> Who spend their whole time in thinking,
> I'le ne're busy my pate
> With secrets of State.
>
> (1:143)

In this the royalist concurs, but his response is surprisingly more cynical than that of his counterpart. His willingness to profit from the folly of those with some estate or wealth—to "squeeze" them with fines and fees—supports perhaps an intentional irony directed at current parliamentarian practices of sequestration and taxation. "The Royalists Answer," in any case, is not as forthright as "The Cheerful heart," a poem that cheerfully endorses flattery in the secure belief that the powerful will eventually fall, and "We will serve them at last, / As they serv'd those that have been above 'um" (1:158). In the end the royalist echoes the Leveller's desire

> To live quiet and free,
> To drink sack and submit,
> And not shew our wit
> By our prating, but silence, and thinking.
>
> (1:145)

The full cup once again commands the only true allegiance, and the rhythm of the round redefines the circularity of the threatening times: "He that drinks well, does sleep well, he that sleeps well doth think well, / He that thinks well, does do well, he that does well, must drink well" (1:145).

The ideal in these poems is self-sufficiency. Brome's speakers agree with the commentary on Ecclesiastes "that in all occurēces and chaunces of thys lyfe, we should liue cōtented wyth our present estate" secure with "tranquility of minde" and at ease with a "chearfulnesse of heart."[24] Their search for the safety enjoyed by Lucian's "wise contented man" acknowledges the long tradition of living within modest means and according to reason, but characteristically the poems of this period express unmistakable pragmatism. The "wise man" envisioned in "The Safety" can accept the security of an indifferent and insignificant estate because he has learned over the last years "I am never the better which side gets the battel" (1:130). As long as he can enjoy the quiet pleasures of friendship and wine, the struggles of 1648 and 1649 to fill the vacuum of power and to promote the safety of the government are irrelevant. His assertion "Let the three kingdoms fall to one of the prime ones, / My mind is a Kingdom and shall be to me" (1:129) is not Lovelace's Stoic resolve. An inspiring faith in the royalist cause is nowhere apparent, and the unconquerable domain of the mind is not exalted. The speaker's assurance "I'm as happy with one" kingdom depends upon the practical condition "If I could but injoy it."

Attempts in other poems to define the kingdom of the mind in the traditional terms of inner strength and outward constancy are not very convincing. "Satisfaction" offers the fullest definition of this desired soul and mind, but the catalogue of commonplaces the speaker ascribes to the "honest, pure and just" individual willing to risk his life for his principles is less satisfying than the poem's extended recognition that humans are by nature their own "God-smiths." The tagged and lifeless ideal again strains the conclusion of "The New Gentry," when its speaker repeats the argument in "The Leveller" that honor should be accorded only the "noble, pow'rful, wise, and just" who struggle in the service of their country. "Upon the Kings imprisonment" reverses this tendency toward generality yet gains little additional conviction. The virtues dramatized in Charles's response to his months of imprisonment at Carisbrooke constitute the patient, unmovable heroism of a righteously indignant monarch who scorns the treason of his subjects. The royal ire, however, lacks conviction, and the drama of the situation becomes artificial and strained. Charles's unshakable, even Stoic fortitude is lame; and the conclusion is more notable for its unintentionally prophetic flourish than for its conventionally paradoxical view:

> Alas though I'm immur'd, my mind is free,
> I'l make your very gaol my liberty.
> Plot, do your worst, I safely shall deride
> In my Crown'd soul, your base inferiour pride,
>     And stand unmov'd, though all your plagues you bring,
>     I'll dye a Martyr, or I'll live a King.
>
> (1:294)

Reduced to its simplest terms in "The safe Estate," happiness for many in those poems depends upon a deliberate contempt for the mutable times. Those who can confine their thoughts to their estates and their pleasures to their friends are encouraged to sit back in safety and "privately laugh" at the inevitable fates of all who are caught in state affairs. As the speaker of "The New Gentry" argues, since the upstarts derive much of their importance from the awe and fear their wealth and position create, the proper response is to ignore them whenever possible and to "live content and jolly / Laughing at their painful folly" (1:157). Scorn and indifference, Brome's poems are careful to point out, presuppose a moderate, unobtrusive, and self-sufficient estate; within this world, however, they often blithely and simply declare that life can fulfill its own uncomplicated rhythms with little concern for either fate or fortune:

> He may sing, he may laugh,
> He may dance, he may quaffe,
> May be mad, may be sad, may be jolly,
> He may sleep without care,
> And wake without fear
> And laugh at the whole world, and its folly.
>
> (1:177)

At its most earnest the attitude implicit in this laughter verges toward George Daniel's sense of *contemptus mundi*. Two similar poems of loss, one on the calamitous progress of the war and the other on the death of Charles I, move inexorably to the conclusion that faith provides the only consolation in an otherwise perilous world. The continued repetition of the phrase "Trust not" in both the meditation "On the loss of a Garrison" and the elegy "On the Kings death" emphasizes the bleakness royalists confronted at the end of the first civil war and in the aftermath of Charles's execution. In their attempts to put defeat and death into perspective, each poem fortifies the soul with the belief that uncertainty and betrayal are inevitable parts of life. A relentlessly pessimistic voice unusual in Brome's poetry stridently proclaims the vanity of wealth, honor, and policy; not even loyalty to friends or the actions of kings can escape treachery and transience. Only one refuge remains:

> Our only trust is in the King of Kings,
> To wait with patience the event of things;
> He that permits the Fathers tumbling down,
> Can raise, and will, the Son up to the crown.
>
> (1:298)

For someone who had seen the revolution challenge and destroy the established church and government, the wisdom of Ecclesiastes seems inescapable; and Brome might naturally agree with seventeenth-century commentators that "the drift of Solomon in this Book" confirms that "true happinesse here in this life cannot be attained by the enjoyment of any thing in the world."[25] Patience and faith are the logical reactions to troubled times—reactions suitable to the meditative and elegiac modes in which the speakers contemplate the loss of the garrison and the death of Charles.[26] But *contemptus mundi* does not necessarily reflect Brome's ultimate response to the 1640s.

In their desire to make the best of a difficult time without losing perspective or disengagement, Brome's poems of this period try various stances. One

moment the traditional ideals of patience and faith appear desirable, and at
another the escapism of sack and the pragmatism of temporizing predomi-
nate. Even the earliest poems, however, stress the futility of the civil conflict,
and time seems to deepen the awareness that "war is become a trade." With
this bitter knowledge, the poems written near the end of the 1640s tend to
abandon their lightheartedness and to develop the skeptical questioning of
Lucian and Ecclesiastes. But although their moods and resolutions change,
the poems are not completely despondent and cynical. In their marked
preference for the good fellowship of the safe estate, the speakers generally
favor an indifference firmly based upon practicality. Plots to gain power and
laws to suppress treasonous statements are at best secondary to state decrees
raising the price of wine. Although implicit in this attitude is a certain
selfishness and venality, Brome does not always fulfill his introductory promise "to lash them smilingly." The preference for personae and for companion
pieces allows Brome to entertain less socially responsible positions without
entirely disowning them. When the mask seems to drop, as it does in the
straightforward "Satisfaction" and "The Advice," Brome endorses the importance of conventional moderation, nobility, and honesty; but in other poems
he does not always undercut speakers bent upon expediency or answer
arguments designed for self-promotion. Despite the obvious posturing in so
many of the poems of this period, they ultimately reflect their author's doubts
about the value of commitment. Brome's ambivalence is unambiguous in his
subsequent attempts to survey the later course of the civil revolution and to
accept the social instability he finds disturbing and threatening.

Increasingly the poems written during the Interregnum stress the bank-
ruptcy of the parliamentary cause. In the months following the king's execution, the reality "we that are loyal" must face is clear:

> the red-coated Saints domineer,
> Who with liberty fool thee,
> While a Monster doth rule thee,
> And thou feelst what before thou didst fear.
>
> (1:95)

The speaker in "Upon the Cavaleers departing out of *London*" knows that the
center of royalist opposition must now suffer the folly of its actions, but the
loyalists banished by the 1650 parliamentary decree enforcing laws against
delinquency are the more immediately affected victims. Though the speaker
consoles his fellow Cavaliers with the earlier poems' assurance that the
oppressors cannot ultimately escape retribution, the injustice and dislocation
associated with laws against delinquents are particularly troublesome to
Brome. Ordinances enacted in 1643 empowered the government to se-
quester the property of royalist supporters, and by 1645 committees were
assessing fines for those who agreed to compound. The involved and uneven

course of composition favored those with substantial estates or wealth, and the Cavalier speaker in "The Murmurer" is not alone in his resentment:

> 'Tis only the petty Delinquent
>   With whom the matter goes hard;
> Where ever much boldness and Chink went,
>   There honour's bestow'd and reward.
>
> (1:110)

Further laws in 1650 and 1655 increasing the burdens upon the defeated royalists also caused a social redefinition Brome considers even more disturbing. The "illgotten store / Of the upstart Mushromes," whom he attacks as a class in "The New Gentry," represents the success of the entrepreneurs, moneylenders, and soldiers who profited from the misfortunes of royalists forced to borrow money or lose their holdings. The rise of the opportunists at the expense of the old order understandably dismayed many royalists, who scorn them as "upstart gentlemen," but Brome seems especially sensitive to the ways in which the beneficiaries of the nation's misery exploit the institutions of society for personal gain.[27]

To the embittered speaker of "The Reformation," the years of upheaval have merely advanced the greedy and unscrupulous. His long survey of the nation's welfare in 1652 dismisses the pretexts of reform as nothing more than opportunity to gain greater wealth and power:

> Our expence of blood and purse
>   Has produc'd no profit.
> Men are still as bad or worse,
>   And will be what e're comes of it. . . .
> Yet spite of all our pains and skill,
> The knaves all in the pack are still,
> And ever were and ever will.
>
> (1:162)

The fatalism leads the speaker in the end to the indifference sought in the safe estate, but sack and laughter are no longer sufficient. In a world in which might is a license to right, Brome stresses the helplessness of the "low and little," who are destroyed by the offices and laws designed ostensibly to protect them. Though the weakness of "Cobweb lawes" and the avariciousness of the legal system had long been recognized, Brome joins the growing criticism among the proponents of legal reform by specifically emphasizing the opportunism of lawyers and judges who build their own landed fortunes at the expense of those delinquents and litigants forced into their hands by the uncertain times.[28] A lengthy portrait of the rising tradesman further reveals Brome's preoccupation with the hypocritical and ambitious exploiters who capitalize upon the social mobility the war has encouraged.[29] The would-be squire who rises through oppression and extortion only to leave his ill-gotten gains to a prodigal heir illustrates the expectation and betrayal that characterize the religious reforms as well. Like law and business, the church has also become in the poem's judgment another source of corruption where ambition and money once again govern all.

Wealth and power assume still greater primacy in the other long survey of this period, "The Satyr of Money." This loose and sweeping catalogue follows by about a year the sardonic emphasis of "The Reformation" on the madness of the nation's changes, but it less subtly proclaims "The wonders that now in our dayes we behold." Brome's declaration that money is "the soul of the world, and the worlding too" challenges the essence of both public and private values. The venality of the Rump Parliament and the Interregnum government is a standard royalist complaint, and satires of lawyers and Puritan preachers also had a good deal of currency. Brome, however, characteristically stresses the relativity of all principles, and he accentuates the social upheaval endemic in a period driven by wealth. Lawyers and preachers effortlessly assume all sides of an issue because truth, beauty, and virtue all lie in the purse. Honor and respect are also at the command of money, and much of the satire confronts the bitter knowledge:

> For money mens lives may be purchas'd and sold,
>   'Tis money breaks laws and that mends 'um again;
> Men venture their quiet and safety for gold,
>   When they wont stir a foot their rights to maintain.
>
> (1:181)

Those who buy their freedom from the law seem to disturb Brome less in this poem than the dull, pompous individuals who have suddenly emerged as social superiors. Though the satire again affects indifference, the concluding gesture in the direction of sack and song is no more successful than the one in "The Reformation": it now appears as a perfunctory response made by an increasingly engaged speaker to a world that favors those "Without breeding, discent, wit, learning or merit."

By the end of Cromwell's rule and in the months of his son's government, the unsettling fortunes of revolution deepened the poems' conservative misgivings and further undermined Brome's earlier stance of indifference. From Thomas Pride's rise to a knighthood and a seat in 1657 among the lords, "The New Knight Errant" concludes, "So when honour is thrown, on the head of a clown, / 'Tis by Parasites held up, and Lyars" (1:205). The satiric account of the man famous for his role in excluding moderate Presbyterians from the parliament that tried the king refuses to dignify him with any mention of his forceful actions in the crucial Pride's Purge of December 1648. By emphasizing instead the colonel's pretenses to the military honors won by his betters and by detailing the high sheriff's later harassment of

Cavaliers, the poem anticipates John Berkenhead's ridicule of "a mundane self-seeker lacking even the affectation of principles."[30] Thomas Pride may merit none of the respect traditionally associated with the royalists' sense of the gentleman, but events nevertheless elevated him to a position his betters no longer occupied:

> Our successour of Kings, like blind fortune flings,
>    Upon him both honour and store;
> Who has as much right, to make *Tom* a Knight,
>    As *Tom* has desert, and no more.
>
> But Fortune that whore, still attended this Brewer,
>    And did all his achievements reward;
> And blindly did fling, on this lubberly thing,
>    More honour, and made him a Lord.
>
> (1:204)

This reality is still more forcefully underscored in the song "On Sir G. B. his defeat" prompted a year later by Sir George Booth's downfall. The poem does not dwell on Booth's abortive royalist uprising in the summer of 1659,[31] and its speaker neither consoles nor bolsters the spirits of the defeated loyalists. With a weariness extreme even in the more cynical pieces, the spokesman for "we Commons" simply refuses to bother himself about the failure to restore the monarchy. The years of frustrated expectations have taught him not to be surprised, "Since that which has been done's no more, / Then what has oft been done before" (1:166), and he knows as well as Brome's other speakers that "there's nothing firm" in the circular pattern of events. Although he too recognizes the exploitation of the nation and again singles out the machinations of the clergy and the lawyers, Brome's speaker dismisses the injustice as he accepts the inevitable truth:

> That side is always right that's strong,
> And that that's beaten must be wrong,
> And he that thinks it is not so,
> Unlesse he's sure to beat 'um too,
>    Is but a fool t'oppose 'um.
>
> (1:168)

Though the poem's bitterness betrays severe disapproval, the wiser individual, it seemingly follows, has no other recourse than to be callously and pragmatically indifferent.

By the spring of the next year, the presence of General George Monck in London offered the weary nation the hope of peace, but in the euphoria that swept the city,[32] Brome's speakers do not entirely lose their detachment. Of the three poems written for the 13 March festivities honoring Monck at the

Clothworkers' Hall, the two songs most unreservedly catch the spirit of celebration recorded by contemporary diarists and other poets. The revelers in "For the Generalls entertainment" abandon their cares and welcome the promise of peaceful abundance with the expectation that the "sprightly melody" of the nation's "well-tun'd souls" will restore a harmony lost in the discord of the trumpets and drums. The other song's call to rejoice also anticipates a peaceful era where self-ruin is part of the past and religious upstarts are ignored. All of England will then become the safe estate enjoyed by the wise and fortunate few:

> We'l eat, and we'l drink, we'l dance and we'l sing,
>    The Roundheads and Cave's no more shall be nam'd;
> But all joyn together to make up the ring,
>    And rejoyce that the many-headed dragon is tam'd.
> 'Tis friendship and love, that can save us and arme us,
> And while we all agree, their is nothing can harme us.
>
> (1:175)

The desired circle can be formed, however, only "while we all agree"; and earlier in the song the speaker's proviso "If these sad Lands by this / Can but obtain the blisse" further tempers unrestrained celebration. This reservation emerges forcefully in the much longer and more thoughtful work, "A speech made to the Lord General *Monck,* at *Clotheworkers-Hall* in *London* the 13. of March, 1659 [1660]."

Although much of the poem greets Monck as a redeemer who "*Atlas*-like" will support the country, the praise is often couched in negative terms. By assuring Monck that as a military leader he will never compromise his nobility and will never ignore the dangers accompanying high position, the speech voices the misgivings that troubled Brome's contemporaries.[33] In March the enigmatic general appeared to some to be poised to take the crown, and other poets were driven in their ingenuity to remind him that George Monck is actually an anagram for "Come ore King."[34] The fears of Brome's speaker might well be, then, the natural reaction of a royalist anxious to restore the monarchy and to avoid another Cromwell, but they surely also reflect the realities described in the poem's rueful account of the nation's misguided attempts to better itself. Without minimizing Monck's great qualities or discouraging his role in the country's restoration, the speaker, who identifies himself as a rustic, voices the wariness of those who have never intended to alter the church and government. Religion, law, liberty, and peace appear to him not to have been the motives for the war; its only discernible purpose has been the desire to take other people's estates. His experience, the lesson of two revolutionary decades, comes at an exorbitant price:

Our truth, our trade, our peace, our wealth, our freedom,
And our full Parliaments, that did get, and breed 'um,
Are all devour'd, and by a Monster fell.

(1:339)

The possibility that Monck will become a new St. George and will slay this
dragon is too fashionable at this time to be in the end ignored, but the poem
described by one contemporary as a "loyal Congratulatory / And daring
Speech" (1:63) does not blunt the criticism with fulsome flattery. The cycle
of events has confirmed once again the vanity of human existence, and Brome
resists the temptation to indulge in hopeful sentiment.

Two months later the restoration of Charles II occasions a still more
forceful denunciation of the folly of revolution. "To the Kings most Sacred
Majesty, on his miraculous and glorious return 29. May, 1660" shares the joy
and expectation of the other poets who rushed to celebrate the return of
monarchy, but Brome's contribution contains noticeably less panegyric than
most others. The longest of his poems devotes less than a third of its four
hundred lines to the restored monarch, and this praise extols mainly the
patience Charles has developed in his twelve years of suffering.[35] Though the
exiled young king has had, of course, no other choice, the poem transforms
his decade of royalist defeat into victory:

> you that did endure
> What e'r the Wit or Malice of your foes
> Could lay on you or yours, yet stoutly chose
> To suffer on, rather than to requite
> Their injuries, and grew Victorious by't;
> And by your patient suffering did subdue
> The Traytors fury, and the Traytors too.

(1:360)

Brome is less interested than Lovelace, however, in praising the fortitude of
triumphant patience; the traitors, not the king, dominate the center of the
poem. The language and concerns of its lengthy summary draw into familiar
focus the earlier poems' contempt for the unconscionable few who made the
nation's misery "their trade." Brome recognizes the ease with which "silly
souls" were drawn by their hopes and fears into the grasp of the unscrupulous, and he stresses at length the roles of the pulpit and law courts in
duping the easily misled. In uncompromising terms he scorns the newly
created gentry and justices who arose from the "scum" of society and spread
their contagion through the lands and offices. "Now they'l all wheel about,"
the poem bitterly concludes,

> and be for you,
> For (like *Camaelions*) they still change their hue,

> And look like that that's next them; they will vow,
> Their hearts were alwaies for you, and are now.
> 'Tis no new Wit, 'tis in a Play we know,
> Who would not wish you King, now you are so?
>
> (1:365)

But the anger does not demand reprisals; his is the loyalists' resolve that appeals instead to the "unconquer'd patience" of the king and counsels him to display mercy and love. The poem's desire for reconciliation overcomes strong misgivings about the trustworthiness of former rebels and recalls the wishes Carew and the earlier Caroline writers once addressed to Charles's father. Wishes appropriate to the spirit of restoration sound a final note of hope as the poem welcomes the prospect of a peace and prosperity founded on the return of "true Religion" and "sacred Laws."

By the end of the year, however, Brome's poems lose their optimism as they confront anew the political realities. Disturbed by the royal proclamation of pardon issued in August, the speaker in "The Cavalier" expresses the sense of betrayal and injustice common in the first months of the Restoration among the loyalists who had "laid all at stake / For his Majesty's sake" (1:111).[36] Their complaints about the lack of suitable rewards are intensified by their feelings that those "were observed to be most importunate who had deserved least." The Cavalier in Brome's song is not only certain that the most vociferous have, in Clarendon's words, not "borne the heat of the day"; they have managed once again to "creep into profit and power."[37] The earlier poems' conviction that the rising rebels must inevitably fall has proven unfounded, for now that "the times are turn'd about," the power of ill-gotten wealth remains undiminished:

> And so come what will,
> They'll be uppermost still;
> And we that are low,
> Shall still be kept so
> While those domineer and devour.
>
> (1:111)

The loyal Cavalier clings only to the hope that his time will come before his patience is gone; the speaker in "A New Ballad" cannot find even this minimal consolation. His embittered response to the Restoration fortunes of the "poor Caveliers" is the persistent theme of Brome's poetry: money does buy preference in peace as well as in rebellion, and principles are secondary to self-centered pragmatism. "Knaves that have lived upon sequestration, / And sucked the blood of the best of the Nation" have in his view undergone "a new translation" and made their peace with the king; the "fools" are left to bear the renewed brunt of their oppression.[38] The fears and expectations of the past twenty years seem for the wise man to lead inexorably to one conclusion:

> If the times turne about 'tis but to comply,
> And make a formal submission,
> And with every new power to live and die,
> Then they are in a safe condition.
>
> (1:216)

Where indifference and conviviality once formed the "safe Estate," compromise now constitutes the essence of a "safe condition."

Brome himself may not, however, finally succumb to this temptation of timeserving. His own position, which remains indirectly voiced in these ballads, songs, and longer poems, emerges in the epistles written *in propria persona* during the last years of the Interregnum and the beginning of the Restoration. These poems to Cotton, Steynings, and others are familiar, urbane, and playful. Brome shows no reluctance, for example, to chide his friend when he invites Steynings and his "beloved *Sue*" to Taunton:

> My *Mat.* and I will meet with her and you.
> And though my *Mat's* no Poet, you shall see,
> She'l sit and laugh with or at us, that be.
> I'll make thy Lady merry, and laugh untill,
> She break that belly, which thou canst not fill.
>
> (1:250)

He also gossips about the fortunes of acquaintances as well as the affairs of state, and his friends respond in kind with pointed comments on Brome's legal profession and his busy pursuit of the law. Invitations to share the unbounded spirits of wine and company are also exchanged, though the exuberant celebration and cutting criticism are noticeably muted. The wit and raillery mask less obviously Brome's central concern throughout his poetry, a desirable "safety and delight."

An epistle written to Charles Steynings in early 1660 distinguishes this safe estate from the expedient compromise the times have encouraged. Recognizing that loyalties cannot and perhaps need not be decided immediately, the epistle questions the possibility of any commitment to the just side:

> You always took that side that's right,
> But when *Charles* with himself did fight,
> Pray of which side were you?
>
> (1:251)

For his own part Brome confesses, "I've been for th'midle twenty years." His willingness to adjust this position to the whims of the moment carries the conviction that "wiser men then me" cannot find the right among the misguided forces that have prevailed. Those mindful of their well-being, it follows, will not overly trouble themselves with the changing pageant:

> Let the times run, and let men turn,
> This is too wise an age to burn,
>     Wee'l in our Judgment hover,
> Till 'tis agreed what we must be.
>
> (1:253)

Brome's nonchalance is, of course, partly banter, and he does not condone political opportunism. His survey of the rapid succession within the year of Richard Cromwell, Arthur Haselrig, and John Lambert underscores the need for prudent detachment in such unsettled times, but the epistle has no sympathy for the "Grandees" who "turn with every wind / Yet keep like Corks above." Brome's compliance reflects the common sense of the middle ground; his advice to Steynings cautions the care of an individual trying to survive these difficult decades. This preoccupation in the other epistles with personal fulfillment and "safe Estate" becomes the blunt advice: "'Tis better to mind what will cloath ye, and feed ye" than to get caught up in state affairs "too weighty and high, / For such mean private persons as thou art, and I" (1:259).

Survival does not necessarily presuppose the cynical indifference some of the songs and ballads espouse. Though Brome cannot resist the opportunities to remind his friends "he that's strongest is best" and "Stick to the strongest side, and think, and laugh," he commends his colleagues' efforts to aid their fellow citizens. When Steynings decides to stand for Parliament in 1659, Brome reminds him that the "wiser sort" are content to remain uninvolved, particularly since the office will add to neither their wealth nor their reputation; but this pessimism does not prevent Brome from counseling his friend to pursue at home the love and honor that elude politicians. After Steynings's unsuccessful bid for the parliamentary seat, Brome consoles,

> But be content, let them do what they will,
> Be thou a Justice I'm Atturney still.
> A poor Attourney is a safer thing
> Now, then to be Protector or a King.
>
> (1:248)

When political circumstances then force Steynings to leave his position as justice of the peace, Brome contemns the failure to appreciate a wise, valorous magistrate and writes him half seriously,

> Let me advize thee (*Charles*) be as thou art,
> A poet, so thou needst not care a———
> For all the turnes of time: who ere did know,

> The Muses sequestred? or who can shew,
> That ever wit paid taxes, or was rated?

(1:249)

Nevertheless Brome advises his friend to continue serving the law by writing a book "where Justices may look, / And learn their trade" (1:249). On another occasion he promotes his own twenty years of unstinting legal service and praises the ministrations of Sir Robert Foster, the lord chief justice who suffered through the misfortunes to become

> Great *Atlas* of our lawes and us, whose will
> Is alwayes active, back'd by unmatch'd skill;
> To rule the Nation, and instruct it too,
> And make all persons live, as well as know.[39]

(1:261)

Similar praise also dominates many of the pieces Brome writes to commemorate the deaths and publications of personal friends and public figures.

In the elegies traditional praise and consolation reflect the revolutionary era. The poems commonly laud the dead as virtuous individuals "Who durst be good when goodness was a crime" and who "scorn'd to live when peace and truth were killed." Not surprisingly, Charles I stands out in "this impious time" as the inspiration for the loyal soul eager to join him in death. "On the death of King CHARLES" develops the commonplace contemporary parallel between the martyred king and his Redeemer, both of whom died for the sins of others. Charles lives on, as well, in the immense popularity of *Eikon Basilike,* a book Brome insists

> shews affliction quells not majesty.
> Yet still Crown, dignity and self deny'd,
> It helps to bear up courage though not pride;
> Trodden humility in robes of state,
> Meekly despising all the frownes of fate.

(1:295)

The educators, magistrates, and divines remembered in the other elegies also manifest less spectacularly a triumphant patience and courage.

Faced with an unsympathetic, even an alien world, these principled individuals display in their lives a selfless devotion to duty at odds with a country "out of course." In stressing once again the corruption in religion and law that favors hypocrisy and greed at the expense of integrity and zeal, the elegies accentuate the "industrous labour" of unidentified or lesser figures who bettered the lives of people around them by shouldering the burdens others had ignored. The unknown schoolmaster W. H. and physician Dr. Hearne appear the Atlases of their world because they tirelessly supported learning and health without concern for their own advancement. They stand in the company of Reverend Josias Shute, "No whirlegig Lect'rer of the times" ready to ignore the ideals of divinity or to encourage the nation's discord. Together they exemplify the purpose epitomized in Richard Aubrey, a man of religion and law who was

> Constant to's principles; and though the times
> Made his worth sin, and his pure vertues crimes,
> He stood unmov'd spite of all troubles hurl'd,
> And durst support but not turn with the World.
>
> (1:299)

All reveal the same quiet heroism Cartwright celebrates in his poetry; steadfast, they understand that the welfare of the nation lies in a willingness to serve the well-being of its people. Each in his own way meets this responsibility with the resoluteness of Aubrey:

> He did what nature had design'd him to
> In his due time, while he had strength to do.
> And when decay and age did once draw nigh,
> He'd nothing left to do but only dye.
>
> (1:299)

The same commitment also characterizes the individuals commemorated in another group of poems, the verses written to commend a variety of publications. Some of these contributions are justly forgotten among the numerous undistinguished poems occasioned by Humphrey Moseley's editions, and others are interesting mainly for the relationships they suggest between Brome and such diverse writers as Thomas Stanley, James Shirley, and Henry Bold. Brome lacks Cartwright's facility in this mode, and his critical judgments do not rise above the commonplace; he reveals, however, considerable sensitivity to the plight of writers alienated from the "barbarous dayes." Poems written during the period of crisis and into the first years of the Restoration complain that "in this envy'ous and ill-natur'd time, / Verse is a scandal, and to print a crime" (1:385). The complaint carries some of the concern writers commonly voice about insensitive readers, but the lament further emphasizes the onerous position of the author caught up in the "strange twirle of Times." Pieces for the Richard Lovelace and Richard Brome editions laud particularly the fearless poet who accepts his "ancient right" and stands defiantly against the suppression of truth. Other, slighter poems express Brome's faith in writers who refuse to condone the abuses of the pulpit, and they express his encouraging hope, "Walk wisely on: Time's changeable, and what / Was once thrown down, is now again reacht at" (1:285). In a warm, witty tribute "To his ingenuous Friend Mr. IZAAK WALTON on his *Complete Angler*," Brome appreciates also the "safe joy" and "true contentment" Walton offers those who follow his example and leave ambitious cares behind for a world in which "Thy mind's thy Kingdom, and content's thy Crown" (1:382). But the most extensive expression of Brome's values is found in his poems to the obscure scholar Edward Sparke.

The commendatory pieces of the 1652 and 1660 editions of *Thysiasthrion vel Scintilla-Altaris* praise their author's undaunted dedication to the established church and its traditions. The first of these poems places Sparke among the "wiser few" who "stood still" in the destructive whirlwinds unleased against the centuries of sacred practices by the "rude Vulgar" and the "Pseudo-levites." By invoking the humanist image of the poet/orator who fulfills the ancient obligation to profit and delight, Brome honors the "milder temper" with which Sparke moved his readers. Sparke's commitment to all that is "constant, pure and true" appears in the second poem as the "rare issue" of a minister who refused to compromise his church and his principles. Brome stridently scorns the "factious crue" and the "vip'rous brood of *Levi*" who gnawed through their parents' bowels and now are devoured by the offspring of their own "lewd designes." The image of perverted generation graphically expresses the greed and pride Brome commonly attributes to the zealots, and his poem aims its derision as well against the newly powerful who encouraged this ambition through the clerical livings they controlled. With unusual vigor and conviction, the dedicatory verse sets Edward Sparke above such self-interest by virtue of his tireless commitment to tradition. Now that the revolution has run its course and the times have turned again, the value of this constancy is unmistakable:

> Thanks to such lights as you are, who have stay'd
> In that firm truth, from which they fondly stray'd,
> Endur'd reproach, and want, all violent shocks
> Which rowl'd like Billows, while you stood like Rocks,
> Unmov'd by all their fury, kept your ground,
> Fix'd as the poles, whiles they kept twirling round.
>
> (1:287–88)

Brome's favorite conceit appropriately defines a constancy consistent with his support of moderation. Like many of his countrymen who turned with the times, Brome acknowledges the wisdom of caution and foresight; unlike them, however, he never changes his allegiance or ceases to admire traditional values. Although the virtues of heroic fortitude and patient suffering are usually encountered in the elegies and commemorations, where the form traditionally sanctions extreme praise, his poems value both in the abstract and in individuals the ability to accept all things with Lucian's "equal mind" and, in the words of Ecclesiastes, to "rejoice in his own works." When his poems seem to qualify this wisdom or when Brome appears to opt for the safety of the "middle" himself, the shift is toward survival and not cynicism. His poems favor a disengagement based perhaps on fatalism but not on defeatism. The diversity of his writing reflects, in short, the misgivings of a realist who recognizes how readily peace and order are sacrificed for misguided principles and personal ambition. The social upheaval that results threatens his conservative disposition particularly, and at times his poems tend towards Hobbes's view of human nature, but in the end they accept accommodation rather than compromise. One of his last poems, an epistle to Charles Steynings, may well be an apologia for this position. "We might have better spent our time," Brome concedes,

> if we
> Had like the world employed it thrivingly,
> If we much wealth and greatness had affected,
> And stead of versifying had projected,
> You might have been a Knight, and I a Squire,
> Titles which now the World does much admire.
>
> (1:344)

Mindful that others might not condone the life of wine, wit, and friendship the epistle celebrates, Brome avows his own contentment:

> You think they'r fools, and they think we are so,
> But both perhaps are fools for ought we know,
> Now since all men are fools, who would be none,
> Let him think what he will, I think he's one.
>
> (1:345)

This final gesture of unconcern affects the calculated indifference reminiscent of the safe estate; the same sensibility, without contradiction, also admires the few who stand and in their own capacities serve.

In coming to terms with the reality that "In this round World, / All things are by a revolution hurl'd" (1:336), Brome's poems in effect embrace anew the wisdom of this paraphrase of Ecclesiastes. His middle ground offers little room for the heroic flight Daniel envisions, and the steadfastness he admires seems closer to Cartwright's ideal than to Lovelace's. Though Brome's insistence on recognizing mutability and his sensitivity to the corruption of religion might easily lead to a decidedly Christian patience, like Cartwright he expresses little overtly religious reaction to the world's vanity and vexation. The light, witty songs commonly associated with Brome convey untroubled easiness readily summarized in the famous lines from Ecclesiastes, "Then I commended mirth, because a man hath no better thing under the sun, than to eat, and to drink, and to be merry." But taken as a whole, the poems reveal a deeper understanding of this biblical wisdom. Skeptical and realistic, lighthearted and facile, Alexander Brome is a writer whose various moods and forms gloss in poetic terms the knowledge stressed in sixteenth- and seventeenth-century biblical commentaries on this passage: "Therefore mocke thou the worlde as it mocketh thee. Dooe thine endeauour and duety, and let goe cares and sorrowfulness. Be of good cheare & meary, knowing that the world useth not to rewarde & consider the good."[40]

# 6

# Abraham Cowley and the "Soule Compos'd of th'Eagle and the Dove"

WHILE Alexander Brome in his epistles accepts without apology a life of accommodation, Abraham Cowley attempts in an autobiographical account "Of My self" to find continuity in a career that began auspiciously in the 1630s at Westminster, led in the 1640s and 1650s to the centers of royalist power at Oxford and Paris, then ended in the tranquil Kentish countryside. The last of his eleven *Discourses by way of Essays, in Verse and Prose,* and perhaps his final work, insists that the young schoolboy consumed with the poetry of Horace and Spenser "was then of the same mind as I am now (which I confess, I wonder at my self)."[1] Stormy years of civil disruption and distinguished service with Lord Jermyn at the exiled court of Henrietta Maria only confirmed, in Cowley's recollection, a natural aversion to turbulence and vanity. Though he wryly admits his beloved tranquillity has proven an elusive mistress, his essay expresses no misgivings about its worth. He would have his readers believe that Abraham Cowley pursued throughout his life and without regret the cheerful equanimity and moderate estate Horace and Martial deem the essence of happiness.

But modern readers share increasing reservations about the accuracy of this view. To many the foremost poet of his day appears to be an ambitious writer who compromised his royalist beliefs during the bleakest years of the Interregnum and then retired with embittered feelings from a Restoration court that would not forget his indiscretion. Subtle analyses discern "political despair," "fatalistic pessimism," and "profoundly pessimistic skepticism" in the poet's reaction to Cromwell's ascendency and his own imprisonment.[2] Before concluding, however, that Cowley came to terms with his life, if at all, only in retirement at Barn Elms,[3] the direction of his literary career should be reassessed. He is, in effect, the compleat loyalist poet whose writing expresses the essential concerns of the writers in this study. From its auspicious beginnings at Westminster and Cambridge, Cowley's poetry shared Cartwright's humanist interest in worthy individuals committed to their nation's well-being. His early occasional pieces also reveal an ambition that later sustains the attempts to write heroic, even epic poetry. When the outbreak of war provided the inspiration for this soaring muse, Cowley could not surmount the problems that frustrated the less-accomplished George Daniel. Defeat and exile forced him, as it had Lovelace, to reconsider the nature of heroic virtue and to comment often indirectly on his nation's tragedy. During the years of Interregnum government, he accepted the political realities by maintaining Brome's distinction between accommodation and compromise. Without contradiction he then welcomed the Restoration and its con-firmation of his growing faith in the nobility of the human spirit and in the direction of history. Through national and personal misfortune, Cowley had realized that in time's cyclical rhythm suffering is inescapable and providence supreme. Accepted with patient fortitude, both lead to victory.

The wisdom acquired in the decades of conflict quite understandably tempers the optimism that is first apparent in *Sylva, or, Divers Copies of Verses, Made upon sundry occasions*. Included with the second edition of *Poetical Blossoms*, this 1636 miscellany displays the precocious talent of a young writer who finds at times a genuine voice amid an often commonplace praise and ridicule. The "immature and immoderate love" of classical poets Cowley later saw in these poems[4] perhaps shapes an untroubled acceptance of the poet's role in the celebration of traditional values. In the odes "Upon the shortnesse of Mans life" and "On the praise of Poetry," Horace's *Carmina* inspires faith in the orphic powers of the poet. The Roman poet's disdain for worldly ambition and pretense is also echoed in poems ridiculing Puritans, lawyers, and courtiers. An ode "On the uncertainty of Fortune" sounds too much like an unconvincing sermon glibly praising the individual who lives a full life in spite of adverse fortune, and the consolation "I have liv'd today" in "A Vote" lacks the resonance of its classical source. But their young author would come to understand the storms that moved Horace to a heroic defiance of tomor-row. Even in these *sylvae*, or hastily produced works in need of further shaping and polishing,[5] the enduring preoccupations of his poetry are never-theless already established.

Among them the Caroline writers' desire for peace and a personal fear of tyranny are unmistakable. An ode commending the king's peaceful reign adapts the prospect of a golden age envisioned in Horace's fourth book of odes. In praising the "blest peace" England alone enjoys among her Euro-pean neighbors, much of the poem describes the beneficent powers of a ruler who has transformed an iron age. This seminal Caroline myth of unbounded prosperity recurs prominently throughout Cowley's writing; and as this ode indicates, the myth's underlying fear of war or "civill slaughter" once again motivates the celebration of peace. Later misgivings are also anticipated in his response to the king's 1633 journey to Scotland. "On his Majesties returne out of *Scotland*" welcomes Charles as a ruler greater than Alexander or Caesar because he reigns "with equall ballance" between mercy and justice. While Cowley probably intends no specific allusions to royal policies enacted after the dissolution of Parliament, the tyranny the poem associates with unchecked pride and ambition troubled Cowley throughout his life. At this point, however, the poems' imitation of the praise current in court masques and university panegyric raises no doubts about their author's earnest traditional loyalties to the crown's just rule.

The Bishops' Wars and the threat of civil upheaval challenged these accepted commitments, and the next group of poems reflects more complicated allegiances. *Miscellanies* is an impressive collection of poems written largely during Cowley's university years at Cambridge amid the widening political crisis. The first of its poems forthrightly reasserts a desire for enduring poetical fame; but in his disavowal of all that might impede the conquests of "the *Muses Hannibal*," Cowley seems to reflect an increased concern with social issues. An imitation of Martial reaffirms the attractiveness of "*Books, and wise Discourse, Gardens* and *Fields*, / And all the joys that *unmixt Nature* yields" (1:39); but many of the miscellaneous poems develop Cartwright's similar praise of individuals who confront increasingly inimical fates without retreating.

The first poems commemorate this humanist ideal in three men of markedly different accomplishments, Lord Falkland, Sir Henry Wotton, and John Jordan. Cowley may have formed friendships or at least acquaintanceships at Great Tew with the brilliant Falkland and the renowned Wotton, and he revered Jordan as his Westminster teacher. When Falkland joined the 1639 expedition against the Scots and when death claimed Wotton and Jordan, Cowley's response on each occasion reveals a fundamental and lifelong commitment to learning. Falkland reigns for all who know him as the "great *Prince* of *Knowledge*"; Wotton has ventured through his foreign missions into "the utmost *Bounds* of *Knowledge*"; and Jordan has "built up *Men* against the future times." Cowley extols at length and with feeling the selfless commitment to knowledge Jordan displayed, but he honors all three individuals for their noble, even heroic quest for wisdom. The boundless memory and the "unbounded Breast" admired in these poems create the desirable inner harmony and self-containment implied at the very least in *Sylva* and now openly espoused. The concern for Falkland's safe return from the ill-fated Bishops' War and the desire to shelter men of his rare caliber also reflect a new fear of war and its wanton destruction, a reality further apparent in the elegy for Jordan and its passing reference to "all the *English Blood* those wars have cost" (1:21).

This fear underlies Cowley's next occasional poem, "On his Majesties Return out of *Scotland*." Included among the seven English poems Cambridge University added to its volume commemorating Charles's second Scottish journey, the tribute written in late 1641 thinly conceals a sense of relief. Unlike the visit to Edinburgh in 1633, when Charles returned from his Scottish coronation with the crown, the uncertain end of this journey created a good deal of apprehension.[6] The English lived in the king's absence with the possibility that Charles would gain Scottish help in imposing his royal will upon the restive country, and when he returned without a new alliance, both Cambridge and Oxford poets hailed the triumphant conqueror's blood-less victory.[7] Cowley avoids their stress on Charles's healing touch, but he complements their visions of peace in his sensitivity to war's disastrous effects. The poem's tribute to the king's godlike ability to bring harmony out of apparent chaos emphasizes the folly of civil war. Its insistence that every-body loses when the nation consumes itself with "mad quarrels" and "proud hopes" is not that of a pacifist, for the poem ends with an appeal to the glory awaiting the English on the battlefields of Europe. Eager to laud heroic prowess and to confirm royal majesty, Cowley nevertheless has no illusions about the toll war exacts. Until the events of the next year fulfill the poem's fears about the game in which "we *Bet all,* and yet for *nothing Play*" (1:23), he welcomes the "happy *Concord.*"

In the interim, "To the Bishop of *Lincoln,* Upon his Enlargement out of the Tower" responds to the growing division with an increasingly complex allegiance and a new awareness of heroic virtue. The congratulatory poem to Archbishop Laud's rival struck the unknown compiler of *Wit and Loyalty Reviv'd* (1682) as "unworthy" of Cowley's name, and modern scholars con-tinue to find the commemoration of John Williams "Inconsistent" with the allegiances of a staunch royalist.[8] The generous tribute to the bishop of Lincoln, however, should not be confused by issues of loyalty. Although Williams was certainly not beyond reproach, this strong-willed, independent clergyman remained firm in his commitment to orthodoxy, and his con-finement to the Tower had less to do with justice than with a long-standing struggle for power involving Archbishop Laud. Since Williams would not sue for release on Laud's terms, which demanded in part the forfeiture of some ecclesiastical offices, he remained confined to the Tower for almost four years, steadfast in his principles.[9] When the House of Lords finally secured the bishop's release in late 1641, the occasion not surprisingly commanded Cowley's poetic talents. While a student at Westminster, he had dedicated his first poems to Dean John Williams, the head of the public school, and to his "very loving master" Lambert Osbaldeston, both of whom were later linked in Star Chamber charges. In all likelihood Cowley also valued Williams's extensive patronage of scholars and respected his policy of moderation. But personal friendship and political principle play no immediate role in the tribute; Cowley admires instead the bishop's heroic stand against adverse fortune.

For the first time in his poetry, the unmistakable ideal is Stoicism. The central comparison likening Williams to Cicero combines traditional human-ist associations of eloquence and state service with still greater emphasis on the unbreakable spirit. Cicero was, for the Renaissance, closely linked with Roman Stoicism; however, in equating Williams's imprisonment with

Cicero's exile, Cowley elevates the "constant and *stedfast*" bishop above his classical counterpart. In a similar world of "Fate," "injurious Chance," and "*ill Fortune*," the Bishop had achieved more than happiness:

> Had your *Prosper'ity* always clearly gon
> As your high *Merits* would have led it on,
> You'had *Half* been lost, and an *Example* then
> But for the *Happy*, the *least part* of men.
>
> (1:29)

Though the lines have never been identified, they are clearly indebted to Seneca's assurance, "to triumph over the calamities and terrors of mortal life is the part of a great man only. Truly, to be always happy and to pass through life without a mental pang is to be ignorant of one half of nature."[10] Appropriately, the poem's discussion of the powers of fortune, fate, and chance also complements the passage's classical source, "On Providence." In this important moral essay, Seneca argues that the good man must submit to forces he cannot control: "We should offer ourselves to Fortune in order that, struggling with her, we may be hardened by her."[11] Seneca's moral, "Disaster is Virtue's opportunity,"[12] becomes Cowley's consolation,

> For a clear *Conscience* and *Heroick Mind*
> In *Ills* their *Business* and their *Glory* find.
> So though less worthy stones are drown'd in *night*,
> The faithful *Diamond* keeps his native *Light*,
> And is oblig'd to *Darkness* for a ray
> That would be more *opprest* then *helpt* by *Day*.
> Your *Soul* then most shew'd her unconquer'd power,
> Was stronger and more armed then the *Tower*.
>
> (1:29–30)

Because he has endured adversity with grace and fortitude, the bishop has found the freedom Seneca offers those few who understand the maxim, "your good fortune is not to need good fortune."[13] The paradox in Cowley's concluding couplet promises, "*Fortune* henceforth will more of *Provi'dence* have, / And rather be your *Friend*, then be your *Slave*" (1:30).

The paradoxical and witty triumph over fortune leaves uncertain the extent to which Cowley intends a Senecan rather than Christian providence, but the importance of Stoic self-containment is unmistakable. Though its praise may at first seem somewhat studied, the poem marks an important development in Cowley's understanding of heroism. Its celebration of the bishop's release confronts openly the sense of fate abstractly conceived in *Sylva* and unobtrusively present in the poems to Falkland and Jordan. With the growing threat of political upheaval, the self-containment seen in the earlier occasional pieces of *Miscellanies* as well as in the other loyalist poems of this study

appears an increasingly desirable response to the stormy years. The outbreak
of civil war deepens misgivings about conventional heroism, and the aftermath of defeat raises questions about the providential universe; they also
enrich Cowley's understanding of the heroic patience described in the poem
to Bishop Williams. At first in satire and then in heroic verse, his support of
royalist fortunes leads him to an increasingly complex sense of loyalist resolve.

Within a few months of the first battles, probably early in 1643, Cowley
turned to satire and sustained attack in *The Puritan and the Papist*. By then,
presumably, he was with the royal party at Oxford and shared their optimism
about the opening military successes.[14] Without looking too closely at the
extent to which Catholicism influenced the royal family and the court,
Cowley capitalizes on the popular fear that Catholics and Puritans alike
threatened to subvert the crown's authority.[15] Though the lengthy satire
purports to be about both Puritans and Papists, it exploits the alleged
similarity between them to expose primarily Protestant extremism in worship
and manners. Addressing the Puritans with increasing directness, the loosely
structured catalogue lists their shortcomings in a topical satire whose wit
depends largely upon the dexterity with which the couplets turn Puritans
into Catholics. Cowley has little of Alexander Brome's ironic detachment,
and he is not above charging Pym with bribery or stressing Holles's sexual
indiscretions. This specific ridicule bolsters an indictment of ignorance, hypocrisy, and greed typical of the attack that flourished on both sides when
censorship broke down, and it is rather misleading to emphasize the "sav-
ageness of the satire."[16] From Cowley's royalist position the Puritans are
wordmongers who lead the unwary through lies and distortions to their own
self-serving ends. Their goal, the satire claims, is to impose an absolute will,
for in their insatiable greed they reveal themselves as "boundlesse *Tyrants*"
who have made a mockery of the shibboleths "publique good" and "publique
faith." To the embattled royalist they threaten the essential order: "To the
*Kings will* the *Lawes* men strove to draw; / The *Subjects will* is now become the
*Law*" (2:156). Basic to Cowley's distinction between will and law are his
fundamental assumption that any government should ensure the rights to
justice and property and his humanist belief that all "ought to follow Nature
as our guide, to contribute to the general good."[17] This fear of tyranny and
this desire to better society, seen earlier in the juvenalia and miscellaneous
poems, influence the major account he began of the civil conflict soon after
the completion of *The Puritan and the Papist*.

The three books of *The Civil War* leave unfinished Cowley's ambitious
attempt to narrate the epic dimensions of the royalist struggle. Begun in the
late summer of 1643, the poem abandons its chronicle of the war soon after
the king's forces faltered in the September battle at Newbury. Cowley never
published the incomplete poem, implying in his 1656 Preface that he had

destroyed the manuscript; and it may well be, as Allan Pritchard suggests in his fine modern edition, that Cowley considered the work only a rough draft.[18] But even in its incomplete form, the poem's extremes of exaltation and denigration reveal Cowley's growing struggle to find the heroic mode and values suited to the nation's crisis. At the same time that it memorializes "Ye *Sonnes of Warre*, by whose bold Acts we see, / How great a thing *exalted man* may be" (p. 84), *The Civil War* also records "well-writ Infamy." To a degree unusual in the traditional epic, the heroic and satiric combine in an unstable relationship of praise and blame. Central to both extremes is an elegiac mood.

The mixed genre reflects the complexity of Cowley's commitment. From the outset he recognizes once again that bloody national division will crown the victors with sorrow only. The alternatives suggested in the extended appeal to the nation's heroic spirit stress again the fears and promise of the poem commemorating the king's second Scottish journey. With obvious dismay and growing irony, Cowley recalls the unrivaled years of Stuart prosperity so many refused to appreciate. Though he sarcastically blames militant clergy for encouraging the discontent, he fears the "strang *fancy*" and "sencelesse Clamours" that have seized the nation and threaten to destroy its institutions. His reaction, however, is not the "bewilderment" of a poet "who can neither escape from the conflict nor take sides in it."[19] When the king rallied supporters at Nottingham and the war began, he did so, in the poem's view, both with his followers' "desires to right / Abusd *Mankind*" as well as with divine aid. Despite his misgivings about civil war, Cowley joined those who "promised noble pens the Acts to write" (p. 79) because he too believed in the principles Charles upheld. Unlike the rebels who allegedly "fight they knew not why," Cowley does not blindly follow the king's standard. His account of the ensuing warfare raises questions about the royalist strategy and grudgingly acknowledges the enemies' courage, but it also never forgets why the battles are being fought. Rebellion against the anointed ruler appears from his vantage point as an attempt to destroy "Gods Image stampt on Monarchs" (p. 108), and the poem remains adamant in its belief that even weak men such as John and Richard II must be obeyed as kings. In the work's account of the first important battle at Edgehill, entangled conflicts are reduced to an emblematic lucidity: angels, Religion, Loyalty, Truth, Learning, and Arts face on the other hill the opposing forces of fiends, Schism, Sedition, Perjury, and Lies. The irreconcilable opposition, reechoed in the final battle of Newbury, pits forces sanctioned by tradition against those consumed with the dream of "sick Fancies."

Cowley sidesteps specific issues of polity or doctrine as he ultimately views the conflict as a struggle for civilization. The end of the first book contemptuously dismisses the rebels' contradictory claims to uphold liberty, property, and religion with the statement that "*Madnesse* onely" explains their destructive course. More insistently and effectively than in *The Puritan and the Papist,* this satire sees in the enemy's deranged ambition and blind ignorance their maniacal desire to destroy all that frustrates their rapaciousness. Portrayed as barbaric hordes of Goths, Huns, and *"Religious Vandalls"* who would sweep away all learning and arts, the rebels become in their voraciousness cannibals who consume their noble victims. In another basic conceit their leaders parody Genesis as they bring chaos out of the nation's "goodly frame" and make confusion art. Their pride and envy are the darkness and madness confronted in the second book's epic descent into hell. Cowley's lifelong fear of tyranny is graphically seen in the duplicitous figure of Rebellion and in the nightmarish confusion Satan creates as he transforms London into "our Night of Hell" (p. 105). The chaotic energy of Book III's vision of a city maddened by a demonic desire to obliterate "All ornaments of Nature, Art, or Grace" (p. 107) creates a powerful version of apocalypse. Tumultuous spirits engulf like another deluge the reason and truth that are the hope of peace.

Against this tempestuous madness stands Charles I. Although the king does not dominate the epic action, his royal presence is felt throughout the poem. He is the reluctant warrior and *"gentle Conquerour"* who embodies the harmony, creativity, and love celebrated during the previous decade in the Whitehall masques. Contraries form within him a *concordia discours*: the king of love and wrath, he appears "Furious as *Lightning* when Warrs *Tempest* came, / But Calme in *Peace,* calme as a *Lambent flame*" (p. 75). A "cheerful anger" marks his regal countenance, while from the "same beames of his *Majesticke* Eye" flow life to his loyal subjects and death to his enemies. Reunited with his queen on the fields of Kineton in a "Scene" of love and war, he holds with her the promise of restoration shown so often in the scenes at the Banqueting Hall. Charles's role on the battlefield, similarly, becomes one of "wise and comely care," as he instills "Soule and Fire" in his followers both through his presence and his encouragement. When he stands before his troops at the critical battle of Newbury and appeals to the order and continuity embodied only in the established church and monarchy, Charles stands a symbol of the truth, justice, and tradition that the poem upholds.

The men he leads defend traditions fundamental to Cowley's view of civilized society. In the poem the military campaigns they conduct and the courageous acts they perform are not as significant as the characters of the men who rally to the king's support. Battles are occasions for commemorating the royalist leaders, and set pieces often resemble those found in Caroline commemorative verse. Book I, for example, deliberately balances the satiric portrait of the prominent rebel John Hampden with the lavish tribute to William Cavendish. The mock encomium of the parliamentary leader contemptuously tags Hampden a "wretched *Man*! curst by *too good a Wit*" (p.

84). The commander of the royalists' northern forces, in contrast, embodies the king's creative spirit:

> every *grace* and every *Muse*,
> Kist at his birth, and for their owne did choose.
> Soe good a *Wit* they meant not should excell
> In *Armes*; but now they see't, and like it well.
> So large is that rich *Empire* of his heart,
> Well may they rest contented with a part.
> How soone forc'd Hee the *Northerne Clouds* to flight?
> And strooke *Confusion* into *Forme* and *Light*.
> Scarce did the *Power divine* in fewer Dayes,
> A peacefull *World* out of wilde *Chaos* raise.
>
> (p. 87)

Unlike the divided and unfulfilled rebels, the nobility aspire to the harmonious completion attained by Henry, Lord Jermyn,

> In whom Wit, Judgment, Valour, Goodnesse joyne,
> And all theise through a comely Body shine,
> A Soule compos'd of th'Eagle and the Dove;
> Which all men must admire, and all men love.
>
> (p. 113)

Men like Jermyn and Cavendish, however, can only illustrate the superiority of the royalist cause; its success ultimately depends upon divine providence. Heaven sanctions Charles's decision to take a military stand, and its vengeance directs the actions of the king's supporters. Throughout the poem's deference to the overriding roles of fate and chance, Cowley, more so than George Daniel, leaves no doubt that the civil conflict is essentially a lesson in God's providence. Honest men and nature are allied in Book I with the side "*God* fought himselfe," and the narrative exalts triumphs achieved through divine intercession. With the greater epic scope of the next book, the war increasingly becomes a battle between the supernatural forces of good and evil. Dehumanized rebels reduced to frenzy now appear "*sencelesse Sinners*" caught up in the plagues of a wrathful God's avenging angels. When the demonic figures released in Book III attempt to fulfill Satan's fondest dreams of power, God's presence becomes all the more urgent. Charles, "like his God," brings everywhere among his troops new life and spirit, but "Gods wrath" and "Heavens Justice" determine at Newbury "The acts of Fortune, and of Providence" (p. 116).

The battle's outcome severely tests the poem's faith in providence, its very thesis. Midway through the last book, the turn of events threatens for the first time the absoluteness of the opposing principles. As victory eludes the royalists and the furies strengthen the rebels' resistance, Cowley tries to attribute this "strange" course to heaven's just will, dismissing his misgivings with the assurance that a loving God "Punisht our Sinnes, yet did our Cause approve" (p. 117). Significantly, Cowley now includes the royalists among the sinners, and the poem's insistence on the unquestioned rectitude of the king's position falters. Although a scathing characterization of the parliamentary forces vehemently reasserts the difference between those nameless wretches and the noble royalists, the animus does not dispel the fleeting yet crucial doubt. Falkland's suicidal charge into deadly musket fire shatters the poem's confidence. The death of the "Man in whom all Virtues grew" is rebellion's gain and civilization's loss:

> They killd a Man, whose Knowledge did containe,
> All that the Apple promis'd us in vaine.
> The farthest lands of Art did hee invade,
> And widestretcht Nature was his Triumph made,
> What unjust weights into this Scale were hurl'd?
> Wee gain'd a Feild, and lost in him a World.
>
> (p. 122)

The loss of the arts and virtues idolized in Falkland underscores the worst fears of the poem, and the elegy's efforts to transcend them offer little solace. The elegiac tribute to Falkland praises the generosity, love, and learning that flourish only in peace. In recalling Falkland's grief at the spectacle of this national folly and in suggesting that Falkland welcomed death, Cowley perhaps betrays his own despondency. Although the penultimate verse paragraph defiantly proclaims that the rebels will never conquer learning and virtue and that Falkland will always live in inspired royalists, the further promise of vengeance reveals Cowley's sense of painful loss. The last lines, however, recognize that revenge is not in keeping with Falkland's spirit, and they acknowledge, instead, England's fallen nature. The prayerful ending implores God to "Thinke on our sufferings" and to accept Falkland as atonement: "Our Sinnes are great," Cowley abruptly ends, "but Falkland too is slaine" (p. 124).

These realities prove inescapable. Lament for the fallen royalists and derision of their enemies are possible only as long as royalist values are unquestioned.[20] Initially Cowley's faith in the king's cause had overcome his abhorrence of civil war, and he accepted the poet's obligation to uphold truth. Despite his deep-seated fears that war may consume men of Falkland's and Jermyn's sensibilities, he proclaims in his first books the nobility of their souls. Those like Grenville who fall in battle, he agrees with Cartwright, are more alive in their inspiring deaths than the inhuman rebels who defy providence. But as the carnage mounts and the royalist victory falters, themes of divine wrath and vindication no longer seem appropriate. Once the purpose of the civil conflict is questioned, all are sinners who merit punishment, and only the New Testament "Father of Peace, mild Lamb, and gaullesse Dove" can reconstruct the ruined nation. A satire suited to militant certainty loses its effectiveness, and elegiac praise assumes overtones of defeat. Even before the disheartened royalist forces abandon their drive toward London and return to Oxford, the poem's heroic ambitions have lost direction. Unable to sustain Cartwright's faith in the ennobling example of the valorous, yet unwilling to consider Daniel's criticism of the king's diminished majesty, Cowley has in effect lost the assurance as well as the optimism central to the Caroline vision the poem tries to evoke. Soon he joins the retreat from England, following Lord Jermyn and the exiled court to France. In exile and defeat his reconsideration of heroic verse will lead him to revalue the Stoic self-possession he has praised in Bishop Williams. Years of uncertainty and frustration will teach him, as they did Daniel, Lovelace, and Brome, the importance of a patient and heroic fortitude.

Away from the tumult of the war, Cowley gives new dimension to his undiminished interest in the heroic muse. The verses occasioned around 1650 by the appearance of Davenant's *Gondibert* praise once again a heroic poetry that celebrates *"Man in Mans chief work"* (1:42). The experience of *The Civil War,* however, may have confirmed his later recognition that "a warlike, various, and a tragical age is best to *write of,* but worst to *write in"* (1:7), for he has no reservations about Davenant's decision to avoid the present strife and to praise "past things." The elegy "On the Death of Mr. *Crashaw"* also admires with fervor and conviction the "boundless *Godhead"* that is the theme of the poetry written by Cowley's Cambridge friend. Sincere, independent judgment characterizes the poem's commemoration of Crashaw's sacred muse, and no false note sounds in Cowley's identification with those militant poets who recognize the difficulties and dignity of the poetic vocation. His desire to soar with Crashaw's inspiration toward heavenly knowledge will not be realized, but the poem most scholars consider his next major work attempts on its own terms to "learn of things *Divine"* (1:49). The *Davideis* celebrates the wisdom of divine providence at least in part by also following Davenant's lead: in the manner of Daniel's and Lovelace's narratives, Cowley's most ambitious poem resorts to the indirection and distance these loyalists developed in defeat.

The epic narrative of Israel's first monarchy moves away from the immediate conflicts of *The Civil War* to the heroic struggle between Saul and David. Saul's kingship and David's succession seem, however, to parallel indirectly seventeenth-century English history, and the poem has often been interpreted as a thinly disguised commentary on the Cromwellian rise to power. But the *Davideis* has not been dated with any certainty, despite the recent and widespread assumption that Cowley probably wrote this poem after 1650. Supposition and not evidence challenge the traditional notion that Cowley completed much of his epic while at Cambridge and that he worked on the revision in the years before its 1656 publication.[21] The absence of precise data about its stages of composition, in any case, does not diminish the significance of Cowley's decision to publish the unfinished work and its extensive notes. Without the obvious partisanship and satire of the civil-war narrative, his biblical epic uses the first book of Samuel somewhat self-consciously to fulfill seventeenth-century strictures about the "Divine Poem." The four books completed add to the familiar council scene in *The Civil War* prophetic visions and historical summaries designed to enhance heroic magnitude. At the risk of fragmenting narrative unity, the episodic work explores the course of divine providence in the sweep of biblical history. More diversely and ambitiously than *The Civil War*, the *Davideis* seeks to understand in the conduct of its central figures and in the institutions of their society the implications of God's design and the limits of heroic virtue.

The poem's proposition establishes the essential conflict. Cowley invokes the "blest rage" of Christ's inspiration ostensibly to celebrate David's triumph:

> I Sing the *Man* who *Judahs Scepter* bore
> In that right hand which held the *Crook* before;
> Who from best *Poet*, best of *Kings* did grow;
> The two chief *gifts Heav'n* could on *Man* bestow.
> Much danger first, much toil did he sustain,
> Whilst *Saul* and *Hell* crost his strong fate in vain.
> Nor did his *Crown* less painful work afford;
> Less exercise his *Patience*, or his *Sword;*
> So long her *Conque'ror Fortunes* spight pursu'd;
> Till with unwearied *Virtue* he subdu'd
> All homebred Malice, and all forreign boasts;
> Their strength was *Armies*, his the *Lord of Hosts*.
>
> (1:242)

The most popular Old Testament hero in Renaissance epic poetry,[22] David was "the greatest *Monarch* that ever sat on the most *famous* Throne of the whole Earth" (1:12). The 1656 Preface further contends, "whom should a *Poet* more justly seek to *honour*, then the highest Person who ever *honoured* his Profession" (1:12). But David's rise from humble origins to great glory does not involve merely his struggle against Saul and Satan. Thomas Rhymer unwittingly expresses Cowley's main concern when he objects, "*David* is made King, but this is the work of Heaven, not any atchievement of his own."[23] David's "unwearied *Virtue*" and his "strong fate" conquer fortune through the intercession of the "*Lord of Hosts*." While his enemies rely upon military might, David suffers adversity with "*Patience*" and faith. The *Davideis* is after all subtitled *A Sacred Poem of the Troubles of David*, and again Rhymer misses the point when he complains, "I think the *Troubles of David* is neither title nor matter proper for an *Heroick* Poem, seeing it is rather the *actions* than his sufferings that make an *Heroe.*"[24] War may be the conventional inspiration for heroic poetry, but like Milton, who also challenges traditional heroism, Cowley proposes to sing "the better fortitude / Of patience."

David offers an appropriate focus. Seventeenth-century tradition readily associated the virtue of patience with this famous poet and monarch. Numerous sermons welcoming the Restoration find in the second book of Samuel a specific "Register of our times,"[25] and they commonly stress in the parallel between David's return to Jerusalem and Charles's to England "the Providence of God, who thus afflicts the King to try his Patience, to exercise and improve his Graces, to prepare him for the greater Glory, and make him the greater blessing and more welcome to his people."[26] David's relationship with Saul and Jonathan in the first book, moreover, also readily exemplifies throughout the seventeenth century the "wonderfull providence of God."[27] John Marbeck and Andrew Willet typically emphasize in quite different works the same "godly and wholsome lessons" contained in 1 Samuel: "that is: to haue sure patience in persecution, due obedience to our Prince without rebellion: and also the true and most faithfull dealings of friendes."[28] Others commonly insist that Saul's unjust actions and David's patient suffering prepared the young man to be a better ruler, and they sometimes further note, "as *David* endured many troubles, persecutions and sufferings before he entred into his kingdome, so did Jesus Christ here on earth before he entred in his."[29] Although Cowley does not moralize as blatantly upon the values of "*Patience* and *dependence upon God* even in our lowest ebbe of fortune,"[30] his narrative agrees with the seventeenth-century commentators who recognize in David's struggles with Saul that heroic virtue begins with conformity to the divine will and grows through adversity.

This moral assumption explains the poem's inescapable sense of fate. From the abrupt beginning *in medias res,* where Saul's fear of David's "mastring Fate" is immediately established, the *Davideis* recognizes the larger forces shaping human actions. Book I quickly overbalances hell, Satan, and Envy with heaven, God, and angels, pitting the archtyrant who "knew himself too weak / The smallest Link of strong-wrought *Fate* to break" (1:245) against the source of all being from whom "th' *effect* of our weak *Action* flows." The ironic narrative of Saul's futile efforts to fulfill Satan's will may defer to epic tradition in its references to fortune, chance, and fate, but Cowley reminds his readers in a note, "The *Fates;* that is, according to the *Christian Poetical* manner of speaking, the *Angels,* to whom the *Government* of this *world* is committed" (1:316). When an angel does indeed deflect the spear meant to kill David, the narrator further moralizes, "How vain Mans pow'er is! unless God command" (1:255). In the narrative even the baser spirits who fail to see the angels hovering around the defeat of Goliath and who attribute David's victory to chance are given ample opportunity to see God's absolute mastery.

Understood correctly, His purposeful control is the greatest cause for celebration.

Through David He will manifest His wondrous power, for David is
destined in the *Davideis* to be a redeemer. God declares in His first speech that
Saul will undo himself with his own hand and, more important, that David
will "expiate the disgrace" the king has brought to the throne. The second
book unfolds the magnitude of David's role more extensively in the history of
Abraham and the vision of David. Both episodes draw heavily upon Old
Testament history to suggest the fate of Israel. Among the ten tapestries
depicting Abraham's "painful, but well-guided Travels," the sacrifice of Isaac
strikingly illustrates a heroic suffering borne "patiently" out of the love, faith,
and obedience that David and then later Christ will express. Although in the
tapestries Cowley develops no correlation between biblical type and antitype,
the subsequent vision David has of the future makes the traditional relationship between David's and Christ's redemptive roles explicit. Cowley's
often tedious chronology from Kings and Chronicles traces in the fate of
David's descendents the same benevolent providence seen later in Book IV's
account of the four hundred years before Saul's reign. Throughout both
chronicles of ambition, treachery, and violence, a merciful God chooses
"well-form'd Spirits" to free the nation from its suffering and to reestablish
peace. Despite its often bleak and seemingly cyclical pattern, history moves
inexorably in the *Davideis* to complete God's design, "The promis'd *Shilo*, the
great *Mystick King*" (1:305). Toward this end David surpasses Abraham as
the greatest Old Testament figure.

The man of peace and love, he waits patiently to fulfill his destined role.
Others sense in him a future glory and recall his earlier triumphs, but David
exists almost passively in the present. Even when Joab recounts the famous
defeat of Goliath, David appears to be essentially an instrument of divine
majesty who acts out of great love for the nation. For him the single combat
pits his god against Goliath's in a contest David considers a vindication of
divine justice. Against the present enmity of Saul, he shows still greater
willingness to trust in divine intercession. While angels deflect the spears and
befuddle the senses of his enemies, David feigns death and madness, fleeing
from any confrontation with Saul. The narrative of a flight Cowley likens to
Aeneas's escape from Troy never diminishes, however, its praise of David's
undaunted courage or forgets the implications of his actions. Quite probably
when he published the poem Cowley intended in David's patient fortitude an
inspiring example for England's troubled exiles—those who fled the country
and those who, like the other loyalists in this book, found refuge away from
the center of power in the country house and among friends as well as in
prison. And he undoubtedly also raises in David's response to Saul's tyranny
an inescapable seventeenth-century dilemma. Civil war forced many to reconsider David's reluctance to resist Saul, "to stretch forth mine hand against

him, seeing he is the anointed of the Lord," and in the aftermath of Charles's execution, all sides in the conflict reexamined the first book of Samuel.[31] Cowley's part in the debate resists simplification, but his emphasis on David's patience suggests a mature understanding of the conduct that a providential view of history demands.

The account of Israel's monarchy in Book IV is crucial to Cowley's view of providence and the vexing issue of compromise. Although some modern scholars sense in this narrative of Saul's kingship an allegorical commentary on England's political crisis, attempts to equate Cromwell with either Samuel or Saul and to establish a political allegory on the commonwealth have not proved convincing. Nor can it be argued with any certainty that Book IV's comments on the origin and the desirability of the monarchy reflect an erosion of Cowley's royalist beliefs.[32] The political dimensions implicit in David's narrative of "the *Motives* for which the people desired a *King*" (1:364) are at best general. His account of Samuel's and Saul's reigns raises unavoidable questions about the best form of government, but they too are less pressing than the basic issues about the nature of government. Cowley's foremost concern in this complex narrative remains the fundamental differences between the responsible and tyrannical uses of power.

Nowhere does he unequivocally confirm Samuel's warning: "Cheat not your selves with *words*: for though a *King* / Be the mild Name, a *Tyrant* is the *Thing*" (1:371). As David points out in response, Samuel confuses what may occur with what will occur. The embittered Samuel has, to be sure, considerable warrant for his misgivings. David's history of the peaceful years under the Judges recounts a proud, restless, and assertive people's willingness to forsake Samuel's humble guidance for the glitter and pomp they envy in the eastern potentates. But the narrative's obvious approval of the Judges' plain, direct rule also concedes the people's just dissatisfaction with the weak sons an indulgent Samuel has chosen to succeed him. While the narrative faults the people for losing faith in "*Common Means*" and later considers their desire for a king a rebellion against God, the history never condemns the form of government promised the Israelites in the prophecies of Moses and Abraham. The *Davideis* maintains both the nation's right to be governed justly and its obligation to observe divine will. Under Samuel the Israelites mistook "*Powers* true *Source*" when they demanded the trappings of the office and despaired of God's help.

The monarchy they receive need not inevitably prove to be a tyranny. Samuel's impassioned description of the suffering a king will inflict upon the helpless Israelites presupposes that the monarch will be an "*unbounded Man*" led by his "*Guidless Passion*." Cowley's note, in contrast, endorses no such absolutism: "It is a vile opinion of those men," he demurs, "and might be punished without *Tyranny,* if they teach it, who hold, that the *right* of *Kings* is set down by *Samuel* in this place" (1:396). Closer to his position is Moab's reproof. Moab's succinct rejoinder limits political power to an unspecified degree: "*Laws guid,* but cannot *reign;* / And though they *bind* not Kings, yet they *restrain*" (1:372). To this objection David simply responds, "'Tis true"; the *Davideis* clarifies no further the distinction between "bind" and "restrain." It exemplifies, instead, the difference between king and tyrant in the narrative of Saul's attempts to establish his authority.

God chooses through heaven's lot a man worthy to be king. The son of Kis appears in Book IV as an exceptional man of great beauty, courage, and wit. The lavish praise of his noble nature is not, as Samuel Johnson later objects, a lapse in decorum and characterization. Cowley gives Saul, in Johnson's words, "both the body and mind of a hero"[33] because they suit the poem's understanding of authority. Later Cowley will argue that "all men who are the effecters of extraordinary mutations in the world" must possess "excellent parts of nature, and mixture of Merit with their Vices" (2:360, 363); now, like George Daniel, he contends that the crown brings to its wearer an aura of majesty but that the office alone cannot command unquestioning obedience. Once the Israelites have their king, few follow Saul with any loyalty; the king must command their allegiance by leading them to war. His actions justify his rule: "The *Oyl,* the *Lot,* and *Crown* less *crown'd* him King." When the assembled people present the crown again, Samuel now leaves little doubt about Saul's regal nature:

> Behold his Beauty, Courage, Strength and Wit!
> The *Honour* heav'en has cloath'd him with, sits *fit*
> And comely on him; since you needs must be
> Rule'd by a *King,* you'are happy that 'tis *He.*
> Obey him gladly, and let him too know
> *You* were not made for *Him,* but he for *You,*
> And both for *God.*
> Whose gentlest yoke if once you cast away,
> In vain shall *he* command, and *you* obey.
>
> (1:382)

Saul merits the office and the office will become him as long as all understand the monarch's authority. But Cowley has no illusions about the difficulties the powers and fortunes of office bring to even the noblest rulers. Saul in his tyranny becomes an almost tragic study of the burdens of a crown.

His downfall begins when he usurps the priestly office and offers in Samuel's absence prayers and sacrifices. His motives are more complex than the simple act of supplication described in the first book of Samuel. In the poem's interpretation of the biblical text, Saul incurs the wrath of God because he is "Impatient ere Gods time Gods mind to know" (1:383). Cowley's note underscores this point: "I confess I incline to believe, that it was not so much *Sauls* invasion of the *Priestly* office, by offering up the

Sacrifice himself . . . as his disobedience to Gods command by *Samuel,* that he should stay *seven days,* which was the sin so severely punisht in him" (1:400). Saul cannot wait for Samuel, the *Davideis* proposes, because his pride will not endure the shame of military defeat and the affront implied by Samuel's delay. The narrative understands how Saul might naturally assume no limit here to his great power, but it also accepts the magnitude of the transgression. With greater forcefulness than the biblical denunciation, Samuel rebukes in his action the archetypal sin:

> His foul *Ingratitude* to heav'en he chid,
> To pluck that *Fruit* which was alone *forbid*
> To Kingly power in all that plenteous land,
> Where all things else submit to his command.
> And as fair *Edens* violated *Tree,*
> To'*Immortal Man* brought in *Mortalitie:*
> So shall that *Crown,* which God eternal meant,
> From thee (said he) and thy great house be rent,
> Thy Crime shall *Death* to all thine *Honours* send,
> And give thy'*Immortal Royalty* an *End.*

(1:384)

Beginning with this initial unwillingness to trust in God's providence, Saul becomes increasingly uncertain. His attempt to reassert his authority in the battle with the Philistines leads at the end of the fourth book to the impossible dilemma between saving face or sacrificing his son, and from there he is driven by his sense of abandonment to greater acts of tyranny. The paranoia so strikingly apparent in his envy and hatred of his nemesis David exhibits in its intensity the principal force consuming all tyrants: "They doubt the *Lords,* mistrust the *Peoples* hate, / Till *Blood* become a *Principle* of *State*" (1:289). Alienated from both God and subjects, Saul compromises the kingship envisioned in the *Davideis.* But although his reign will end with his suicide, Saul has not destroyed monarchy. Far from being "a work of political despair,"[34] the *Davideis* implies in its use of the fall the promise of redemption seen already in David's vision of the still greater kingdoms to follow. Jonathan's presence in the fourth book as a foil to his father further tempers the effects of the king's fall.

Unlike his father, who violates the king's obligation to serve, Jonathan is remarkably unselfish: "To *Help* seems all his *Power.*" Book IV accentuates the magnanimity and love that characterize his relations with others, and not surprisingly it also stresses the essential obligation: "As never more by *Heav'en* to *Man* was giv'en, / So never more was paid by *Man* to *Heav'en*" (1:378). On the battlefield against the Philistines, this commitment to divine will consumes Jonathan's identity as he becomes one with God. The extensive descriptions of his military feats develop a heroic tenor absent in the cam-

paigns of *The Civil War,* but the man who commands angels in the completion of heaven's design displays his most extraordinary heroism after the
battle ends. When Jonathan unknowingly breaks Saul's prohibition against
eating and stands condemned by his father's rash curse, he surpasses his
previous greatness:

> The *Prince* alone stood mild and patient by,
> So bright his sufferings, so triumphant show'd,
> Less to the *best* then *worst* of fates he ow'ed.
> A victory now he o're *himself* might boast;
> He *Conquer'd* now that *Conqu'eror* of an *Host.*
>
> (1:392)

The son who stands in this final scene for sacrifice reenacts the role Isaac was
fated to play; he also foreshadows, of course, Christ's obedient acceptance of
His father's will. The link with Christ becomes unavoidable when the narrative describes how the Israelites defied Saul and "sav'ed their *wondrous
Saviours* sacred blood" (1:392), but another association is also implicit. In
this final image of unjust suffering and triumphant patience, Jonathan becomes an emblem of the heroism David manifests in the *Davideis.*

This emblematic ending avoids the abrupt incompletion of *The Civil War.*
Though the poem stops with eight of the projected twelve books still
unwritten, the future does not disturb or threaten. Distanced from the very
immediate and destructive course of history, the narrative celebrates divine
providence with a greater assurance of its purpose. Kings betray their office
and tyrants abuse their powers, but the suffering they inflict is part of the
redemptive pattern seen in the patience of heroes and the rhythms of time.
For royalists confronting the bleak prospects of the Interregnum, the *Davideis*
offers in the end a consolation missing in the militant stridency of *The Civil
War.* Without abandoning or even questioning the royalist commitment, the
poem finds in the first book of Samuel the fate that often befalls the well-
intentioned ruler. Responsibilities can at least be considered and fears
lessened with the reassurance that the destruction of one monarchy is not the
destruction of all monarchy. Unlike the uncertain hope of expiation expressed at the death of Falkland, the wonder of God's saving grace is asserted
from the beginning of the *Davideis.* Its heroes are instruments of providence;
their heroic virtues attest above all to the importance of faith and patience.

This patience is severely tested in Cowley's next major work, the *Pindarique Odes.* Cowley's decision to imitate "the noblest and highest kind of
writing in Verse" (1:156) allows him to pursue without the demands of
sustained narrative an exalted vision of poetry. Thus when he returns to the
Old Testament, this time to Isaiah, form and expression may be his paramount concern: "The manner of the *Prophets* writing, especially of *Isaiah,*" he

notes in his commentary on the ode, "seems to me very like that of *Pindar;* they pass from one thing to another with almost *Invisible connexions,* and are full of words and expressions of the highest and boldest flights of *Poetry,* as may be seen in this Chapter, where there are as extraordinary Figures as can be found in any *Poet* whatsoever; and the connexion is so difficult, that I am forced to adde a little, and leave out a great deal to make it seem *Sense* to us" (1:214). The "Sense" he makes, however, often reflects in this and the other Pindaric odes the aftermath of defeat apparent particularly in the poetry of Lovelace and Brome. The destruction God brings upon the "*Rebel World*" in "The 34. Chapter of the Prophet *Isaiah*" and the scourges enumerated so fully in "The Plagues of *Egypt*" touch if only tacitly the England of the 1650s. The tragedy of a "mad *Nation*" ravaged by an "*Epidemick War*" becomes explicit in "To Dr. *Scarborough*," and war's effects are further apparent in the ambiguous tone of the other odes. Their altering moods and varied stances are symptomatic of Cowley's struggle to keep the tragedy in the perspective of the larger forces that shape existence. The most obviously political odes, "Destinie" and "Brutus," seek with troubled spirit the patience and assurance of the *Davideis.*

By likening the civil war to a game of chess, "Destinie" attempts to find a meaningful pattern in the royalist defeat. The rise of the pawn and the actions of the knight at first appear to follow understandable rules:

> Here I'm amaz'ed at th'actions of a *Knight,*
>> That does bold wonders in the fight.
>> Here I the losing party blame
>> For those false *Moves* that break the *Game,*
> That to their *Grave* the *Bag,* the conquered *Pieces* bring,
> And above all, th'*ill Conduct* of the *Mated King.*
>
> (1:192)

Cowley wants to believe that the individual pieces determined their own fate, and he is not unwilling to criticize the strategy of the king's supporters. With remarkable, albeit somewhat ambiguous candor, he also seems to include in his criticism "th'*ill Conduct* of the *Mated King*": the game exempts none from its test of strengths and weaknesses. But this initial certitude dissolves with the "enlightned" observation that "*two Angels* plaid the *Mate*" and "*Desti'ny plays us all.*" Seen in its true light, the game absolves Charles and the losing side from apparent responsibility, for an "*unseen Hand*" determines all the moves. The implications are also unavoidable for the poet who is now forced with new awareness to view the "unlucky *Doom*" of his own career. Cowley overcomes the temptation to indulge in an embittered account of sacrifice and neglect because he sees once more that he is not exempt from playing a part in a larger pattern. Melancholy, sentimentalism, and defeatism have no

place in his resignation. Though his musings lead to the inescapable conclusion, "With *Fate* what boots it to contend," Cowley seeks still greater
solace in a final gesture of defiance:

> Do Thou nor *grieve* nor *blush* to be,
> As all th'inspired *tuneful Men,*
> And all thy great *Forefathers* were from *Homer* down to *Ben.*
>
> (1:194)

The renewed commitment to his destiny reflects the complex attitude of
the poem's epigraph, the famous line from Manilius's *Astronomica, "Hoc
quoque; fatale est, sic ipsum expendere fatum* (This, too, is sanctioned by fate,
that I should thus expound the rule of fate)."[35] In its original context the line
concludes a prooemium on destiny similar in spirit to Cowley's poem.
Manilius contends that all humans are destined by birth and all events are
controlled by fate; but while the good may suffer and the evil prosper, this
inescapable destiny does not, paradoxically, justify a surrender of all responsibility. The lines preceding the epigraph encourage, "Let man's merits,
therefore, possess glory all the greater, seeing that they owe their excellence
to heaven; and, again, let us hate the wicked all the more, because they were
born for guilt and punishment. Crime, whencesoever sprung, must still be
reckoned crime."[36] The book they introduce ends in turn with an exalted
image of man and his rational capacities—an image similar to that Cowley
envisions in "To Mr. *Hobs,*" the tribute to the "great *Columbus* of the *Golden
Lands* of *new Philosophies*" (1:189) written, presumably, immediately before
"Destinie." Cowley joins the tradition "from *Homer* down to *Ben*" without
invoking the larger role of providence or exploring the uncertain limits of
will. The epigraph at the opening and the allusion at the end reach out
instead toward Manilius, Homer, and Jonson for assurance that individuals
can play their parts meaningfully in the game fate oversees. "Destinie" accepts
the poet's fate to set forth fate without pessimism and defeatism;[37] its
defiance, however forced it may seem to some, rests on a Stoicism Cowley has
not abandoned.

"Brutus" reconfirms this resolve in its appeal to a decidedly more Christian
patience. Cowley's defense of the tyrannicide once again encourages specific
political readings,[38] but like similar interpretations of the *Davideis,* they run
the risk of distorting the poem's understanding of divine will. The confusion
arises, in part, when readers interpret the poem in relation to Cowley's
admission in the 1656 Preface: "yet when the event of battel, and the
unaccountable *Will* of *God* has determined the controversie, and that we have
submitted to the conditions of the *Conqueror,* we must lay down our *Pens* as
well as *Arms,* we must *march* out of our *Cause* it self, and *dismantle* that, as
well as our *Towns* and *Castles,* of all the *Works* and *Fortifications* of *Wit* and

*Reason* by which we defended it" (1:455).[39] Too often Cowley's submission to divine will is seen as a confirmation of his apostasy, and the ode is then read as an allegorical support of Cromwell's rule. Both Cowley and his first biographer, however, denied that he had ever written anything against the king. After his return to England and his arrest in 1655, according to Thomas Sprat's biography, "He therefore believed that it would be a meritorious service to the King, if any man who was known to have followed his interest could insinuate into the Usurpers minds, that men of his Principles were now willing to be quiet, and could perswade the poor oppressed Royalists to conceal their affections for better occasions."[40] Although Cowley was later willing to "acknowledge and repent them as an error," he insisted that he intended in the lines no disloyalty to the king, "whose service I always accounted the chief duty, and favour the chief happiness, of my life. . . . I am fully satisfied in conscience of the uprightness of my own sense in those [two] or three lines which have been received in one so contrary to it, and . . . I am sure all my actions and conversation in England have commented upon them according to that sense of mine, and not according to the interpretations of others."[41] Clarendon may have been unwilling to accept Cowley's distinction, but in the opinion of an eminent modern historian of the Interregnum, "there is no evidence to convict him. . . . Cowley conformed peacefully enough, and justified himself in print, but went no further than a realistic, Hobbesian acceptance of the existing power."[42] The poem in praise of Brutus does not contradict this claim. Cowley's study of limited virtue and necessary accommodation praises the heroic fortitude of those who struggle to remain accountable to "the unaccountable Will of God."

Brutus's defeat confirms this heroism. Throughout the ode Cowley defends "Excellent *Brutus*" against all detractors, only to admit in the end the inevitable failure of this great Roman. The panegyric of this noble man insists almost defensively upon a flawless life of virtue unswerving in its values. The ode expresses no doubts about Brutus's need to rid the country of the tyrannical Caesar, and it has only praise for the man who selflessly comes to the aid of the nation and courageously defies the spirit of Caesar. But when "wretched *Accidents*" conspire with "*Ill men*" to defeat "The best *Cause* and best *Man* that ever drew a *Sword*" (1:196), the bitterness and dejection are palpable:

> What can we say but thine own *Tragick Word*,
> That *Virtue*, which had worshipt been by thee
> As the most solid *Good*, and greatest *Deitie*,
>> By this fatal proof became
>> An *Idol* only, and a *Name*.

(1:197)

The tragedy of Brutus is not, however, as it would seem, the failure of all
virtue. Caught up in the magnitude of Brutus's loss, the reader can easily
forget the initial description of him as "The best till *Nature* was improv'ed by
*Grace*" (1:195). Without faith and grace Brutus must fail, a failure the poem
acknowledges when it abruptly turns away from the pain of Brutus's defeat
and counsels restraint:

> The *Time's* set forth already which shall quell
> Stiff *Reason,* when it offers to *Rebell.*
> > Which these great *Secrets* shall unseal,
> > And new *Philosophies* reveal.
> A few years more, so soon hadst thou not dy'ed,
> Would have confounded *Humane Virtues* pride,
> > And shew'd thee a *God crucifi'ed.*
>
> > > > (1:197)

Cowley does not agree with *An Harmonie vpon the First Book of Samvel* that
Brutus's self-destruction does "not much mooue vs,"[43] but he does recognize
a similar impatience in the noble Roman's actions. Guided solely by "Stiff
*Reason,*" Brutus appears a rebel; had he restrained himself, the final lines
conclude, he could have lived to witness in the crucifixion the ultimate
undoing of "*Humane Virtues* pride" and the vindication of patience, humil-
ity, suffering, and faith.

Time also brings the despondent royalists the only consolation. Later
Cowley looked back upon the years of civil war and recognized the futility of
any action:

> In such a time it was as this, that not all the wisdom and power of the
> Roman Senate, nor the wit and eloquence of *Cicero,* nor the Courage and
> Virtue of *Brutus* was able to defend their Country or themselves against the
> unexperienced rashness of a beardless Boy, and the loose rage of a volup-
> tuous Madman. The valour and prudent Counsels on the one side are
> made fruitless, and the errours and cowardize on the other harmless, by
> unexpected accidents (2:361).

"Brutus" struggles with this reality. Resisting suicidal despair, the ode accepts the prospect of further suffering with the patience and faith of the
*Davideis.* Passivity, however, is not capitulation. Both poems explore the
limitations of unaided virtue, and through trust in a providential future, each
overcomes the need to defy tyranny. Seen in the larger course of events,
David's willingness to flee and Jonathan's readiness to obey are preferable to
Brutus's defiance. Cowley obviously sympathizes with the virtuous, patriotic
instincts of the noble Roman, but at a bleak moment in his country's history,
he also understands the wisdom of accepting the design of providence. His is
the consolation Lipsius finds at another period of civil upheaval: "yeeld to

God, and giue place to the time. And if thou be a good citizen or common-
wealths-man preserue thy selfe to a better and happier end. The liberty which
now is lost, may be recouered againe hereafter; and thy decayed country may
flourish in another age: why doest thou loose al courage & fal into dispair?
Of those two Consuls at the battel of *Cannes,* I account *Varro* a more
excellent citizen, who escaped, than *Paulus* that was slain."[44]

Accommodation again preoccupies Cowley in the next of the Pindaric
odes, "To Dr. *Scarborough.*" In a movement parallel to that of the previous
poem, great praise yields ultimately to a recognition of inevitable limitation.
Through five of the six stanzas, Cowley lauds the extraordinary achievements
of a physician friend who seems sent by God to heal the nation's tragic
wounds. As another Apollo, "not, only," Cowley notes, "the *God* of *Physick,*
but of *Poetry,* and all kind of *Florid Learning*" (1:201), Scarborough expresses humanism at its best; and the ode draws parallels in suitably heroic
allusions to the realms of conquest and discovery. Like his counterpart in "To
Mr. *Hobs,*" he has made all nature his province, and in his short life he has
mastered many of its secrets. And yet, the final stanza admits, Scarborough's
"noble *Reparations*" must be undone. The poem's military imagery draws
sadly toward its conclusion:

> Like *Archimedes,* hon'orably in vain,
> Thou holdst out *Towns* that must at last be *ta'ne,*
> And *Thou* thy self their great *Defender* slain.
>
> (1:200)

Mortality, naturally, will undo all that Scarborough has fought to preserve,
but as Cowley's note suggests, the allusion to Archimedes' death at the siege
of Syracuse suggests treachery, betrayal, and indifference. In the battle
against fate, Cowley, like Brome, can only urge his friend to "*compound,* and
for the *Present Live*" (1:200). Acceptance is not surrender, for the ode advises
Scarborough to use only some of the time for pleasure before the long
campaign ends. But the final couplet makes no attempt to conceal the jarring
reality: "Let *Nature,* and let *Art* do what they please, / When all's done, *Life is
an incurable Disease*" (1:200). The pessimistic dimensions of the last line
threaten the positive tenor of the ode's praise, and in doing so they replicate
the tensions of "Destinie" and "Brutus." Their strained tone of consolation
introduces the somber cast of Cowley's next grouping, the four odes on the
vanity of human existence.

"Life and Fame," "The Extasie," "To the New Year," and "Life" develop
traditional Christian attitudes, often with brutal candor. Relentlessly Cowley
assaults the delusions of life, scorning human pretensions and offering little
hope against the passage of time. In effect the odes become extensions of the
epigraph in "Life," "*Nascentes Morimur.*" Manilius's assertion that "At birth

our death is sealed" serves in the odes to encourage the only response: "Set free your minds, O mortals, banish your cares, and rid your lives of all this vain complaint."[45] When "To the New Year" suppresses the natural inclination to consider the future, Cowley may have in mind as well the Stoic belief that the greatest benefit of virtue is "the quality of not needing a single day beyond the present, and of not reckoning up the days that are ours."[46] His resolve to plunge into the *"Fatal Flood"* has none of the bravado of his juvenile imitation of Horace's similar counsel. The odes find nothing but suffering and emptiness in the "wretched Inn" of life, and their unrelieved tone of *contemptus mundi* reveals in its extremeness the doubts and even despondency Cowley overcomes in the other odes. He yearns, "The Extasie" implies, to gain the transcendent perspective from which the civil war becomes meaningless; here and at the end of "Life," the movement is upward, toward the ideal George Daniel also longed to achieve.

But the poems written in the waning years of the Interregnum and published with one exception in *Verses, Lately Written upon Several Occasions* (1663) avoid the dangers of escapism and pessimism. Although Cowley does not completely resolve his nagging doubts about the life of poetry he seeems fated to pursue, he resists the nihilism of "Life and Fame," drawing renewed inspiration from contemporaries who display a patient nobility. Buffeted in exile by the storms of tyrannous fortune and driven like David to disguise his identity, the duke of Buckingham found in his constant virtue "Home in Banishment" (2:463). In the tempestuous years of ill fortune, the earl of Balcarres also stood "Fixt as an Island 'gainst the waves and wind" (1:415). Cowley extols their inviolability, confident in the certainty that providence will protect the "great Mans Soul" and mindful of the strength that love can create. The same constancy and not wit alone enabled the matchless Orinda, Katherine Philips, to stand unmoved above all worldly vanities, the "tender Goodness of her Mind" (1:443) invulnerable to the assaults that befell less harmonious individuals. Like William Harvey, who "sought for Truth in Truth's own Book" (1:417), the subjects of Cowley's praise developed the sense of self-sufficiency lauded at greater length in Cartwright's poetry: despite often threatening circumstances, they are still concerned with restoring the well-being of others. Their qualities are idealized in the collection's most ambitious praise, the ode celebrating the Restoration.

The return of the Stuarts brings renewed hope in the earlier Caroline certainty of a future glory based upon the monarchy's commitment to St. George and Christ.[47] The triumphant ode "Upon His Majesties Restoration and Return" likens the civil war once again to a second fall, but now it sees in the dark confusion of the last years another genesis, for "Loe, the blest *Spirit* mov'd, and *there was Light*" (1:424). The ode traces the *"Almighty's hand"* and the *"Almighty Mercy"* in familiar Old and New Testament patterns of suffering and restoration. God's direction and the monarchy's right are manifest in the royal family's journey through their *"rough Red sea"* and in their years of wandering in a "fatal *Wilderness.*" Though a divine and "unerring hand" guides them to the promised glory, their right is assured through the blood of the martyred king. Unequivocally the ode avers that nothing can withstand the "sacred force" exerted in the union of "the *naked Truth,* and the *unarmed King*" (1:426). Years of rage and folly are dismissed as an unavoidable and necessary means to virtue. With understated simplicity the ode understands and even accepts the horror of the previous decades:

> Man ought his *future Happiness* to fear,
>     If he be always *Happy here*
>     He wants the *bleeding Mark of Grace,*
> The *Circumcision of the chosen race.*
>
> (1:427)

Suffering and glory are inextricably united in the poem's celebration of a *"Heroick* worth," the epic roots of which are firmly set in the world of Virgil and Homer as well as in the Bible. The vision of redemption apparent to Cowley in the "wisest *Poets*" of the classical world sanctions the ode's belief that only the chosen few can form through the storms of adversity and loneliness the virtue required to rebuild a nation. Suitably protected by their heavenly arms, a sign for Cowley of their absolute dependency upon divine aid, these Aeneases prove even to the heavens the greatest heroism:

> No show on Earth can sure so pleasant prove,
>     As when they *great misfortunes* see
> With *Courage* born and *Decency.*
>
> (1:429)

From this perspective the dark days of disguise and flight following the royalist defeat at Worcester and the unhappy years of exile at the courts of Europe appear the source of the greatest honor. Purified in these purgatorial fires, Charles II and his brothers already have been graced with a magnificence and glory no restoration celebration can surpass. Together with their sisters, they exemplify the nobility of their mother. In the Caroline splendor of the past, the queen offered in her roles of wife and mother the assurance of a prosperous future; now the *"Daughter of Triumphs, Wife of Martyrdom"* brings anew the hope driven from the nation:

> Thy Princely *Mind* with so much *Courage* bore
> *Affliction,* that it dares return no more;
> With so much *Goodness* us'd *Felicity,*
> That it cannot refrain from coming back to *Thee;*
> 'Tis come, and seen to day in all it's *Bravery.*
>
> (1:431)

The larger pattern of the poem completes the unfinished vision of *The Civil War* and the *Davideis*. The hope they place in Falkland, Jonathan, and David is fulfilled in the sacrifice, patience, and fortitude of the royal family. Though the last stanzas of the ode recognize too the selflessness of General Monck and the other patriotic members of Parliament, its theme of redemption clearly reveals royalist allegiances. With none of the earlier poems' anger, the ode expresses Cowley's belief that divinely guided virtue will triumph in the tragedy of existence. England's fate appears to Cowley in 1660, as it had to Daniel, part of a divine comedy in which suffering and loss assume creative as well as heroic dimensions.

The rejuvenated England in the final poems proves the providential vision. The occasional piece "On the Queens Repairing *Somerset* House," which Cowley wrote some three or four years after Charles II's return, sees in the queen's renovated residence a microcosm of the national restoration:

> She imitates the Kindness to Her shown;
> She does, like Heaven (which the dejected Throne
> At once restores, fixes, and higher rears.)
> Strengthen, Enlarge, Exalt what she Repairs.
>
> (1:433)

In looking from the house's location on the Thames toward the court and town, then beyond the river into the country and out into the ocean, the topological poem proclaims with a nationalistic and even imperialistic note a golden era of prosperity and vigor once only wistfully associated with the past. Although Cowley admits at the poem's outset that he cannot understand why God allowed the forces of evil their years of triumph, he ends with the conviction that the "Kingdom's Happy now at last." The variation of the Virgilian recognition *"O fortunatus nimium"* tempers but does not diminish the familiar Caroline faith in the royal family:

> (Happy, if Wise by their Misfortunes past)
> From hence may Ómens take of that success
> Which both their future Wars and Peace shall bless:
> The Peaceful Mother on mild *Thames* does build,
> With her Son's Fabricks the rough *Sea* is fill'd.
>
> (1:435)

The archetypal rhythm of fall and redemption in "To the *Royal Society*" retraces in equally familiar heroic images Cowley's persistent faith in the divine design that first led the nation through its wilderness of suffering and now leads it into another promised land. The "New Scenes of Heaven" and the "Crowds of golden Worlds" that await exploration and conquest are also unmistakable in *Plantarum,* the long Latin poem Cowley wrote in the last years of his life.

The poem's recollection of the past and its vision of the future reflect the sobering experience of the last decades. Written in large part near the end of his life, when Cowley retired to his Chertsey gardens and their rural solitude, *Plantarum* complements the temperament of the more familiar *Several Discourses by way of Essays, in Verse and Prose*. These essays, which have been aptly described as "the ultimate or essential epic of humble life,"[48] depict in their blend of prose and poetry a life modeled on Virgil, Horace, and Martial. Their willingness to forsake the glory of Rome and their visions of rural happiness earlier inspired many of Cowley's civil war contemporaries to seek a world removed from strife. But Cowley wryly recognizes that this existence has none of "the simplicity of the old Poetical Golden Age," and he qualifies the juvenile enthusiasm expressed in *Sylva*. His translation of a central passage from Virgil reflects his mature understanding:

> Happy the Man, I grant, thrice happy he
> Who can through gross effects their causes see:
> Whose courage from the deeps of knowledg springs,
> Nor vainly fears inevitable things;
> But does his walk of virtue calmly go,
> Through all th'allarms of Death and Hell below.
> Happy! but next such Conquerours, happy they,
> Whose humble Life lies not in fortunes way.
>
> (2:410)

Cowley acknowledges that the "humble Life" is no guarantee of an existence freed from the cares of ambition and secure in the virtue of an untroubled conscience. To a greater extent than Virgil, his translation emphasizes the reality learned in two decades of national uncertainty: happiness depends upon the equanimity with which the "Conquerours" confront daily misfortune calmly and fearlessly. The self-possession or patience, and not the pastoral life itself, has long been Cowley's concern; and when he actually undertakes the study so congenial to contemplation, the subject of nature leads him in the six books of *Plantarum* back to the world of heroic struggle and triumphant patience.

The Latin poem Cowley undertakes as a diversion from "Wearisomeness of human Affairs" praises in the history of herbs, flowers, and trees the divine design apparent even in nature's smallest creations. But as the loosely structured narrative reveals the purposeful roles the humble herbs play in the battle against illness and marvels at the mysteries of reproduction, its lyric account of nature's splendor and value gradually involves the world of state so removed from the garden solitude. At first the poem glances only occasionally at the fate of rulers, content to contrast the short duration of the good prince and the uncertain glory of great figures with nature's unending bounty. With Book III and the empire of flowers, however, the survey touches more directly the concerns familiar to the political poems. The reign of the flowers occasions commentary on the fundamental role virtue must play in sovereignty, and their example serves to warn kings about the folly of waging war against their citizens and of forgetting the mildness central to majesty. A long passage on ambition also included in the essay "Of Agriculture" questions the rewards of power, while the later books stress the honor and peace essential to any just rule. In the commonwealth of flowers and the realm of the trees, Cowley appears both to counsel the restored monarch and to express his own lifelong abhorrence of tyranny. The final book abandons any pretext of indirection and in its effusive narrative of the nation's destiny confronts and summarizes the meaning of the last decades.

The narrative of the civil war and Restoration views the nation's history in the larger mythic rhythm Cowley has come to accept. Enveloping the past and the future in the archetypal pattern of the Fall, the sixth book places the last twenty years in the context of a Saturnine world of peaceful plenty. The poem's fanciful vision of a sylvan state once blessed with Ceres's benevolent guidance has its modern parallel in the golden years of Charles and Henrietta's reign. For the last time Cowley recreates the Caroline image of a peaceful monarch who spread ease and plenty throughout the kingdom, governing a nation far happier than any of the European kingdoms. Within the familiar Caroline adaptation of the halcyon myth, peace built her nest in the only calm amid the tempestuous storms of war; there she hatched the blessings of justice and faith. Once again the Virgilian irony is also unmistakable: "Such was the State of *England*, sick with Ease, / Too happy, if she knew her Happiness."[49] Ignorant of her bliss, the nation blindly pursued a seemingly inevitable destiny: a Parliament driven by envious pride and committed to the popular cry of "Religion, Liberty, and Property" destroyed the "Prince of peace."

With the distance and the perspective of time, Cowley gains no greater understanding of the civil war. Though he continually sees in rebellion's claims of liberty and religion an underlying pride and avarice, Cowley never truly comprehends the political and religious complexities of his nation's tragedy. His account of prolonged suffering accepts the classical and Renaissance commonplace that peace and plenty contain in their luxury and sloth the seeds of self-destruction.[50] The narrative, replete with furies, evil genius, and fate, also resorts to the royalists' derision of fanatic demogogues and misguided citizens consumed by their depraved appetites. The history of uncontrolled ambition comes no closer than the other works in this study to an analysis of the royalist defeat, and it shows no willingness to admit the monarchy's responsibility. Cowley refuses to dwell on the spectacle of the military losses, and he attributes the king's downfall and execution to reasons known only to God. The derisive handling of a tyrannic Cromwell and his avaricious rout indulges a vengeful, gloating animus typical of Restoration

reactions to the Interregnum, and no attempt is made to explore the ig-
nominious years of defeat and suppression. The narrative instead offsets the
nation's fall with the few heroic individuals who outbrave fate and accept
heaven's will.

The son of the martyred king stands foremost. The poem emphasizes the
fortitude with which his father courageously defied the fateful period of
defeat, flight, and death; but the actions of the exiled Charles Stuart command Cowley's attention. The narrative of the abortive attempt in 1651 to
rally English support and the description of the six weeks of hiding after the
battle of Worcester prove the young king's heroic virtue. In his saga of the
military defeat and the king's efforts to elude his pursuers at Boscobel,
Cowley follows the numerous publications of the 1660s that rushed to
proclaim the Royal Miracle and to sing the praises of God's mercy and
providence;[51] his account, however, gives Charles's patience and fortitude a
prominence well beyond its competing versions. Their passing allusions to
David's flight from Saul and to Job's unwarranted suffering touch less
directly the essential truth: "to Heaven's Favourites Loss is Gain, and that
*Patience* is a Crowning vertue."[52] From the bitter disappointment of Worcester and the long weeks of flight, Charles gains a triumphant nobility:

> Thou greatest now of Kings indeed, while yet
> With all the Miseries of life beset,
> Thy mighty Mind cou'd Death nor Danger fear,
> Nor yet even then of Safety coud despair.
> This is the Virtue of a Monarch's Soul,
> Who above Fortunes reach can all her Turns controul;
> Thus if Fate rob you of your Empires Sway,
> You by this Fortitude take hers away;
> O brave Reprisal! which the Gods prefer,
> That makes you triumph o'er the Conqueror.
> The Gods who all day will this Justice do
> Both make you Victor and Triumpher too.[53]

The victory recalls Lovelace's poems of "griefe triumphant," although the
value of patient fortitude is shared in principle by all the writers in this study.
It is a victory over fortune Cowley gives equally to the king and to God.

In this triumph the golden past is restored. The future anticipated in
Charles's courage at Boscobel brings the return of peace. The scene of
welcome reminiscent of the Caroline masques envisions the descent of a
snowy-winged peace attended by noble ladies, who usher in a train of
allegorical figures suited to "a just Prince's Reign" (*"sub Rege viget quae
maxima justo"*). Appropriately, Henrietta Maria resumes the role she played
so often in the Whitehall masques. Charles shares this victory once again, as
he does in the Restoration ode, with the woman who stood unbowed in

harrowing circumstances: "your Mind was all your own; / The giddy World roll'd round you long in vain, / Who fix'd in Virtues Centre still remain."[54] Theirs is the triumph of mind and virtue that all of Cowley's noblest figures strive to achieve. It is the victory of the self-possessed or centered individual admired by each of the poets in the previous chapters.

With the return to peace, Cowley envisions flourishing religion and learning, released from the tyranny of the rebellion; he also anticipates the glory waiting beyond the nation's shores. The poem's final episode foreshadows in its description of the 1665 naval engagement with the Dutch at the Battle of Lowenstoft the glory the legendary Brutus embarked upon when he was given sovereignty over all the seas. The battle with a foreign enemy over English rights expresses in brief the heroic energy thwarted in the self-destructive years of civil war. Behind this English naval prowess lie the traditions of Columbus and Drake, and in the military conquest appears the assertiveness prominent in the tributes to those who assault the frontiers of knowledge. With a chauvinism shared by many who welcomed the new national unity, Cowley eagerly embraces the heroism traditionally associated with arms and empire. But the future fame it promises crown and country is possible only because of those individuals who patiently endured the oppression of tyranny and heroically accepted the guidance of providence.

Firmly committed to the humanist values of virtue and eloquence, Cowley sustains to the end a Renaissance faith in the human ability to extend its sovereignty over nature, but he ultimately believes even more firmly in the unconquerable human spirit. During periods of great distress and uncertainty, the poems test and affirm the fundamental worth of love and goodness, the resiliency of the human spirit, and the purposefulness of history. Their epic accounts of the undaunted will may never regain the esteem with which they were once held, but the poems remain a valuable testimony to the courage other contemporaries found at some of the nation's bleakest moments. Not all the writers in this study accepted Cowley's faith in a larger and finally unknowable course of providential history, and most did not live to see the resolution of the conflict and the restoration of monarchy, but each faced the future with similar resolve. Though they lived in different social milieus and possessed different poetic talents, Cartwright, Daniel, Lovelace, Brome, and Cowley share a common distinction between withdrawal and retreat. The banks of the river Devia, the warmth of the country-house hearth, and the safety of exile variously offered places of refuge and not escape. Within these enclosed worlds of recreation and re-creation, even the most skeptical of the writers appreciates the "mind that is free, lofty, fearless, and steadfast." Such an individual "stands like a center unmoved."

# Notes

## Introduction

1. Harry Coningsby, "The Preface and Occasion of this Melancholick Divertisement," in *The Consolation of Philosophy*, trans. Thomas Coningsby (London, 1664), sig. A5r. The entry in the *Dictionary of National Biography* for Harry Coningsby contains biographical information about his father drawn largely from this preface.

2. Coningsby, "Preface," sig. A4v.

3. Ibid., sig. A6r.

4. Ibid., sigs. A6r, A8r.

5. Seneca, "On the Happy Life," in *Moral Essays*, trans. John W. Basore, The Loeb Classical Library, 3 vols. (Cambridge: Harvard University Press, 1935), 2:109.

6. Boethius, *The Consolation of Philosophy*, trans. Richard Green (Indianapolis, Ind.: Bobbs-Merrill, 1962), p. 9.

7. Joseph Hall, "Of a Patient Man," in *Heaven vpon Earth and Characters of Vertves and Vices*, ed. Rudolf Kirk (New Brunswick, N.J.: Rutgers University Press, 1948), p. 155.

8. Joseph Hall, "Character of the Wise man," in Kirk, *Characters of Vertves and Vices*, p. 148.

9. Justus Lipsius, *Two Bookes Of Constancie Written in Latine by Iustus Lipsius, Englished by Sir John Stradling*, ed. Rudolf Kirk (New Brunswick, N.J.: Rutgers University Press, 1939), p. 79.

10. Cicero, *De Officiis*, trans. Walter Miller, The Loeb Classical Library (New York: G. P. Putnam's Sons, 1928), p. 281.

11. Gerard Verbeke, among others, considers the earlier traditions of Stoicism in *The Presence of Stoicism in Medieval Thought* (Washington, D.C.: The Catholic University of America Press, 1983). A discussion of the early humanists' indebtedness to Stoicism and an extensive bibliography are found in George M. Logan's *The Meaning of More's Utopia* (Princeton: Princeton University Press, 1983).

12. Rudolf Kirk surveys the classical editions and translations in "Stoic Writings Anglicized," a section of the introduction to his edition of Lipsius, *Two Bookes Of Constancie*, pp. 13–32.

13. Gordon Braden, *Renaissance Tragedy and the Senecan Tradition: Anger's Privilege* (New Haven: Yale University Press, 1985), p. 71. The basic principles of Renaissance Stoicism are clearly presented in Kirk's edition of Hall; Isabel Rivers, *Classical and Christian Ideas in English Renaissance Poetry* (London: George Allen & Unwin, 1979); and Jason Lewis Saunders, *Justus Lipsius: The Philosophy of Renaissance Stoicism* (New York: The Liberal Arts Press, 1955).

14. See, for example, the bibliographic citations in Braden's notes as well as such studies as T. S. Eliot, "Seneca in Elizabethan Translation" and "Shakespeare and the Stoicism of Seneca," in *Selected Essays, 1917–1932* (New York: Harcourt, Brace and Company, 1932); Sam H. Henderson, "Neo-Stoic Influence on Elizabethan Formal

185

Verse Satire," in *Studies in English Renaissance Literature,* ed. Waldo F. McNeir (Batton Rouge, La.: Louisiana State University Press, 1962), pp. 56–86; and Morris W. Croll, *"Attic" & Baroque Prose Style,* ed. J. Max Patrick, Robert O. Evans, and John M. Wallace (Princeton: Princeton University Press, 1966).

15. Gerald J. Schiffhorst observes in *The Triumph of Patience* (Orlando, Fla.: University Presses of Florida, 1978), "Though Justus Lipsius saw that Stoic indifference precludes Christian hope, he and Erasmus, Elyot, Du Vair, and others were generally unclear in drawing distinctions between the cold, proud, defiant patience of the ancients and the humble, ardent, submissive Christian virtue" (p. 7). Braden also considers the Christian reservations concerning Stoicism in *Renaissance Tragedy,* pp. 92–98.

16. Lipsius, *Two Bookes Of Constancie,* pp. 83–84.

17. Guillaume Du Vair, *The Moral Philosophie of the Stoicks, Englished by Thomas James,* ed. Rudolf Kirk (New Brunswick, N.J.: Rutgers University Press, 1951), p. 127.

18. Several studies of the humanist attitude are particularly relevant. In *The Meaning of More's Utopia,* George M. Logan emphasizes the humanist dilemma of service, pp. 89–111. Katharine Eisaman Maus's chapter "Jonson and the Roman Social Ethos" in *Ben Jonson and the Roman Frame of Mind* (Princeton: Princeton University Press, 1984) is also valuable. Maus's discussion of the Roman moralists and their influence on Jonson also provides a good sense of some classical traditions central to the following study of loyalism. Less immediately relevant but nevertheless important is Harry Berger's essay, "The Renaissance Imagination: Second World and Green World," *The Centennial Review* 9 (1965):36–78.

19. Cicero, *De Officiis,* p. 157.

20. Ibid., p. 21.

21. Seneca, "On Leisure," 2:187.

22. Seneca, "On Tranquillity of Mind," 2:233–35.

23. Lipsius, *Two Bookes Of Constancie,* p. 127.

24. Du Vair, *Moral Philosophie,* p. 55.

25. Seneca, "On Leisure," 2:187.

26. Braden writes about Renaissance Stoicism: "Virtus in its fight against fortuna grades naturally, almost inevitably, into *virtù:* inner resource translating itself back into public action at a new pitch of self-confidence" (*Renaissance Tragedy,* p. 80). See also Michael O'Loughlin's sensitive discussion of "civic and retired leisure" in *The Garlands of Repose* (Chicago: The University of Chicago Press, 1978). O'Loughlin's analysis of Horace, in particular, emphasizes "leisurely innocence not in an earthly paradise given to an improbable *beatus ille* but as a condition of mind achieved in tension with the real world, as the personal experience of a profoundly characterized ego" (p. 80). The individual "who liberates himself by containing himself" creates "the center of calm" and the "paradise within the mind." "At home within himself," he is freed through the "festivity and the power of the imagination."

27. Earl Miner, "Patterns of Stoicism in Thought and Prose Styles, 1530–1700," *PMLA* 85 (1970):1023–34.

28. Maren-Sofie Røstvig, *The Happy Man,* 2 vols. (Oslo: Norwegian Universities Press, 1954, 1962); Earl Miner, *The Cavalier Mode from Jonson to Cotton* (Princeton: Princeton University Press, 1971). Røstvig's 1962 edition considerably revises her first edition; Miner's suggestion, however, that the revision deletes much of the "pattern of stoicism" is debatable (p. 1025 of "Patterns of Stoicism"). Though A. D. Cousins's survey is necessarily much narrower, his essay "The Cavalier World and John Cleveland," *Studies in Philology* 78 (1981):61–86, also offers valuable insights.

The first two chapters of Isabel Rivers's *The Poetry of Conservatism, 1600–1745* (Cambridge, England: Rivers Press, 1973) are also very relevant.

29. Miner, "Patterns of Stoicism," pp. 90, 91. See also O'Loughlin, *Garlands of Repose*, pp. 53–154.

30. Conrad Russell, "Introduction," in *The Origins of the English Civil War*, ed. Conrad Russell (New York: Barnes and Noble, 1973), p. 1; Conrad Russell, "The Nature of a Parliament in Early Stuart England," in *Before the English Civil War*, ed. Howard Tomlinson (New York: St. Martin's Press, 1984), p. 124; Anthony Fletcher, *The Outbreak of the English Civil War* (New York: New York University Press, 1981), p. xxx.

31. R. W. Harris, *Clarendon and the English Revolution* (Stanford: Stanford University Press, 1983), p. 110. John Morrill, "Introduction," in *Reactions to the English Civil War, 1642–1649*, ed. John Morrill (New York: St. Martin's Press, 1983), p. 5. Brian Manning, "What Was the English Revolution?" *History Today* 34 (March 1984):18–19.

32. Morrill, "Introduction," p. 17; Morrill, *The Revolt of the Provinces* (London: Allen and Unwin, 1976), p. 42; Harris, *Clarendon*, p. 95; Fletcher, *The Outbreak of the English Civil War*, pp. 264–282; Manning, "What Was the English Revolution?" p. 19; Ian Roy, "The English Civil War and English Society," in *War and Society*, ed. Brian Bond and Ian Roy (New York: Holmes and Meier Publishers, 1975), pp. 24–43; and Derek Hirst, *Authority and Conflict: England, 1603–1658* (Cambridge: Harvard University Press, 1986), pp. 223–30.

33. Surveys of this debate are found in R. C. Richardson, *The Debate on the English Revolution* (New York: St. Martin's Press, 1977), pp. 126–45; Lawrence Stone, *The Causes of the English Revolution, 1529–1642* (London: Routledge & Kegan Paul, 1972), pp. 26–43; Howard Tomlinson, "The Causes of War: A Historiographical Survey," in *Before the English Civil War*, pp. 16–26; Austin Woolrych, "Court, Country and City Revisited," *History* 65 (1980):236–45.

34. "In fact," John Morrill observes, "the principal determinant of allegiance in 1642 is proximity to the King's person or to Westminster" (p. 12 of "Introduction"). In *Revel, Riot, and Rebellion* (Oxford: Clarendon Press, 1985), David Underdown stresses the allegiances to church and monarchy associated with local traditions of festival culture. His earlier study *Pride's Purge: Politics in the Puritan Revolution* (Oxford: Clarendon Press, 1971) offers a very good analysis of the evolving and shifting commitments in the 1640s.

35. Peter W. Thomas, "Two Cultures? Court and Country under Charles I," in *The Origins of the English Civil War*, pp. 168–93; and Thomas, "Charles I of England: The Tragedy of Absolutism," in *The Courts of Europe*, ed. A. G. Dickens (New York: McGraw-Hill, 1977), pp. 191–211.

36. C. V. Wedgwood, *Poetry and Politics under the Stuarts* (Cambridge: Cambridge University Press, 1960).

37. Thomas, "Two Cultures?" p. 182; Thomas, "Charles I of England," p. 204.

38. Fletcher, *The Outbreak of the English Civil War*, p. 283.

39. *The foure Ages of England: Or, The Iron Age. With other select Poems* (London, 1648), p. 51. The title page attributes this poem to "Mr. A. Cowley," but no modern scholar has accepted the attribution.

40. In *Destiny His Choice: The Loyalism of Andrew Marvell* (Cambridge: Cambridge University Press, 1968), John M. Wallace makes another distinction: "whereas the obedience of the royalist was to the king's person, the loyalist's was to his office and authority" (p. 5).

41. Derek Hirst notes that John Morrill uses the term to describe a number of

historians who have supported the conclusions of Conrad Russell; "Revisionism Revised: The Place of Principle," *Past and Present* 92 (1981):79–99. Warning that the revisionists are too diverse to be considered a school, Howard Tomlinson nevertheless concedes "their researches have all questioned the power of parliament, the extent to which there was a permanent opposition in the Commons and whether the raising of major issues was not more influenced by court intrigues, local pressures and war than matters of principle or grand constitutional design" ("The Causes of War," in *Before the English Civil War*, p. 24). They have, moreover, challenged the Whig view of the seventeenth century, and they offer a valuable corrective to those historians who view the seventeenth century with the hindsight of the civil war. The following study is particularly indebted to Conrad Russell and Kevin Sharpe, but it also reflects the views of historians such as J. P. Kenyon, G. R. Elton, and G. E. Aylmer who are not usually associated with the revisionists. Criticism of the revisionists may be found in the Hirst essay and in the bibliography Morrill provides in *Reactions to the English Civil War*, particularly p. 219. Revisionist ideas are sensitively developed in a literary context by Martin Butler, *Theater and Crisis, 1632–1642* (Cambridge: Cambridge University Press, 1984).

42. Lipsius, *Two Bookes Of Constancie*, p. 98.

43. Abraham Cowley, "Preface" to his 1656 edition in *The English Writings of Abraham Cowley*, ed. A. R. Waller, 2 vols. (Cambridge: Cambridge University Press, 1905–1906), 1:7.

44. As such, this study offers an alternative to Christopher Hill's *The Experience of Defeat* (New York: Viking Penguin, 1984), which "illustrates not only reactions to the defeat of the English Revolution, but also acceptance of the fact of revolution itself" (p. 27).

## Chapter 1. The Caroline Circle of Peace

1. Charles I, *Eikon Basilike*, ed. Philip A. Knachel (Ithaca: Cornell University Press, 1966), p. 39.

2. Graham Parry, *The Golden Age Restor'd: The Culture of the Stuart Court, 1603–42* (New York: St. Martin's Press, 1981), p. 197; C. V. Wedgwood, *Poetry and Politics under the Stuarts* (Cambridge: Cambridge University Press, 1960), pp. 44–45; Peter W. Thomas, "Two Cultures? Court and Country under Charles I," in *The Origins of the English Civil War*, ed. Conrad Russell (New York: Barnes and Noble, 1973), pp. 175, 179; Perez Zagorin, *The Court and the Country* (New York: Atheneum, 1970), p. 71.

3. Joshua Sprigg, *Anglia Rediviva* (London, 1647), p. 1; Lucy Hutchinson, "The Life of Mrs. Lucy Hutchinson," in *Memoirs of the Life of Colonel Hutchinson*, ed. James Sutherland (London: Oxford University Press, 1973), p. 279; Tom May, *The History of the Parliament of England: Which began November the third, M.DC.XL.* (London, 1647), part 1, p. 21. The information on the contemporary histories is drawn from Raymond A. Anselment, "Clarendon and the Caroline Myth of Peace," *The Journal of British Studies* 23 (1984):37–54.

4. Edward Hyde, earl of Clarendon, *The Life of Edward Earl of Clarendon*, 3 vols. (Oxford, 1759), 1:70; Clarendon, *The History of the Rebellion*, ed. W. Dunn Macray, 6 vols. (Oxford: Clarendon Press, 1888), 1:93.

5. Sir Philip Warwick, *Memoires Of the reigne of King Charles I* (London, 1701), p. 46.

6. Hamon L'Estrange, *The Reign of King Charles* (London, 1656), p. 143.

7. J. P. Kenyon, *Stuart England* (New York: St. Martin's Press, 1978), p. 118. In

*Rebellion or Revolution? England, 1640–1660* (Oxford: Clarendon Press, 1986), G. E. Aylmer further cautions, "there is a general problem of evidence in relation to the policies of the Personal Rule" (p. 7).

8. Hugh F. Kearney, *The Eleven Years' Tyranny of Charles I* (London: Routledge & Kegan Paul, 1962); cf. J. P. Kenyon, *Stuart England;* Conrad Russell, *Parliaments and English Politics, 1621–1629* (Oxford: Clarendon Press, 1979); and Kevin Sharpe, "The Personal Rule of Charles I," in *Before the English Civil War,* ed. Howard Tomlinson (New York: St. Martin's Press, 1984), pp. 53–78.

9. *Calendar of State Papers Venetian, 1632–1636,* ed. Allen B. Hinds et al., 38 vols. (London: His Majesty's Stationery Office, 1921), 23:499; 24 (1636–1639): 223.

10. Kenyon, *Stuart England,* pp. 10–11; John Morrill, "Introduction," in *Reactions to the English Civil War, 1642–1649,* ed. John Morrill (New York: St. Martin's Press, 1983), pp. 3–4; and Morrill, "What Was the English Revolution?" *History Today* 34 (March 1984):11–12. Morrill, it should be noted, does not view Charles sympathetically; Derek Hirst also develops a critical view of him in *Authority and Conflict: England, 1603–1658* (Cambridge: Harvard University Press, 1986).

11. Conrad Russell, *Parliaments and English Politics,* p. 426. Too often overlooked is the reality, in G. E. Aylmer's words, that "We have in fact no means of telling whether or not the King had ever intended to rule without Parliament indefinitely" (p. 7). Other studies that recognize the era of peace include J. H. Elliott, "England and Europe: A Common Malady?" in *The Origins of the Civil War,* pp. 246–57; G. M. D. Howat, *Stuart and Cromwellian Foreign Policy* (London: Macmillan, 1974); John Morrill, *The Revolt of the Provinces* (London: Allen and Unwin, 1976); J. P. Kenyon, *Stuart England;* and Kevin Sharpe, "The Personal Rule of Charles I."

12. Clarendon, *History,* 1:94; David Lloyd, *Memoires of the Lives, Actions, Sufferings & Deaths of those Noble, Reverend, and Excellent Personages* (London, 1668), p. 13.

13. Lloyd, *Memoires of the Lives,* p. 13; Warwick, *Memoires Of . . . Charles I,* p. 62; Clarendon, *History,* 1:96. In his account of Charles I, Lloyd also observes, "His own people could not wish for more happinesse than they enjoyed, unless it were the addition of grace to understand their happinesse" (*Memoires of the Lives,* p. 174).

14. Clarendon, *The Life,* 1:71.

15. John Davies, *The Civil Warres of Great Britain and Ireland* (London, 1661), p. 1.

16. Virgil, *Georgics,* trans. Abraham Cowley, *The English Writings of Abraham Cowley,* ed. A. R. Waller, 2 vols. (Cambridge: Cambridge University Press, 1905–1906), 2:409.

17. Simon Adams offers the best account in "Spain or the Netherlands? The Dilemmas of Early Stuart Foreign Policy," in *Before the English Civil War,* pp. 79–101. See also Bernard Capp, "The Political Dimension of Apocalyptic Thought," in *The Apocalypse in English Renaissance Thought and Literature,* ed. C. A. Patrides and Joseph Wittreich (Ithaca: Cornell University Press, 1984), pp. 93–124; and, more generally, Per Palme, *Triumph of Peace* (Stockholm: Almqvist and Wiksell, 1956), pp. 7–40, and Katharine R. Firth, *The Apocalyptic Tradition in Reformation Britain, 1530–1645* (Oxford: Clarendon Press, 1979).

18. *Calendar of State Papers Venetian, 1636–1639,* 24:296–97.

19. Charles Carlton quotes the king's letters in his discussion of Charles's foreign policy; pp. 173, 170 of *Charles I: The Personal Monarch* (London: Routledge & Kegan Paul, 1983). Conrad Russell develops this interpretation in *Parliaments and English Politics;* see particularly pp. 70–84.

20. Adams, "Spain or the Netherlands," pp. 99–100; Pauline Gregg, *King Charles I* (Berkeley and Los Angeles: University of California Press, 1984), pp. 197, 260.

21. Peter Paul Rubens, *Letters,* trans. and ed. Ruth Saunders Magurn (Cambridge: Harvard University Press, 1955), p. 320.

22. D. J. Gordan reproduces this painting in "Roles and Mysteries," in *The Renaissance Imagination,* ed. Stephen Orgel (Berkeley and Los Angeles: University of California Press, 1975), p. 2.

23. Kevin Sharpe, "The Personal Rule of Charles I," pp. 58–63; Robert Ashton, *The English Civil War* (New York: W. W. Norton, 1979), p. 30; David Mathew, *The Social Structure in Caroline England* (Oxford: Clarendon Press, 1948), pp. 35–36; Peter W. Thomas, "Charles I of England: The Tragedy of Absolutism," in *The Courts of Europe,* ed. A. G. Dickens (New York: McGraw-Hill, 1977), pp. 193–94; Kevin Sharpe, "Faction at the Early Stuart Court," *History Today* 33 (October 1983):43; and Gregg, *King Charles I,* pp. 246–47, 254–55.

24. Paul Slack, "Books of Orders: The Making of English Social Policy, 1577–1631," *Transactions of the Royal Historical Society,* 5th ser., 30 (1980):1–22.

25. G. E. Aylmer, *The King's Servants* (London: Routledge & Kegan Paul, 1961), p. 462. Kevin Sharpe is even more positive in "The Personal Rule of Charles I."

26. Stephen Orgel and Roy Strong, *Inigo Jones: The Theatre of the Stuart Court,* 2 vols. (Berkeley and Los Angeles: University of California Press, 1973), 1:58. In *Van Dyck: Charles I on Horseback* (New York: The Viking Press, Inc., 1972), Roy Strong contends, "Charles and Henrietta are the first English royal couple to be glorified as husband and wife in the domestic sense" (p. 70).

27. Ben Jonson, *Love's Triumph through Callipolis,* ed. Stephen Orgel and Roy Strong, in *Inigo Jones: The Theatre of the Stuart Court,* 1:405. Unless noted, all of the masques cited in the text are from this edition.

28. Thus among the essays edited by David Lindley in *The Court Masque* (Manchester: Manchester University Press, 1984): Lindley, "Introduction," p. 3; Jennifer Chibnall, "'To that secure fix'd state': The Function of the Caroline Masque Form," pp. 80–83; and Helen Cooper, "Location and Meaning in Masque, Morality, and Royal Entertainment," p. 147. Stephen Kogan's recent book *The Hieroglyphic King: Wisdom and Idolatry in the Seventeenth-Century Masque* (Rutherford, N. J.: Fairleigh Dickinson University Press, 1986) argues at length that "the transcendental visions of the previous generation gave way to the glorification of privilege and power" (p. 38). The Caroline masques of the 1630s, he contends, "Like the king himself, . . . would no longer be treated as emblems of a higher 'intelligence,' but would now convey the idea that he and the queen were inherently divine and that the court was a perfect world all its own" (p. 127). His belief that the Platonism of the Caroline masque attempts "not to elevate reality but to deny it altogether" (p. 208) should be compared with Joanne Altieri's position that "it seems legitimate to emphasize less the Platonism" than the "practical connections to the real life of the time—both the writers' and the culture's at large" (p. 74), a reading she develops in another recent study, *The Theatre of Praise: The Panegyric Tradition in Seventeenth-Century English Drama* (Newark, Delaware: University of Delaware Press, 1986).

29. Adams, "Spain or the Netherlands," p. 91.

30. In their seminal work on the Caroline masque, Orgel and Strong accept too readily the Whig notion of Charles's "unparalleled assumption of royal power"; they see the masques as means to reenforce "Charles's autocracy" (1:52). Stephen Orgel more sweepingly contends in *The Illusion of Power* (Berkeley and Los Angeles: University of California Press, 1975), "The 1630s saw the most complete consolidation of royal power in British History" (p. 78).

31. Frederick Schloer, *The Death of the Two Renowned Kings of Sweden and Bohemia* (London, 1633), p. 27; Robert Monro, *Monro His Expedition* (London, 1637), part 2, p. 167; Alexander Gill, *The New Starr of the North* (London, 1632), p. 22.

32. Nathanial Butter and Nicholas Bourne chronicle Gustavus's triumphs and death in *The Swedish Intelligencer,* a series that Joseph Frank says began publication in January 1632 (*The Beginnings of the English Newspaper, 1620–1660* [Cambridge: Harvard University Press, 1961], p. 15). In addition to the contemporary reactions recorded in this series, a sense of the English response can be found in Ethel Seaton, *Literary Relations of England and Scandinavia in the Seventeenth Century* (Oxford: Clarendon Press, 1935), pp. 73–90; and Marvin A. Breslow, *A Mirror of England* (Cambridge: Harvard University Press, 1970), pp. 124–38.

33. Samuel R. Gardiner, "Futile Diplomacy," in *History of England from the Accession of James I. to the Outbreak of the Civil War, 1603–1642,* 10 vols. (London: Longmans, Green, and Co., 1884), 7:169–219.

34. A Star Chamber decree on 17 October 1632 prohibited the printing of all English newspapers. Folke Dahl suggests in "Amsterdam—Cradle of English Newspapers," *The Library,* 5th ser., 4 (1949–50), that Charles imposed the censorship because he felt reports about Gustavus "were, in a way, tacit reproaches to his own policy and his person" (p. 174).

35. William Gouge, *The Saints Sacrifice* (London, 1632), p. 284, as quoted by Breslow, *A Mirror of England,* p. 131.

36. *Calendar of State Papers, Domestic Series, Charles I (1631–1633),* ed. John Bruce, 23 vols. (London: Her Majesty's Stationery Office, 1862), 5:454; and Simonds D'Ewes, *The Autobiography and Correspondence of Sir Simonds D'Ewes,* ed. James Halliwell, 2 vols. (London: Richard Bentley, 1845), 2:86.

37. L. C. Knights, "The Social Background of Metaphysical Poetry," in *Further Explorations* (London: Chatto and Windus, 1965), p. 118; Margaret Whinney and Oliver Millar, *English Art, 1625–1714* (Oxford: Clarendon Press, 1957), p. 72; Seaton, *Literary Relations,* p. 85.

38. Peter W. Thomas, "Two Cultures? Court and Country under Charles I," in *The Origins of the English Civil War,* pp. 179, 175. Despite his reservations about "The fatal separation of this gorgeous world of art from the world of political actuality," Louis L. Martz deems Carew's answer a "superb poem," in *The Wit of Love* (South Bend, Ind.: University of Notre Dame Press, 1969), p. 73. Stephen Kogan develops at greater length the suggestion that "Carew's poem expresses a typical Caroline sentiment that beauty can somehow turn reality around and melt away all harshness and adversity" (*The Hieroglyphic King,* p. 132). Lynn Sadler's short discussion in *Thomas Carew* (Boston: Twayne Publishers, 1979) concludes that Carew's "Royalism has overriden his common sense" (p. 85). Michael P. Parker, on the other hand, offers a sympathetic and sensitive reading of the poem in "Carew's Politic Pastoral: Virgilian Pretexts in the 'Answer to Aurelian Townsend,'" *John Donne Journal* 1 (1982):101–16. In her reading of the poem in "Responses to a Waning Mythology in Carew's Political Poetry," *Studies in English Literature* 26 (1986):107–24, Joanne Altieri contends that Carew's "ambivalence" undercuts the poem.

39. Francis Quarles, "Eclogve X," in *The Shepheards Oracles; The Complete Works in Prose and Verse of Francis Quarles,* ed. Alexander Grosart, 3 vols. (Edinburgh: T. and A. Constable, 1880), 3:231.

40. Quarles, "Eclogve X," 3:232.

41. Aurelian Townshend's poem "Aurelian Tounsend to Tho: Carew vpon the death of the King of Sweden" is included in Appendix D of *The Poems of Thomas Carew,* ed. Rhodes Dunlap (1949; rpt. Oxford: Clarendon Press, 1970). This edition is hereafter cited in the text.

42. John Saltmarsh, "To his ingenious *Friend* Master *Russell,* upon his Heroick *Poem*"; John Russell, *The Two Famous Pitcht Battels of Lypsich, and Lutzen* (Cambridge, 1634), sig. ¶¶3v, p. 33.

43. Dudley North, "An Incentive to our Poets upon the Death of the victorious King of *Swedeland*," in *A Forest Promiscuous* (London, 1659), p. 72.

44. Parker and Altieri also stress the poem's movement. The following reading does not agree with Altieri that "Carew's maneuver failed rhetoric's final test: it did not work" ("Responses to a Waning Mythology," p. 116). More subtly than Quarles, who places Charles at the center of a poem describing the rise and fall of Gustavus, Carew implicitly praises the king.

45. John Russell, *The Two Famous Pitcht Battels*, pp. 34–35; Robert Gomersall, *Poems* (London, 1633), sigs. O3r–4r; William Camden, *Remaines Concerning Britaine* (London, 1637), pp. 399–400; Nathanial Butter and Nicholas Bourne, *The Swedish Intelligencer. The Third Part* (London, 1633), pp. 155, 181–98; and the following poems in this issue: Henry King, "An Elegy," sig. ¶4r; Anon., "On the King of Sweden," sig. ¶¶¶2v; and Anon., "Upon the King of *Sweden*," sigs. ¶¶¶3r–v.

46. Michael Roberts suggests in *Gustavus Adolphus: A History of Sweden, 1611–1632*, 2 vols. (London: Longmans, Green, 1958), "The end of his life heralded the closing of an epoch; the epoch which had begun with the Reformation; and though England was still to produce, in Cromwell, Gustav Adolf's epigone, on the continent the influence of religion upon politics was waning fast" (2:773).

47. *Calendar of State Papers, Domestic Series, Charles I (1631–1633)*, 5:293–94; James Howell, *Dodona's Grove, or the Vocall Forrest* (London, 1644), p. 117; and Simonds D'Ewes, *The Autobiography*, 2:85.

48. Rhodes Dunlap suggests in his edition of Carew that "the description which follows . . . fits exactly Townshend's masque *Tempe Restord*" (p. 252). Erica Veevers uses a fragment of a masque in the Huntington Library to argue that Carew actually had in mind "A masquing accompaniment to *The Shepherd's Paradise*" that Townshend wrote for a performance of Montague's play; while Paulina Palmer counters with the suggestion that Carew "may be referring equally well to Townshend's poem 'On hearing her Majesty sing' "—see their exchange, "A Masque Fragment by Aurelian Townshend," *Notes and Queries*, n.s., 12 (1965):343–45, and "Thomas Carew's Reference to 'The Shepherd's Paradise,' " *Notes and Queries*, n.s., 13 (1966):303–4. Unable to match all of Carew's description with *Tempe Restored*, Louis L. Martz in *The Wit of Love* develops the suggestion of a masque intended for Montague's play: "Has Townshend perhaps used some of the themes, along with the costumes, settings, and machinery, from his masque of the previous year, in order to enhance the beauties of *The Shepheards Paradise*" (p. 89)? But the link between Montague's play and Townshend's poems remains, at best, conjectural; and the passages Martz cannot fit into *Tempe Restored* are not out of place if they are interpreted figuratively.

49. Francis Bacon, "Of Masques and Triumphs," in *The Works of Francis Bacon*, ed. James Spedding, Robert Ellis, and Douglas Heath, 14 vols. (London: Longman and Co., 1858), 6:467–68.

50. [R.] Malcolm Smuts, "The Political Failure of Stuart Cultural Patronage," in *Patronage in the Renaissance*, ed. Guy Fitch Lytle and Stephen Orgel (Princeton: Princeton University Press, 1981), pp. 165–87. Judith Richards considers Charles's tendency to distance himself from his subjects in " 'His Nowe Majestie' and the English Monarchy: The Kingship of Charles I before 1640," *Past and Present* 113 (1986):70–96.

51. Altieri, "Responses to a Waning Mythology," p. 119.

52. Clarendon, *The Life*, 1:71.

53. Howard Erskine-Hill, *The Augustan Idea in English Literature* (London: Edward Arnold, 1983), p. 172.

54. In his essay "Carew's Politic Pastoral," Parker also suggests that "The phrase 'our *Halcyon* dayes' signifies in its widest sense an indeterminate period of calm and

peace. . . . Carew's choice of phrase, I believe, reflects his own recognition of how tenuous the *pax carolina* really was" (p. 113).

55. This reading is closer to Altieri, *The Theatre of Praise,* pp. 79–87, than to Kogan, *The Hieroglyphic King,* pp. 183–205. Altieri concludes that the Caroline masque consciously requires "the dismissal of Momus, the abandonment of the satirical eye that sees and understands prosaically, for the idealizing verse of Mercury and his songs and revels" (p. 87). Kogan, on the other hand, believes "the masquers have not tried to reach knowledge" (p. 204); he sees in the masque "the full expression of the Caroline temper, which is both arrogant and seductive" (p. 205).

56. The preface to *Britannia Triumphans,* Orgel and Strong, 1:71.

57. The discussion of the paintings reflects the following studies: D. J. Gordon, "Rubens and the Whitehall Ceiling," in *The Renaissance Imagination,* pp. 24–50; Oliver Millar, *Rubens: The Whitehall Ceiling* (London: Oxford University Press, 1958); John Charlton, *The Banqueting House Whitehall* (London: Mansell Limited, 1983); and Palme, *Triumph of Peace,* pp. 225–62. In 1972 the paintings were rearranged to reflect the original intention. The change in perspective, John Charlton suggests, heightens the impact: "When, for example, an ambassador to be received by the King passed through the tall entrance doorway and approached the throne he would see on the ceiling above (the right way up to him) first *The Apotheosis of James I* and then, above the throne, the blessings of his reign, flanked by figures representing Royal Bounty and Wise Government. The King, looking the other way towards the entrance would see (the right way up to him) *The Union of England and Scotland,* with Hercules crushing Envy on one side and Minerva Ignorance on the other. Meanwhile if the courtiers lining the hall looked up beyond the crowds in the balconies they would see depicted processions of cherubs carrying to his subjects the benefits of the King's wise rule" (p. 23).

58. Gordon, "Rubens and the Whitehall Ceiling," p. 35.

59. Walter Forbes, "A Panegyricke to the High and Mighty Monarch Charles," in Walter Forbes, *The Entertainment of the High and Mighty Monarch Charles* (Edinburgh, 1633), p. 35.

60. R. M[alcolm]. Smuts, "The Puritan Followers of Henrietta Maria in the 1630s," *English Historical Review* 93 (1978):35–37.

61. *Calendar of State Papers Venetian, 1632–1636,* 23:444.

62. Conrad Russell, *Parliaments and English Politics, 1621–1629,* p. 426. Austin Woolrych, it should be noted, does not accept this view in "Court, Country and City Revisited," *History* 65 (1980):240. Another favorable assessment of Charles's reign during the 1630s is Kevin Sharpe, "The Personal Rule of Charles I."

63. From a letter of 12 March 1638, as quoted by Gordon, "Rubens and the Whitehall Ceiling," p. 29, and in Rubens, *Letters,* pp. 408–9.

64. Conrad Russell, "The Nature of a Parliament in Early Stuart England," in *Before the English Civil War,* p. 148.

65. Kevin Sharpe, "The Personal Rule of Charles I," pp. 76–78; Russell, "Introduction," in *The Origins of the English Civil War,* pp. 12–13, 27–28; Russell, "The Nature of a Parliament in Early Stuart England," pp. 148–49; Morrill, "Introduction," in *Reactions to the English Civil War, 1642–1649,* pp. 5, 12; and Brian Manning, "What Was the English Revolution?" *History Today* 34 (March 1984):18.

66. Thomas Heywood, *Londoni Status Pacatus: Or, Londons Peaceable Estate* (London, 1639), sig. B3r.

67. Theodore B. Leinwand, "London Triumphing: The Jacobean Lord Mayor's Show," *Clio* 11 (1982):140–42.

68. Heywood, *Londoni Status Pacatus,* sig. c2r.

69. Ibid., sig. c3v.

70. Charles I, *Eikon Basilike*, p. 122.

71. Michael P. Parker also emphasizes the masque in "'To my friend G. N. from *Wrest*': Carew's Secular Masque," in *Classic and Cavalier*, ed. Claude J. Summers and Ted-Larry Pebworth (Pittsburgh: University of Pittsburg Press, 1982), pp. 171–91.

72. Parker suggests that "In view of the earl's death in November 1639, Dunlap's tentative dating of the poem to March 1640 should probably be revised to the summer or autumn of the preceding year" ("Carew's Secular Masque," p. 189). But the dating remains uncertain, and Carew could conceivably have known the masque.

73. Seneca, "On Leisure," in *Moral Essays*, trans. John W. Basore, The Loeb Classical Library, 3 vols. (Cambridge: Harvard University Press, 1935), 2:187.

74. John Gauden, *The Love of Trvth and Peace* (London, 1641), p. 41.

75. Henry Glapthorne, "White-Hall," in *The Plays and Poems of Henry Glapthorne*, ed. John Pearson, 2 vols. (London, 1874), 2:248.

76. James Turner surveys the nostalgic reaction in *The Politics of Landscape* (Cambridge: Harvard University Press, 1979), pp. 85–115. See also Raymond A. Anselment, "Clarendon," pp. 51–52.

## Chapter 2. William Cartwright

1. When William Cartwright's poems were published posthumously in 1651, tributes from more than fifty Caroline writers prefaced the first edition of his collected works. No other English poet had been printed with so many contemporary eulogies, and the publisher Humphrey Moseley claims somewhat defensively in his prefatory remarks "To the Reader" that the numerous verses reflect the love and admiration due "high Abilities" and "vertuous Modesty." When G. Blakemore Evans published the Cartwright tercentenary edition in 1951, he judged the poetry in the established context of seventeenth-century schools. "Cartwright's verse," he concluded, "has all the impersonality and some of the polish and ease of Jonson, the metaphysical conceit gone stale of Donne, and the conventionality of the born courtier, all tempered by the mental attitude of an age on the defensive" (*The Plays and Poems Of William Cartwright*, ed. G. Blakemore Evans [Madison: The University of Wisconsin Press, 1951], p. 35; hereafter cited in the text). The new interest in Jonson's nondramatic poetry together with the growing emphasis on Donne's commemorative verse has prompted a reassessment of longer, nonlyrical poems, but the ground-breaking studies of occasional poetry have not displaced Evans's impression that "no one of Cartwright's poems in this genre falls below the common standards of such poetry—poetry which, never of a very high order, can easily degenerate into a rant of hyperbole not worthy the name of verse" (pp. 38–39). Peter W. Thomas's more negative view of the university wits who formed an Oxford coterie during the 1630s and 1640s is found in "Charles I of England: The Tragedy of Absolutism," in *The Courts of Europe*, ed. A. G. Dickens (New York: McGraw-Hill, 1977), p. 211; and Peter W. Thomas, "Two Cultures? Court and Country under Charles I," in *The Origins of the English Civil War*, ed. Conrad Russell (New York: Barnes and Noble, 1973), p. 179.

2. One English poem did appear in the 1622 volume for Henry Savile and three were published in the 1614 volume for George St. Paul, but these are the rare exceptions. The role Oxford played in the development of English commemorative poetry is discussed by Raymond A. Anselment, "The Oxford University Poets and Caroline Panegyric," *John Donne Journal* 3 (1984):181–201.

3. "To the Queen," *Vitis Carolinæ Gemma Altera* (Oxford, 1633), sig. I1r.

4. David Lloyd, *Memoires of the Lives, Actions, Sufferings & Deaths of those Noble, Reverend, and Excellent Personages* (London, 1668), p. 422.

5. Moseley, "To the Reader," p. 832; Lloyd, *Memoires of the Lives,* p. 598.

6. Moseley records Jonson's judgment in "To the Reader," p. 831.

7. Menander describes the characteristics of the arrival speech or epibaterion in *Rhetor,* trans. and ed. D. A. Russell and N. G. Wilson (Oxford: Clarendon Press, 1981), pp. 95–115. James D. Garrison briefly discusses Cartwright's contribution in terms of the verse panegyric in *Dryden and the Tradition of Panegyric* (Berkeley and Los Angeles: University of California Press, 1975), pp. 98–99.

8. George Puttenham, *The Arte of English Poesie,* ed. Gladys Doidge Willcock and Alice Walker (Cambridge: Cambridge University Press, 1936), pp. 49–50.

9. Lester K. Born's translation of Erasmus's well-known observation in "The Perfect Prince According to the Latin Panegyrists," *American Journal of Philology* 55 (1934):35. Several of the following works cite this passage in their observations about the poetry of praise written during this period: Warren L. Chernaik, *The Poetry of Limitation* (New Haven: Yale University Press, 1968); James D. Garrison, *Dryden and the Tradition of Panegyric;* O. B. Hardison, Jr., *The Enduring Monument* (Chapel Hill: The University of North Carolina Press, 1962); Barbara K. Lewalski, *Donne's Anniversaries and the Poetry of Praise* (Princeton: Princeton University Press, 1973); and Ruth Nevo, *The Dial of Virtue* (Princeton: Princeton University Press, 1963).

10. Ben Jonson, "To Sir William Iephson," in *Ben Jonson,* ed. C. H. Herford and Percy and Evelyn Simpson, 11 vols. (1947; rpt. Oxford: Clarendon Press, 1954), 8:75.

11. Katharine Eisaman Maus stresses Jonson's indebtedness to the Roman moralists' attitudes toward inheritance, nobility, and virtue in *Ben Jonson and the Roman Frame of Mind* (Princeton: Princeton University Press, 1984), particularly pp. 123–26.

12. Aurelian Townshend, *Albion's Triumph,* in *Inigo Jones: The Theatre of the Stuart Court,* ed. Stephen Orgel and Roy Strong, 2 vols. (Berkeley and Los Angeles: University of California Press, 1973), 2:457.

13. Livy, *The History of Rome,* in *Livy,* trans. B. O. Foster, The Loeb Classical Library, 13 vols. (Cambridge: Harvard University Press, 1939), 1:245.

14. William Davenant, *Salmacida Spolia,* in Orgel and Strong, *Inigo Jones,* 2:733.

15. Jonas A. Barish, *Ben Jonson and the Language of Prose Comedy* (Cambridge: Harvard University Press, 1960), p. 244—from a longer passage quoted by Stephen Orgel in *The Jonsonian Masque* (Cambridge: Harvard University Press, 1965), p. 108.

16. Jonson, *Timber: or, Discoveries,* 8:597.

17. Ibid., 8:640 and 595.

18. W. H. Herendeen, "Like a Circle Bounded in Itself: Jonson, Camden, and the Strategies of Praise," *Journal of Medieval and Renaissance Studies* 11 (1981):137–67.

19. Horace, "Satire II. 7," in *The Satires and Epistles of Horace,* trans. Smith Palmer Bovie (Chicago: The University of Chicago Press, 1959), p. 148. In The Loeb Classical Library edition *Satires, Epistles and Ars Poetica,* (Cambridge: Harvard University Press, 1928), H. Rushton Fairclough translates this passage, "The wise man, who is lord over himself . . . is a whole, smoothed and rounded, so that nothing from outside can rest on the polished surface, and against whom Fortune in her onset is ever maimed" (pp. 231–33).

20. Thomas M. Greene discusses Jonson's view in "Ben Jonson and the Centered Self," *Studies in English Literature* 10 (1970):325–48. Richard S. Peterson also provides valuable commentary on this theme as well as on the importance of standing in Jonson's poetry; see his chapters "The Full Circle: Poet as Vessel" and "The Stand: Noble Natures Raised," in *Imitation and Praise in the Poems of Ben Jonson* (New Haven: Yale University Press, 1981). None of the other Caroline poets uses either metaphor with Cartwright's consistency, although occasionally the figurative circle

and standing are developed, particularly by those Jonson influenced. See, for example, Thomas Randolph's "To Mr. Feltham on his booke of Resolves," in *The Poems of Thomas Randolph,* ed. G. Thorn-Drury (London: Frederick Etchells & Hugh Macdonald, 1929), pp. 75–78; and Edmund Waller's "Epitaph on the Lady Sedley," in *The Poems of Edmund Waller,* ed. G. Thorn-Drury, 2 vols. (New York: Charles Scribner's Sons, 1901), 2:114–16.

21. Peterson, *Imitation and Praise,* p. 70, and in general his chapter "The Stand: Noble Natures Raised."

22. Jonson, "To Sir Iohn Radcliffe," 8:60.

23. On naming in Jonson see Herendeen, "Like a Circle Bounded in Itself," pp. 149–57; Edward Partridge, "Jonson's *Epigrammes:* The Named and the Nameless," *Studies in the Literary Imagination* 6 (1973):153–98; and David Wykes, "Ben Jonson's 'Chast Booke'—The *Epigrammes,*" *Renaissance and Modern Studies* 13 (1969):76–87.

24. See Achsah Guibbory, "The Poet as Myth Maker: Ben Jonson's Poetry of Praise," *Clio* 5 (1976):315–29.

25. William Knowler, *The Earl of Strafforde's Letters and Dispatches, with an Essay towards his Life, by Sir George Radcliffe,* 2 vols. (London, 1639), 1:363. Raymond A. Anselment, "The Countess of Carlisle and Caroline Praise: Convention and Reality," *Studies in Philology* 82 (1985):212–33, surveys contemporary reactions to the countess.

26. Anthony Fletcher, *The Outbreak of the English Civil War* (New York: New York University Press, 1981), p. 318.

27. Peter W. Thomas, *Sir John Berkenhead, 1617–1679* (Oxford: Clarendon Press, 1969), p. 134.

28. Evans, *The Plays and Poems Of William Cartwright,* p. 741.

29. Peterson, *Imitation and Praise,* pp. 20–21.

30. William Davenant develops a similar tribute in his "Epitaph. On Mr. John Sturmy," in *The Shorter Poems, and Songs from the Plays and Masques,* ed. A. M. Gibbs (Oxford: Clarendon Press, 1972), p. 151.

31. Cicero, *De Officiis,* trans. Walter Miller, The Loeb Classical Library (New York: G. P. Putnam's Sons, 1928), pp. 23–25.

32. Ibid., p. 21.

33. Ibid., p. 69.

34. Samuel R. Gardiner, *History of the Great Civil War, 1642–1649,* 4 vols. (London: Longmans, Green, 1894), 1:93–95; Carola Oman, *Henrietta Maria* (London: Hodder and Stoughton Limited, 1936), pp. 139–41.

## Chapter 3. George Daniel

1. Seneca, "On Leisure" and "On Tranquillity of Mind," in *Moral Essays,* trans. John W. Basore, The Loeb Classical Library, 3 vols. (Cambridge: Harvard University Press, 1935), 2:185, 223.

2. Seneca, "On Leisure," 2:195.

3. Seneca, "On the Happy Life," 2:141; Boethius, *The Consolation of Philosophy,* trans. Richard Green (Indianapolis: Bobbs-Merrill, 1962), pp. 63, 92; Justus Lipsius, *Two Bookes of Constancie Written in Latine by Iustus Lipsius, Englished by Sir John Stradling,* ed. Rudolf Kirk (New Brunswick, N.J.: Rutgers University Press, 1939), p. 105.

4. George Daniel, *The Selected Poems of George Daniel of Beswick, 1616–1657,* ed. Thomas B. Stroup (Lexington, Ky.: University of Kentucky Press, 1959), p. 38.

Stroup's edition will hereafter be cited in the text by page; citations by volume and page are from *The Poems of George Daniel, Esq., of Beswick, Yorkshire (1616–1657)*, ed. Alexander Grosart, 4 vols. (Boston, Lincolnshire: R. Roberts, 1878).

5. Apparently Suckling's poem was written in 1637 and circulated in manuscript before its publication in 1646; see Thomas Clayton's discussion of the poem in *The Works of Sir John Suckling*, ed. Thomas Clayton and Lester A. Beaurline, 2 vols. (Oxford: Clarendon Press, 1971), 1:266–78.

6. In his edition Stroup supplements the biographical information gathered by Grosart. John T. Cliffe describes Daniel's father as a man of "comparatively modest estate," "a suspected papist who had a recusant wife," in *The Yorkshire Gentry* (London: The Athlone Press, 1969), pp. 6, 185.

7. "The local diaries of the period," Derek Hirst observes, "show how well informed people in the country often were of the scandals and failings of the court, and even of the complexities of parliamentary developments," in "Revisionism Revised: The Place of Principle," *Past and Present* 92 (1981):92. Movement between the country and London continued despite Charles I's attempts to keep the gentry at home; and Clive Holmes suggests that ballads, corantos, government proclamations, the mails, and gossip kept country inhabitants abreast of the London news—"The Country Community in Stuart Historiography," *Journal of British Studies* 19 (1980):61.

8. In her revised edition of *The Happy Man*, 2 vols. (Oslo: Norwegian Universities Press, 1962), Maren-Sofie Røstvig briefly discusses Horace's influence upon Daniel, "whom he often seems to have imitated at two removes, i.e. through the mediation of Ben Jonson, Thomas Randolph, or William Habington" (1:114–17).

9. This manuscript dating is probably Old Style, and the poem should therefore be dated 1639/40.

10. Boethius, *The Consolation of Philosophy*, p. 104.

11. Seneca, "On Tranquillity of Mind," 2:225.

12. In likening the Puritan reformers to Henry VIII, Abraham Cowley's *The Puritan and the Papist* (*The English Writings of Abraham Cowley*, ed. A. R. Waller, 2 vols. [Cambridge: Cambridge University Press, 1905–1906], 2:156) summarizes the contemporary view:

> O let not such loud *Sacriledge* begin,
> Tempted by *Henries* rich successefull sinne.
> *Henry* the *Monster* King of all that age;
> Wilde in his *Lust,* and wilder in his *Rage.*

Charles I was, according to Brendan O Hehir, obsessed with the idea that "he was paying the price of Henry VIII's crimes against the Church," from *Harmony from Discords: A Life of Sir John Denham* (Berkeley and Los Angeles: University of California Press, 1968), p. 86. See also O Hehir's notes on Henry VIII in his critical edition of John Denham's *Coopers Hill, Expans'd Hieroglyphicks* (Berkeley and Los Angeles: University of California Press, 1969).

13. See, for example, C. V. Wedgwood, *Oliver Cromwell and the Elizabethan Inheritance* (London: Jonathan Cape, 1970); Anne Barton, "Harking Back to Elizabeth: Ben Jonson and Caroline Nostalgia," *ELH* 48 (1981):706–31; and Dolores Palomo, "The Halcyon Moment of Stillness in Royalist Poetry," *Huntington Library Quarterly* 44 (1981):205–21.

14. Lipsius, *Two Bookes Of Constancie,* pp. 135, 136.

15. Ibid., p. 136.

16. In his edition Stroup suggests "It is perhaps a reference to Oliver Cromwell" (p. 194).

17. Francis Quarles's *The Shepheards Oracles* was published in 1644, although the epistle to the reader states "the Authour had some years before his lamented death, compos'd, review'd, and corrected these Eglogues"; *The Complete Works of Francis Quarles,* ed. Alexander Grosart, 3 vols. (Edinburgh: T. and A. Constable, 1880), 3:202.

18. Henry Vaughan's "The King Disguis'd" also expresses fears about trusting the Scots; he is hopeful, however, that the sun will again shine. John Cleveland seeks a typological reassurance in "The Kings Disguise." An entry for 2 May 1646 in the Essex clergyman Ralph Josselin's diary succinctly complements Daniel's fears: "newes that the King in a disguise was gone from Oxford: sic transit gloria mundi." See Henry Vaughan, *Poetry and Selected Prose,* ed. L. C. Martin (Oxford: Clarendon Press, 1963), p. 398; John Cleveland, *The Poems of John Cleveland,* ed. Brian Morris and Eleanor Withington (Oxford: Clarendon Press, 1967), p. 7; and Ralph Josselin, *The Diary of Ralph Josselin, 1616–1683,* ed. Alan MacFarlane (London: Oxford University Press, 1976), p. 59.

19. The different translations of Smith Palmer Bovie, *The Satires and Epistles of Horace* (Chicago: University of Chicago Press, 1959), p. 263, and Charles E. Passage, *The Complete Works of Horace* (New York: Frederick Ungar Publishing Co., 1983), p. 353. *"Nemus"* and *"umbra"* are simply "grove" and "shade" in H. Rushton Fairclough's translation, *Satires, Epistles and Ars Poetica,* The Loeb Classical Library (Cambridge: Harvard University Press, 1928), p. 431.

20. One whose views are at times similar to Daniel's is Mildmay Fane, earl of Westmoreland, *Otia Sacra (1648),* ed. Donald M. Friedman (Delmar, New York: Scholars' Facsimiles & Reprints, 1975).

21. See, for example, *A True Relation of that Memorable Parliament, which wrought Wonders* (London, 1641); *The Life and Death of King Richard the Second* (London, 1642); *The iust reward of Rebels, or The Life and Death of Iack Straw and Wat Tyler* (London, 1642); *A Mis-led King* (London, 1643); *The Bloody Parliament in the Raigne of an Unhappy Prince* (London, 1643); and John Cleveland, *The Idol of the Clownes, or, Insurrection of Wat Tyler* (London, 1654).

22. Lipsius, *Two Bookes Of Constancie,* p. 98.

## Chapter 4. Richard Lovelace

1. Robert Herrick, "His Cavalier," in *The Poetical Works of Robert Herrick,* ed. L. C. Martin (Oxford: Clarendon Press, 1956), p. 31.

2. Lovelace's association with Cartwright and the university wits is unknown, but he contributed "Princesse *Katherine* borne, christened, buried in one day" to *Musarum Oxoniensium Charisteria* and "*Clitophon* and *Lucippe* translated" to another Oxford publication, *The Loves of Clitophon and Levcippe.* His more famous poetry, according to Herbert Grierson, contains the "finest expression of honour and chivalry in all the Cavalier poetry," in *Metaphysical Lyrics & Poems of The Seventeenth Century* (Oxford: Clarendon Press, 1921), p. xxxvi. Douglas Bush writes in *English Literature in the Earlier Seventeenth Century, 1600–1660* (New York: Oxford University Press, 1962), "to think of the cavalier spirit is to think first of Richard Lovelace"; "he enshrined the cavalier trinity, beauty, love, and loyal honour" (p. 122).

3. Anthony à Wood, *Athenæ Oxonienses,* ed. Philip Bliss, 4 vols. (London, 1817), 3:460, 462. Andrew Marvell, "To his Noble Friend Mr. *Richard Lovelace,* upon his *Poems,*" p. 9; Francis Lenton, "To the Honorable, Valiant, and Ingenious Colonel

*Richard Lovelace,* on his Equisite *Poems,"* p. 12; John Pinchbacke, "Another upon the *Poems,"* p. 5; in *The Poems of Richard Lovelace,* ed. C. H. Wilkinson (1930; rpt. Oxford: Clarendon Press, 1953). This edition is hereafter cited in the text.

4. In particular, Bruce King, "Green Ice and a Breast of Proof," *College English* 26 (1964–65):511–15. King's essay has been reprinted in the revised edition of *Seventeenth-Century English Poetry: Modern Essays in Criticism,* ed. William R. Keast (New York: Oxford University Press, 1971). In "Comment and Rebuttal," *College English* 31 (1970):637–40, Randolph L. Wadsworth, Jr., justly questions some of King's conclusions. Paulina Palmer's reading of several poems in "Lovelace's Treatment of Some Marinesque Motifs," *Comparative Literature* 29 (1977):300–12, stresses with considerable sensitivity to tone and style a Cavalier "recognition of the bleakness of the human predicament" (p. 309).

5. Later critics have not always heeded H. M. Margoliouth's sensible comment in his review of Wilkinson's edition, "I do not know what evidence there may be for the addition of new matter to books after they had been licensed, but there must be a *prima facie* assumption against any particular poem being later than the date of licensing"; *Review of English Studies* 3 (1927):94. The series of articles Willa McClung Evans wrote in the 1940s relies upon circumstantial evidence for dating. Others commonly assume that *Lucasta* contains poetry written after the execution of Charles I.

6. Seneca, "On Tranquillity of Mind," in *Moral Essays,* trans. John W. Basore, The Loeb Classical Library, 3 vols. (Cambridge: Harvard University Press, 1935), 2:213.

7. Seneca, "On Providence," 1:25.

8. Wilkinson, *The Poems of Richard Lovelace,* p. xlii. C. J. Wortham argues in "Richard Lovelace's 'To Lucasta, Going to the Warres': Which Wars?" *Notes and Queries,* n.s., 26 (1979):430–31, that Lovelace may have been involved in the French wars and that he may never have fought in the English civil war.

9. Wilkinson, *The Poems of Richard Lovelace,* p. 254.

10. George Fenwick Jones believes Lovelace uses honor "in its older sense of reputation or good name"; Lovelace does not, in Jones's opinion, view honor in terms of *honestum,* "integrity, or loyalty to an inner moral law"; pp. 131 and 132 in "Lov'd I Not Honour More: The Durability of a Literary Motif," *Comparative Literature* 11 (1959):131–43.

11. This is closer to H. M. Richmond, "A Note on Professor Holland's Psychoanalytic Approach to Lovelace," *Literature and Psychology* 14 (1964):126, than to Norman N. Holland, "Literary Value: A Psychoanalytic Approach," *Literature and Psychology* 14 (1964):52.

12. Thomas Clayton, ed., *Cavalier Poets: Selected Poems* (Oxford: Oxford University Press, 1978), p. 264; and Alexander C. Judson, "Who Was Lucasta?" *Modern Philology* 23 (1925):80.

13. Margoliouth, "Review of Wilkinson's Edition," p. 94. See also Manfred Weidhorn, *Richard Lovelace* (New York: Twayne Publishers, 1970), p. 71.

14. "The Publique Faith," "Short and Sweet," "A Madrigall on Justice," and "The Times," for example, in *Rump: or an Exact Collection Of the Choycest Poems and Songs Relating to the Late Times* (London, 1662).

15. Douglas Brooks-Davies, *The Mercurian Monarch* (Manchester: Manchester University Press, 1983), pp. 164–65.

16. Seneca, "Epistle XCII: On the Happy Life," in *Ad Lucilium Epistulae Morales,* trans. Richard M. Gummere, The Loeb Classical Library, 3 vols. (New York: G. P. Putnam's Sons, 1930), 2:449.

17. Andrew Clark reproduces the poem in "Merry Thoughts in a Sad Place," *Notes and Queries,* 10th ser., 1 (1904):141. G. Thorn-Drury identifies it as a poem by

Roger L'Estrange in *Notes and Queries*, 10th ser., 1 (1904):250; he also lists a number of seventeenth-century publications of the poem.

18. Seneca, "On Tranquillity of Mind," 2:283.

19. Geoffrey Whitney, *A Choice of Emblemes* (Lyden, 1636), p. 101.

20. Seneca, "On the Happy Life," 2:109, 121.

21. *Æsops Fables* (London, 1655), pp. 124–26; *The Fables of Esop, in English* (London, 1647), p. 91; Leonard Willan, *The Phrygian Fabulist* (London, 1650), pp. 130–31; Whitney, *A Choice of Emblemes*, p. 159.

22. Abraham Cowley, "The Grashopper," in *The English Writings of Abraham Cowley*, ed. A. R. Waller, 2 vols. (Cambridge: Cambridge University Press, 1905–1906), 1:57. Cf. also Kitty W. Scoular, *Natural Magic* (Oxford: Clarendon Press, 1965), pp. 108–10.

23. Thomas Stanley, "The Grassehopper," in *The Poems and Translations of Thomas Stanley*, ed. Galbraith Miller Crump (Oxford: Clarendon Press, 1962), p. 94.

24. Albrecht Dihle, "The Poem on the Cicada," *Harvard Studies in Classical Philology* 71 (1966):110.

25. Thomas Stanley, *Excitations Vpon Anacreon*, in *Poems* (London, 1652), p. 107.

26. Ibid., p. 107.

27. Ibid., p. 107.

28. Don Cameron Allen surveys the grasshopper's meaning in "Richard Lovelace: The Grasse-hopper," in *Image and Meaning: Metaphoric Traditions in Renaissance Poetry* (Baltimore, Md.: The Johns Hopkins University Press, 1960), pp. 80–92. See also Thomas Moffett, *The Theater of Insects*, in *The History of Four-Footed Beasts and Serpents and Insects* (1658), intro. Willy Ley, 3 vols. (New York: Da Capo Press, 1967), 3:994.

29. Moffett, *Theater of Insects*, 3:991–92, 991.

30. Ibid., 3:991.

31. Joachim Camerarius, Emblem XCVI, *Symbolorvm Et Emblematvm Centvriæ Tres* (Nuremberg, 1605), part 3, p. 96r. David Marsh has kindly translated all the passages from Camerarius in this study.

32. Allen, who notes in *Image and Meaning* the traditional associations with the evil north, believes that the poem reflects the period "sometime after the collapse of the great cause and the execution of King Charles" (p. 80). The entry of *Lucasta* in the Stationers' Register suggests an earlier date.

33. Allen interprets the passage in *Image and Meaning*, "So when December comes lamenting the usurping of 'his Raigne,' the 'his' means both the King of England and the King of Christmas" (p. 89). In his sensitive reading of the poem, Earl Miner goes on to demonstrate that "the poem presents us with three realms—those of the Grasshopper King, of King Christmas and of the Royal Friends," in *The Cavalier Mode from Jonson to Cotton* (Princeton: Princeton University Press, 1971), p. 292. Bruce King offers a debatable Christian reading of the poem in "The Grasse-hopper and Allegory," *Ariel* 1 (1970):71–82.

34. Margoliouth has doubts about Wilkinson's suggestion that the poem may be addressed to Endymion Porter ("Review of Wilkinson's Edition," p. 93), but later critics have accepted the identification. In "The Cavalier Country-House Poem: Mutations on a Jonsonian Tradition," *Studies in English Literature* 19 (1979):93–108, Mary Ann C. McGuire emphasizes the private, "distinctly epicurean paradise" (p. 106) Lovelace envisions.

35. Seneca, "Epistle CXXIV: On the True Good as Attained by Reason," 3:437.

36. C. H. Collins-Baker, *Lely and Kneller* (New York: Frederick A. Stokes Co., 1922), p. 17; Ellis Waterhouse, *Painting in Great Britain, 1530–1790* (London:

Penguin Books, 1953), p. 63; Margaret Whinney and Oliver Millar, *English Art, 1625–1714* (Oxford: Clarendon Press, 1957), pp. 170–71.

37. Horace Walpole, *Anecdotes of Painting in England* (London: A. Murray, 1872), p. 226.

38. Cf. Clayton's note, "In the allusion to the beheading of Charles ('the royal captive'), the King's death becomes one of many allegorical elements in this elaborate protest of inadequacy" (*Cavalier Poets*, p. 271). No critic has attempted any allegorical reading; Charles, in any case, was probably still alive when this poem was written.

39. Seneca, "On the Happy Life," 2:169.

40. Cicero, *De Officiis*, trans. Walter Miller, The Loeb Classical Library, (New York: G. P. Putnam's Sons, 1928), p. 81.

41. Wilkinson, *The Poems of Richard Lovelace*, pp. lv–lviii. Arthur E. Waite, "Lovelace," *The Gentleman's Magazine* 257 (1884):475.

42. Aelian, *On the Characteristics of Animals*, trans. A. F. Scholfield, The Loeb Classical Library, 3 vols. (Cambridge: Harvard University Press, 1958), 1:125; Pliny, *Natural History*, trans. H. Rackham, The Loeb Classical Library, 10 vols. (Cambridge: Harvard University Press, 1940), 3:501; Proverbs 6:6.

43. Joseph Frank, *Hobbled Pegasus* (Albuquerque: The University of New Mexico Press, 1968), p. 17, and the descriptive bibliography. See also the next chapter on Alexander Brome.

44. Clayton's notes (*Cavalier Poets*, pp. 306–08) helpfully summarize the possible political allusions Willa McClung Evans explicates in "Richard Lovelace's 'Mock-Song,'" *Philological Quarterly* 24 (1945):317–28.

45. King, "Green Ice and a Breast of Proof," p. 513.

46. Wolfgang Franz, *The History of Brutes* (London, 1670), p. 244.

47. George Wither, *A Collection of Emblemes (1635)*, ed. John Horden (Menston, England: Scolar Press, 1968), p. 19.

48. Randolph L. Wadsworth, Jr., "On 'The Snayl' by Richard Lovelace," *Modern Language Review* 65 (1970):757. This essay develops a rich, allusive reading based on the complex traditions that in the seventeenth century give meaning to the snail.

49. Camerarius, "Emblem XCVII," part 4, p. 97v.

50. Camerarius, "Emblem XCIX," part 4, p. 100r.

51. Seneca, "On Tranquillity of Mind," 2:255.

52. Seneca, "To Helvia His Mother On Consolation," 2:447.

53. Camerarius, "Emblem C," 4:100v. Wadsworth discusses this emblem on pp. 756–57 of "On 'The Snayl' by Richard Lovelace."

54. Seneca, "To Helvia His Mother On Consolation," 2:457–59. The Renaissance neo-Stoics Joseph Hall, Guillaume Du Vair, and especially Justus Lipsius also stress the recognition, "Euery place in the world is a wise mans countrie, or rather no place at all is his countrie. For his habitation is in heauen" (Du Vair, *The Moral Philosophie of the Stoicks, Englished by Thomas James*, ed. Rudolf Kirk [New Brunswick, N.J.: Rutgers University Press, 1951], p. 98).

55. George Turberville, *The Booke of Faulconrie or Hauking* (London, 1575), p. 160. This book contains a picture of the struggle between the falcon and the heron as well as a description of the training necessary to prepare the falcon for the hunt.

56. Samuel Wesley, *Maggots* (London, 1685), in Wilkinson, *The Poems of Richard Lovelace*, p. 307.

57. Camerarius, "Emblem XXXII," part 3, p. 32r. Kitty Scoular also notes this emblem in *Natural Magic*, p. 74.

58. Andrew Marvell, "An *Horatian* Ode upon *Cromwel's* Return from *Ireland*," in *The Poems and Letters of Andrew Marvell*, ed. H. M. Margoliouth and revised by Pierre

Legouis and E. E. Duncan-Jones, 2 vols. (Oxford: Clarendon Press, 1971), 1:93.

59. Henry Peacham, *Minerva Britanna* (London, 1612), p. 94.

60. John Ogilby, "Fable XXXIII: Of the Fly and the Ant," in *The Fables of Æsop,* intro. Earl Miner (Los Angeles and Berkeley: University of California Press, 1965), p. 79. Parallels are also found in *Æsops Fables,* pp. 46–48; *The Fables of Esop,* p. 65.

61. Robert Farley, "*Nocitura peto,*" "Moral Emblem 25," in *Lychnocavsia sive Moralia Facvm Emblemata* (London, 1638), sig. E2r.

62. These cryptic lines are not easily paraphrased; this reading rejects Lynn Beach Sadler's interpretation in "Lovelace's 'A Fly Caught in a Cobweb,'" *Literatur in Wissenschaft und Unterricht* 6 (1973):27, and supports Clayton's interpretation in *Cavalier Poets,* p. 309.

63. Weidhorn, *Richard Lovelace,* p. 43.

64. Aelian, *On the Characteristics of Animals,* 3:377–79; Pliny, *Natural History,* 3:53.

65. Peacham, *Minerva Britanna,* p. 106.

66. Camerarius, "Emblem IV," part 2, p. 6r.

67. Peacham, *Minerva Britanna,* p. 106.

68. Edward Topsell, *The History of Four-Footed Beasts,* 2:726, 783.

69. Franz, *The History of Brutes,* p. 242.

70. See Randolph L. Wadsworth, Jr.'s criticism of Bruce King's reading, "Comment and Rebuttal."

71. Ogilby, "Fable LXVII: Of the Oke and the Reed," p. 170.

72. Peacham, *Minerva Britanna,* p. 165; Ben Jonson, "To William Roe," in *Ben Jonson,* ed. C. H. Herford and Percy and Evelyn Simpson, 11 vols. (1947; rpt. Oxford: Clarendon Press, 1954), 8:81.

73. Clarendon, *The Life of Edward Earl of Clarendon,* 3 vols. (Oxford, 1759), 1:42.

## Chapter 5. Alexander Brome

1. Gerard Langbaine, *An Account of the English Dramatick Poets* (Oxford, 1691), p. 32.

2. J. L. Brooks has established much of the biography in his unpublished dissertation, "Alexander Brome: Life and Works," Ph.D. diss., Harvard University, 1932. Roman R. Dubinski's edition *Alexander Brome Poems,* 2 vols. (Toronto: University of Toronto Press, 1982) also offers a useful summary of Brome's career. Dubinski's edition will be cited in the text.

3. Edward Phillips, *Theatrum Poetarum* (London, 1675), part 2, p. 6.

4. Roman R. Dubinski discusses the "psychological complexity" of Brome's love poetry in "The Scientific Element in Alexander Brome's Love Poetry," *English Studies in Canada* 2 (1976):8–26; and C. V. Wedgwood briefly considers Brome's political poetry in *Poetry and Politics under the Stuarts* (Cambridge: Cambridge University Press, 1960). The recent publication of Dubinski's fine edition, which also considers the political poems (1:22–29), may encourage further study of Brome's poetry.

5. F. J. C. Hearnshaw notes in "Court and Parliament, 1588 to 1688," "Alexander Brome wrote a long series of political songs and ballads which well repay the careful study of those who are seeking to discover contemporary opinion concerning the great schism," in *English History in Contemporary Poetry* (London: The Historical Association, 1926), part 4, p. 28. C. V. Wedgwood, on the other hand, believes Brome's "work deserves study if only for the lamentable comment which it supplies under its apparent lightness on the rotting away of a cause" (*Poetry and Politics,* p. 108).

6. Derek Hirst, *Authority and Conflict: England, 1603–1658* (Cambridge: Harvard University Press, 1986), p. 288.

7. "To Colonel *Lovelace* on his Poems," 1:289–90, and "To C. C. Esquire," 1:227–28.

8. Valentine Oldis, "To his Ingenious Friend Mr. A. B. upon his most excellent Poems," 1:64–65; C. W., "To my worthy Friend Mr. *Alex. Brome*," 1:62–63; Richard Thynne, "On Mr. *Alexander Brome's* Poems," 1:56–58; Richard Newcourt, "On the Death of Mr. *Alexander Brome*, who dyed the 30th. of June, 1666," 1:55; Robert Napeir, "To the Ingenious Author Mr. A. B.," 1:59–60.

9. "To his Mistres affrighted in the wars" (1:94–95) and "Though *Oxford* be yielded" (1:213–14).

10. Brome obviously echoes Suckling's "Why So Pale and Wan Fond Lover" in "The Counsel" (1:73–74) and "Woman's Constancy" in "The Libertine" (1:78–79). Other poems that promote Suckling's wisdom and stress his solipsism include "Plain Dealing" (1:69–70), "To a coy Lady" (1:106), "The Contrary" (1:79–80), "Advice to *Caelia*" (1:108–9), and "The Indifferent" (1:70–71). Dubinski's notes should also be consulted for parallels.

11. Wedgwood, *Poetry and Politics,* p. 108.

12. It is, in the title of one popular poem, "A Mad World, My Masters"; *The Cavalier Songs and Ballads of England from 1642 to 1684,* ed. Charles Mackay (London: Griffin Bohn and Co., 1863), pp. 14–16. The ironic disclosure characterizes a number of the pieces Joseph Frank lists in his descriptive bibliography *Hobbled Pegasus* (Albuquerque, N.M.: The University of New Mexico Press, 1968); see, for example, entries 119, 183, 271, and 311. In his edition (2:76) Dubinski also cites several poems from the *Rump: or an Exact Collection Of the Choycest Poems and Songs Relating to the Late Times* (London, 1662).

13. *Harleian Miscellany,* 5:416–17, as quoted by Robert Ashton, *The English Civil War: Conservatism and Revolution, 1603–1649* (New York: W. W. Norton, 1979), p. 184. Besides Ashton's discussion on pp. 181–84, John Morrill succinctly defines the underlying irony in his "Introduction," in *Reactions to the English Civil War, 1642–1649* (New York: St. Martin's Press, 1983), pp. 6–7.

14. Ashton, *English Civil War,* pp. 13, 20; and the historians earlier cited in the "Introduction," endnote 32.

15. James Howell graphically captures the plight of the country caught in "this unnatural, self destroying war" in *England's Tears for the present Wars* (1644), in *The Somers Collection of Tracts,* 13 vols. (London, 1811), 5:37–46. Ballads and songs expressing a similar dismay can be found in various collections; see, for example, "Thankes to the *Parliament*," "A Godly *Exhortation*," and "Alas poore Trades-men," in *Cavalier and Puritan,* ed. Hyder E. Rollins (New York: The New York University Press, 1923).

16. *The Petition of Right of the Free-holders and Free-men of the Kingdom of England* (1648) as quoted by Robert Ashton, "From Cavalier to Roundhead Tyranny, 1642–9," in *Reactions to the English Civil War, 1642–1649,* p. 195. See also Ashton, *The English Civil War,* pp. 257–60; Donald Pennington, "The War and the People," in *Reactions to the English Civil War, 1642–1649,* pp. 115–35; John Morrill, "The Church in England, 1642–9," in *Reactions to the English Civil War, 1642–1649,* p. 109. Among the poets see, for example, Robert Heath, *Clarastella, Together with Poems occasional, Elegies, Epigrams, Satires (1650),* intro. Frederick H. Candelaria (Gainesville, Fla.: Scholars' Facsimiles & Reprints, 1970) and such poems as "To a Friend wishing peace," pp. 91–92. Among the poets who later describe the loss of peace, Robert Fletcher, *The Poems and Translations of Robert Fletcher,* ed. D. H.

Woodward (Gainesville, Fla.: University of Florida Press, 1970) is particularly interesting.

17. "The Power of the Sword," 1:223–25, and "A Time-Sonnet," 2:263–64, in *A Collection of Loyal Songs Written against the Rump Parliament, Between the Years 1639 and 1661*, 2 vols. (London, 1731); "The Penitent Traytor," in the *Rump*, part 1, pp. 53–57; "The Phanatics Plot Discovered," in *Political Ballads Published in England During the Commonwealth*, ed. Thomas Wright (London: Percy Society, 1841), pp. 234–37.

18. Francis Quarles, *Solomons Recantation, Entituled Ecclesiastes, Paraphrased* (London, 1645), in *The Complete Works in Prose and Verse of Francis Quarles*, ed. Alexander Grosart, 3 vols. (Edinburgh: T. and A. Constable, 1880), 2:171.

19. Joseph Frank annotates the 1649 pamphlet *A Curse Against Parliament-Ale* as "one of the works that marks the shift among Royalist poets toward expressing their grievances in drinking songs rather than in direct political statements" (p. 249). In *The Royalists During the Puritan Revolution* (The Hague: Martinus Nijhoff, 1956), Paul H. Hardacre states, "Men were constantly being apprehended for abusing the Protector or drinking to the king" (pp. 122 and 74).

20. See, for example, Francis Wortley's "The contented Prisoner his praise of *Sack*," which J. Woodfall Ebsworth notes is "the earliest appearance in print, known to us, of this characteristic outburst of Cavalier vivacity," in *Choyce Drollery* (Boston, Lincolnshire, 1876), pp. 93–96, 300. Also noteworthy are the drinking poems by Hugh Crompton, *Poems* (London, 1657); Henry Bold, *Latine Songs, With their English: and Poems* (London, 1685); and Charles Cotton, *Poems of Charles Cotton*, ed. John Buxton (Cambridge: Harvard University Press, 1958). On occasion other poets such as Thomas Flatman, *Poems and Songs* (London, 1674) and Tom Weaver, *Songs and Poems of Love* (London, 1654) develop distinctive tones in their praise of drinking.

21. Thomas Stanley, "Anacreon XXVI," in *The Poems and Translations of Thomas Stanley*, ed. Galbraith Miller Crump (Oxford: Clarendon Press, 1962), p. 85.

22. "A la Mode," pp. 64–70, and "The Lamentation of a bad Market: or, the Disbanded Souldier," pp. 229–33, in Wright, *Political Ballads;* Donald Pennington, "The War and the People," stresses the common complaint against quartering (particularly pp. 117–21).

23. Cf. Tom Weaver's "The Compounders Song," in *Songs and Poems of Love*, pp. 13–15.

24. Martin Luther, *An Exposition of Salomons Booke, called Ecclesiastes or the Preacher* (London, 1573), p. 7r; Thomas Granger, *A Familiar Exposition or Commentarie on Ecclesiastes* (London, 1621), p. 69; and Michael Jermin, *A Commentary, Upon The Whole Booke of Ecclesiastes or the Preacher* (London, 1639), p. 299. See also William Pemble, *Salomons Recantation And Repentance* (London, 1632), p. 14, and John Cotton, *A Briefe Exposition with Practicall Observations upon The Whole Book of Ecclesiastes* (London, 1654), pp. 189–90.

25. Arthur Jackson, *Annotations Upon the Book of Ecclesiastes Or the Preacher,* in *Annotations Upon The five Books* (London, 1658), part 2, p. 2.

26. In one other poem, "The Lamentation," Brome concludes, "To heav'n alone unfold thy want" (1:171). The lament, however, is a set piece modeled after Jeremiah.

27. The information on sequestration is derived from C. H. Firth, "The Royalists Under the Protectorate," *English Historical Review* 52 (1937):634–48; Hardacre, "The Delinquents, 1643–1649," in *The Royalists During the Puritan Revolution*, pp. 17–38; and David Underdown, *Royalist Conspiracy in England, 1649–1660* (New Haven: Yale University Press, 1960).

28. Donald Veall observes in *The Popular Movement for Law Reform, 1640–1660*

(Oxford: Clarendon Press, 1970), "Denunciations of the lawyers in contemporary tracts were legion. They were 'the professors of iniquity who lived on the sins of the people'" (p. 201). The legal profession is also singled out in Thomas Hobbes's *Behemoth: The History of the Causes of the Civil Wars of England,* ed. William Molesworth (New York: Burt Franklin, 1963).

29. In his discussion of the shifting allegiances in the 1640s, David Underdown suggests that "the revolutionaries also seem to have been drawn in a marked degree from families which were insecure ('declining gentry', in a famous phrase), or from outside the traditional political establishment (*nouveaux riches,* lesser gentry, families of obscure and usually urban origins)," in *Pride's Purge: Politics in the Puritan Revolution* (Oxford: Clarendon Press, 1971), p. 4.

30. Peter W. Thomas, *Sir John Berkenhead, 1617–1679* (Oxford: Clarendon Press, 1969), p. 200.

31. Underdown, *Royalist Conspiracy in England,* pp. 254–85.

32. Ibid., p. 314.

33. Godfrey Davies, *The Restoration of Charles II, 1658–1660* (San Marino: The Huntington Library, 1955), p. 307; Maurice Ashley, *General Monck* (London: Jonathan Cape, 1977), p. 205.

34. William Drummond, "Anagram On his Excellency the Lord General *George Monck,*" in *Broadsides of Speeches, Songs, Etc. Delivered in the Presence of General Monck,* in *Illustrations of Early English Popular Literature,* ed. J. Payne Collier, 2 vols. (1863; rpt. New York: Benjamin Blom, 1966), 2:37. See also Thomas Jordan, "A Speech Made to his Excellency *George Monck,* General, &c. The Twelfth day of Aprill, M.DCLX," 2:19–22.

35. Cf. Edmund Waller, "To the King, Upon His Majesty's Happy Return," *The Poems of Edmund Waller,* ed. G. Thorn-Drury, 2 vols. (New York: Charles Scribner's Sons, 1901), 2:37–38; Abraham Cowley, "Upon His Majesties Restoration and Return," chap. 6.

36. Hardacre, *The Royalists During the Puritan Revolution,* pp. 145–69; Underdown, *Royalist Conspiracy in England,* pp. 315–17, 336–38; Thomas Jordan, "The Discontented Cavalier," in *A Royal Arbor of Loyal Poesie* (London, 1664), rpt. J. Payne Collier, *Illustrations of Old English Literature,* 3 vols. (London, 1866), 3:104–7.

37. The quotations from Clarendon are from Underdown, *Royalist Conspiracy in England,* p. 316, and Hardacre, *The Royalists During the Puritan Revolution,* p. 145.

38. The complaint has justification. "There is certainly evidence," G. E. Aylmer notes, "that the rank and file of the Cavalier gentry and perhaps also humbler royalists below them in the social scale recovered less well and, if they had to sell lands in order to pay debts, were less likely to get compensatory benefits under the restored monarchy than their wealthier, better-connected colleagues"; *Rebellion or Revolution? England, 1640–1660* (Oxford: Clarendon Press, 1986), pp. 117–18.

39. Occasionally other poets also recognize the valued few in the often-criticized legal profession; see Owen Felltham, "On *Thomas* Lord *Coventry* . . . who dyed Decemb. *1640,*" in *Lusoria: or, Occasional Pieces,* in *Resolves* (London, 1677), pp. 34–36.

40. Luther, *An Exposition,* p. 143r. For similar interpretations of verse 8:15, see also Jermin, *A Commentary,* pp. 299–301, and Jackson, *Annotations,* part 2, p. 82.

## Chapter 6. Abraham Cowley

1. Abraham Cowley, "Of My self," in *Several Discourses by way of Essays, in Verse and Prose,* in *The English Writings of Abraham Cowley,* ed. A. R. Waller, 2 vols.

(Cambridge: Cambridge University Press, 1905–6), 2:456. Hereafter cited in the text.

2. David Trotter, *The Poetry of Abraham Cowley* (Totowa, N.J.: Rowman and Littlefield, 1979), p. 96; Nicholas Jose, "Ideal Restoration and the Case of Cowley," in *Ideas of the Restoration in English Literature, 1660–71* (Cambridge: Harvard University Press, 1984), p. 82; and Ruth Nevo, *The Dial of Virtue* (Princeton: Princeton University Press, 1963), p. 119. Unlike these more recent critics, Robert B. Hinman emphasizes the optimism of Cowley; his work, *Abraham Cowley's World of Order* (Cambridge: Harvard University Press, 1960), is not concerned, however, with the political dimensions of the poems.

3. The conclusion both Nevo and Jose stress. Nevo contends in *The Dial of Virtue* that Cowley's "melancholy scepticism" led him to "retreat from politics and the world to his own Sabine farm"; she does see Cowley earlier attracted to the possibility that fortune can be overcome only to conclude "There can be no Fortune-quelling hero for him" (p. 122). In *Ideas of the Restoration* Jose suggests Cowley ultimately developed the detachment of a pastoral retirement (p. 94).

4. Cowley, "Of My self," 2:457. The first chapter of James G. Taaffe's *Abraham Cowley* (New York: Twayne Publishers, 1972) discusses Cowley's early classical indebtedness.

5. The definition of *sylva* developed by Cicero and Quintilian. See Annabel M. Patterson, *Marvell and the Civic Crown* (Princeton: Princeton University Press, 1978), pp. 51–52, and Richard S. Peterson, *Imitation and Praise in the Poems of Ben Jonson* (New Haven: Yale University Press, 1981), p. 10.

6. John M. Wallace considers the prevailing tension in "*Coopers Hill:* The Manifesto of Parliamentary Royalism, 1641," *ELH* 41 (1974):510–16.

7. Raymond A. Anselment, "The Oxford University Poets and Caroline Panegyric," *John Donne Journal* 3 (1984):194–96.

8. "To the Reader," in *Wit and Loyalty Reviv'd* (London, 1682), n.p.; Arthur H. Nethercot, *Abraham Cowley: The Muses's Hannibal* (Oxford: Clarendon Press, 1931), p. 71; Trotter, *The Poetry of Abraham Cowley*, pp. 59–60.

9. Biographical information is found in Samuel Rawson Gardiner's life of Williams in the *Dictionary of National Biography*, ed. Leslie Stephen and Sidney Lee, 22 vols. (Oxford: Oxford University Press, 1921–1922), 21:414–20, and H. R. Trevor-Roper, *Archbishop Laud, 1573–1645* (Hamden, Conn.: Archon Books, 1962).

10. Seneca, "On Providence," in *Moral Essays*, trans. John W. Basore, The Loeb Classical Library, 3 vols. (New York: G. P. Putnam's Sons, 1928), 1:25.

11. Ibid., 31.

12. Ibid., 27.

13. Ibid., 45.

14. Abraham Cowley, *The Civil War*, ed. Allan Pritchard (Toronto: University of Toronto Press, 1973), p. 12.

15. Caroline M. Hibbard, *Charles I and the Popish Plot* (Chapel Hill: The University of North Carolina Press, 1983), p. 15.

16. Nethercot, who offers this characterization in *Abraham Cowley*, describes the satire as "one of the most immoderate defences of a moderate position ever written" (p. 82). In *Rebellion or Revolution? England, 1640–1660* (Oxford: Clarendon Press, 1986), pp. 64–66, G. E. Aylmer recognizes the range of expression represented in the twenty thousand works gathered together by George Thomason during the years from 1640 to 1661. John Milton's prose satires and John Cleveland's poetic satires also obviously indicate the tonal extremes on both sides of the conflict.

17. Cicero, *De Officiis*, trans. Walter Miller, The Loeb Classical Library (New York: G. P. Putnam's Sons, 1928), p. 23.

18. Pritchard, *The Civil War,* p. 5. This edition of *The Civil War* will be cited in the text.

19. Trotter, *The Poetry of Abraham Cowley,* p. 10.

20. Cf. Trotter's reading of the poem in *The Poetry of Abraham Cowley,* particularly p. 18.

21. Thomas Sprat records the belief that Cowley "had finish'd the greatest part of it while he was yet a young Student at *Cambridge*"; *An Account of the Life and Writings of Mr. Abraham Cowley* (1668), in *Critical Essays of the Seventeenth Century,* ed. J. E. Spingarn, 3 vols. (1908; rpt. Oxford: Clarendon Press, 1957), 2:133. In his twentieth-century biography, *Abraham Cowley,* Arthur H. Nethercot contends that the *Davideis* published in 1656 is a revised poem "Representing different strata of his work for a period of over fifteen years and revealing many signs of revision" (p. 165); and it suits Nethercot's political reading of the fourth book to date the revisions or writing of this part in the 1650s. An influential article by Frank Kermode, "The Date of Cowley's *Davideis,*" *Review of English Studies* 25 (1949):154–58, rejects the theory of revision and argues that "the whole poem was written after 1650 and finished before 1654" (p. 158). James G. Taaffe (*Abraham Cowley,* pp. 78–79) and David Trotter (*The Poetry of Abraham Cowley,* p. 83) accept Kermode's position, but Ted-Larry Pebworth rightly notes in passing that Kermode's arguments are not "totally convincing," see "Cowley's *Davideis* and the Exaltation of Friendship," in *The David Myth in Western Literature,* ed. Raymond-Jean Frontain and Jan Wojcik (West Lafayette, Ind.: Purdue University Press, 1980), p. 200. Until the new critical edition in preparation resolves the issue of dating, political readings assuming a precise dating must be approached cautiously. The following discussion does not, it should be noted, depend upon the likelihood that Cowley wrote all of the *Davideis* after he finished the pieces to Davenant and Crashaw.

22. Barbara K. Lewalski, *Milton's Brief Epic* (Providence, Rd.I.: Brown University Press, 1966), p. 80.

23. Thomas Rhymer, "Preface to Rapin," in *Critical Essays of the Seventeenth Century,* 2:172.

24. Ibid., 2:171.

25. William Creed, *Judah's Return to their Allegiance: and David's Returne To his Crown and Kingdom* (London, 1660), p. 2.

26. Clement Barksdale, *The King's Return* (London, 1660), p. 2.

27. William Guild, *The Throne of David* (Oxford, 1659), p. 9.

28. John Marbeck, *The Holie Historie of King Dauid* (London, 1579), titlepage; Andrew Willet, *An Harmonie vpon the First Booke of Samvel* (Cambridge, 1607), sig. ¶2v.

29. Guild, *The Throne of David,* p. 3.

30. Creed, *Judah's Return,* p. 18. See also Jeremias Drexel, *The School of Patience* (London, 1640), part 1, p. 55; part 3, pp. 115, 118–19; Richard Vines, *The Posture of Davids Spirit* (London, 1644); and *Davids Three Majesties: Or Soveregnties Three Champions* (Oxford, 1643).

31. See, for example, the works Richard F. Jones cites in "The Originality of *Absalom and Achitophel,*" *Modern Language Notes* 46 (1931):211–18.

32. Nethercot finds "a modern political allegory" in the fourth book (*Abraham Cowley,* p. 153); although he does not develop a sustained reading, Nethercot believes, "The wise Samuel, in whose person Cowley would seem to be flattering Cromwell, apparently voiced Cowley's own opinion when he . . . favoured the retention of the republic" (p. 154). Taaffe can discern "no consistent allegorical scheme" (*Abraham Cowley,* p. 92), and Trotter suggests that the poem should be read "not as a political allegory, but as a political statement" (*The Poetry of Abraham Cowley,*

p. 85). The following analysis does not see the skepticism Trotter stresses in his sensitive and complex reading; nor does it agree with Jose that "the final submission is a weary one" (*Ideas of the Restoration*, p. 79).

33. Samuel Johnson, "Abraham Cowley," in *Lives of the English Poets*, ed. George Birkbeck Hill, 3 vols. (Oxford: Clarendon Press, 1905), 1:54.

34. Trotter, *The Poetry of Abraham Cowley*, p. 96.

35. Manilius, *Astronomica*, trans. G. P. Goold, The Loeb Classical Library (Cambridge: Harvard University Press, 1977), p. 231.

36. Manilius, *Astronomica*, p. 231.

37. This position is closer to Hinman's reading of the poem (*Abraham Cowley's World of Order*, pp. 74–79) than to Trotter's (*The Poetry of Abraham Cowley*, pp. 133–37).

38. Nethercot contends that in this poem "Cowley had gone a long way toward putting himself in countenance with the Cromwellian government" (*Abraham Cowley*, p. 153); and Taaffe more emphatically recognizes "Cowley's passionate support of Cromwell's government" (*Abraham Cowley*, p. 69). Others who also identify Brutus with Cromwell include Paul J. Korshin, *From Concord to Dissent* (Menston, England: Scolar Press, 1973), p. 27; Nevo, *The Dial of Virtue*, p. 119; Pritchard, *The Civil War*, p. 31; and Jose, *Ideas of the Restoration*, p. 81. Two important exceptions are T. R. Langley, "Abraham Cowley's 'Brutus': Royalist or Republican?" *Yearbook of English Studies* 6 (1976):41–52, and James G. Keough, "Cowley's Brutus Ode: Historical Precepts and the Politics of Defeat," *Texas Studies in Literature and Language* 19 (1977):382–91. Both see in Brutus the dilemma of the virtuous individual forced to come to terms with the royalist defeat.

39. This passage appears in the 1656 Preface but not in later editions of Cowley's poetry. Thomas Sprat explains in his biography of Cowley, "Yet seeing his good intentions were so ill interpreted, he told me, the last time that ever I saw him, that he would have them omitted in the next Impression: of which his Friend Mr. *Cook* is a witness"; *Critical Essays of the Seventeenth Century*, 2:126.

40. Sprat, *An Account of the Life*, 2:125.

41. Nethercot reproduces Cowley's letter of 26 December 1659 to Lord Ormonde, *Abraham Cowley*, pp. 189–90.

42. David Underdown, *Royalist Conspiracy in England, 1649–1660* (New Haven: Yale University Press, 1960), p. 318. Underdown's position is at odds with Jose's (*Ideas of the Restoration*, pp. 75–77) and supports those of Keough ("Cowley's Brutus Ode," p. 389) and Langley ("Abraham Cowley's 'Brutus,'" pp. 50–52).

43. Willet, *An Harmonie*, p. 346.

44. Justus Lipsius, *Two Bookes Of Constancie Written in Latine by Iustus Lipsius, Englished by Sir John Stradling*, ed. Rudolf Kirk (New Brunswick, N.J.: Rutgers University Press, 1939), p. 127. Hinman discusses Lipsius's influence upon Cowley at length in his book, *Abraham Cowley's World of Order*; Langley also emphasizes the relevancy of this passage in his reading of the poem, "Abraham Cowley's 'Brutus,'" pp. 48–49.

45. Manilius, *Astronomica*, p. 223.

46. Seneca, "XCII. On the Happy Life," in *Ad Lucilium Epistulae Morales*, trans. Richard M. Gummere, The Loeb Classical Library, 3 vols. (New York: G. P. Putnam's Sons, 1930), 2:463.

47. In a long prose piece written about this time, *A Discourse By way of Vision, Concerning the Government of Oliver Cromwell*, Cowley evokes this expectation with the appearance of Charles I's heir, attired in the ancient symbols of British monarchy. The work reveals Cowley's involvement in the Engagement Controversy.

48. Robert B. Hinman, "'The Pindarique Way': Abraham Cowley's 'Character of

His Own Thoughts' in his *Essays,* Particularly 'Of My Self,'" in *Der Englische Essay,* ed. Horst Weber (Darmstadt: Wissenschaftliche Buchgesellschaft, 1975), p. 86.

49. Cowley, *The Third Part of the Works of Mr Abraham Cowley, Being his Six Books of Plants,* in *The Works of Mr Abraham Cowley* (London, 1688–89), part 3, p. 133. Aphra Behn translated book six, which first appeared in *Poemata Latina* (London, 1668). The Latin lines are: "Talis erat status *Angligenum* tam pulcher & Æger, / Fortunatorum nimium bona si sua nossent [*sic*] (Such was the state of England, so beautiful and sick; among the most fortunate, if they had known their own good)," part 3, p. 316. Marilyn Archibald has provided this and the subsequent literal prose translations.

50. Royce MacGillivray discusses the commonplace in "The Surfeit of Peace and Plenty," in *Restoration Historians and the English Civil War* (The Hague: Martinus Nijhoff, 1974), pp. 237–42.

51. Many of the accounts are gathered together in *The Boscobel Tracts,* ed. John Hughes (Edinburgh: William Blackwood, 1830) and *Charles II's Escape from Worcester,* ed. William Matthews (Berkeley and Los Angeles: University of California Press, 1966).

52. Arthur Brett, *Patientia Victrix: Or, The Book of Job, In Lyrick Verse* (London, 1661), sig. a3r. The frontispiece has pictures of Job and Boscobel. Thomas Blount ends his preface to the second part of *Boscobel; Or, The History of The Most Miraculous Preservation of King Charles II,* "Fear not, for the hand of Saul shall not find thee, and thou shalt be king over Israel," p. 235, in *The Boscobel Tracts.*

53. Part 3, p. 160. The Latin lines are:

> Salve magna Deûm cura, & nunc *Maxime Regnum;*
> Nec te plorantem, nec te rationis egentem
> Horrida tantorum circumstat turba malorum,
> Ille potens verè est, potuit qui tempore tali
> Nec Timuisse *Necem,* nec Desperasse *Salutem.*
> Hoc opus est animi summum Regalis; ademit
> Si Regnum Fortuna tibi, *justissimus ultor*
> Fortunæ tu Regnum adimis, victúsq; triumphas
> Par Superi tantum gaudent committere, sed te
> Donabunt *Rude;* nec longè pulcherrimus ille
> Annus abest; procedet, Iô, procedet Olympo
> Pacatum irradians Astris fœlicibus Orbem.

(Hail, great concern of the gods and now the greatest of kings; while surrounded by the horrible crowd of great evils, you neither wept nor lacked reason; one who is truly powerful, you neither feared death nor despaired of safety. This is the conduct of the greatest royal soul: if fortune took the kingdom from you, as the most just avenger you take the kingdom from fortune. The gods above rejoice to see one who has been conquered triumph, and they will honor your honorable conduct. That most beautiful year is not far away. They will elevate you to Olympian heights, gleaming over the peaceful world with fortunate stars.) (Part 3, pp. 356–57)

54. Part 3, p. 162. The Latin lines are:

> Salve fœminei decus, ô, sexúsq; virilis
> Regina opprobrium! Quam sorte in utraq; decenter
> Lætámque, Tristémque, suiq; in utraq; potentem
> Cernimus, Invidiámq; Deis de Conjuga solo

Conflantem lacrymis, Rota quam circumsonat Orbis
Immiotam, & Centro fixam Virtuitis in ipso.

(Hail, glory of the female sex and, O Queen, disgrace of the male sex. We see you in each fate properly joyous and sad, always self-possessed [powerful of self] and moved to tears only by your spouse. The envy of the gods, as the world turns around, you stand unmoved and fixed in the center of virtue.) (Part 3, pp. 358–59)

# Select Bibliography

The following entries are primarily works cited in the text. The list also includes works selected to suggest a further sense of historical and literary contexts.

## Primary Sources

Aelian. *On the Characteristics of Animals.* Translated by A. F. Scholfield. 3 vols. The Loeb Classical Library. Cambridge: Harvard University Press, 1958–59.

*Æsops Fables.* London, 1655.

Allestree, Richard. *The Art of Patience under All Afflictions.* London, 1684.

Bacon, Francis. "Of Masques and Triumphs." In vol. 6 of *The Works of Francis Bacon,* edited by James Spedding, Robert Ellis, and Douglas Heath. London: Longman and Co., 1858.

Barksdale, Clement. *The King's Return.* London, 1660.

Boethius. *The Consolation of Philosophy.* Translated by Richard Green. Indianapolis: Bobbs-Merrill, 1962.

Bold, Henry. *Latine Songs, With their English: and Poems.* London, 1685.

Brett, Arthur. *Patientia Victrix: Or, The Book of Job, In Lyrick Verse.* London, 1661.

Brome, Alexander. *Alexander Brome Poems.* Edited by Roman R. Dubinski. 2 vols. Toronto: University of Toronto Press, 1982.

Bruce, John, W. D. Hamilton, and S. C. Lomas, eds. *Calendar of State Papers, Domestic Series, Charles I.* 23 vols. London: Her Majesty's Stationery Office, 1858–97.

Butter, Nathanial, and Nicholas Bourne. *The Swedish Intelligencer. The Third Part.* London, 1633.

Camden, William. *Remaines Concerning Britaine.* London, 1637.

Camerarius, Joachim. *Symbolorvm Et Emblematvm Centvriæ Tres.* Nuremberg, 1605.

Carew, Thomas. *The Poems of Thomas Carew.* Edited by Rhodes Dunlap. Oxford: Clarendon Press, 1970.

Cartwright, William. *The Plays and Poems Of William Cartwright.* Edited by G. Blakemore Evans. Madison: The University of Wisconsin Press, 1951.

Charles I. *Eikon Basilike: The Portraiture of His Sacred Majesty in His Solitudes and Sufferings.* Edited by Philip A. Knachel. Ithaca: Cornell University Press, 1966.

Cicero. *De Officiis.* Translated by Walter Miller. The Loeb Classical Library. New York: G. P. Putnam's Sons, 1928.

Clarendon, Edward Hyde, first earl of. *The History of the Rebellion and Civil Wars in England.* Edited by W. Dunn Macray. 6 vols. Oxford: Clarendon Press, 1888.

———. *The Life of Edward Earl of Clarendon.* 3 vols. Oxford, 1759.

Clayton, Thomas, ed. *Cavalier Poets: Selected Poems*. Oxford: Oxford University Press, 1978.

Cleveland, John. *The Poems of John Cleveland*. Edited by Brian Morris and Eleanor Withington. Oxford: Clarendon Press, 1967.

*A Collection of Loyal Songs Written against the Rump Parliament, Between the Years 1639 and 1661*. 2 vols. London, 1731.

Collier, J. Payne, ed. *Illustrations of Early English Popular Literature*. 2 vols. New York: Benjamin Blom, 1966.

Coningsby, Harry. "The Preface and Occasion of this Melancholick Divertisement." In *The Consolation of Philosophy*, translated by Thomas Coningsby. London, 1664.

Cotton, Charles. *Poems of Charles Cotton*. Edited by John Buxton. Cambridge: Harvard University Press, 1958.

Cotton, John. *A Briefe Exposition with Practicall Observations upon The Whole Book of Ecclesiastes*. London, 1654.

Cowley, Abraham. *The Civil War*. Edited by Allan Pritchard. Toronto: University of Toronto Press, 1973.

———. *The English Writings of Abraham Cowley*. Edited by A. R. Waller. 2 vols. Cambridge: Cambridge University Press, 1905–6.

———. *Poemata Latina*. London, 1668.

———. *The Works of Mr Abraham Cowley*. London, 1688–89.

Creed, William. *Judah's Return to their Allegiance: and David's Returne To his Crown and Kingdom*. London, 1660.

Crompton, Hugh. *Poems*. London, 1657.

Daniel, George. *The Poems of George Daniel, Esq., of Beswick, Yorkshire (1616–1657)*. Edited by Alexander Grosart. 4 vols. Boston, Lincolnshire: R. Roberts, 1878.

———. *The Selected Poems of George Daniel of Beswick, 1616–1657*. Edited by Thomas B. Stroup. Lexington, Ky.: University of Kentucky Press, 1959.

Davenant, William. *The Shorter Poems, and Songs from the Plays and Masques*. Edited by A. M. Gibbs. Oxford: Clarendon Press, 1972.

*Davids Three Majesties: Or Soveregnties Three Champions*. Oxford, 1643.

Davies, John. *The Civil Warres of Great Britain and Ireland*. London, 1661.

Denham, John. *The Poetical Works of John Denham*. New Haven: Yale University Press, 1928.

D'Ewes, Simonds. *The Autobiography and Correspondence of Sir Simonds D'Ewes*. Edited by James Halliwell. 2 vols. London: Richard Bentley, 1845.

Draper, John W., ed. *A Century of Broadside Elegies*. London: Ingpen and Grant, 1928.

Drexel, Jeremias. *The School of Patience*. London, 1640.

Du Vair, Guillaume. *The Moral Philosophie of the Stoicks, Englished by Thomas James*. Edited by Rudolf Kirk. New Brunswick, N.J.: Rutgers University Press, 1951.

Ebsworth, J. Woodfall, ed. *Choyce Drollery*. Boston, Lincolnshire, 1876.

Epictetus. *The Discourses as Reported by Arrian, The Manual, and Fragments*. Translated by W. A. Oldfather. 2 vols. The Loeb Classical Library. New York: G. P. Putnam's Sons, 1925–28.

*The Fables of Esop, in English*. London, 1647.

Fanshawe, Richard. *Shorter Poems and Translations*. Edited by N. W. Bawcutt. Liverpool: Liverpool University Press, 1964.

Farley, Robert. *Lychnocavsia sive Moralia Facvm Emblemata.* London, 1638.

Felltham, Owen. *Lusoria: or, Occasional Pieces.* In *Resolves.* London, 1677.

Flatman, Thomas. *Poems and Songs.* London, 1674.

Fletcher, Robert. *The Poems and Translations of Robert Fletcher.* Edited by D. H. Woodward. Gainesville, Fla.: University of Florida Press, 1970.

Forbes, Walter. "A Panegyricke to the High and Mighty Monarch Charles." In *The Entertainment of the High and Mighty Monarch Charles.* Edinburgh, 1633.

*The foure Ages of England: Or, The Iron Age. With other select Poems.* London, 1648.

Franz, Wolfgang. *The History of Brutes.* London, 1670.

Gauden, John. *The Love of Trvth and Peace.* London, 1641.

Gill, Alexander. *The New Starr of the North.* London, 1632.

Glapthorne, Henry. *The Plays and Poems of Henry Glapthorne.* Edited by John Pearson. 2 vols. London, 1874.

Gomersall, Robert. *Poems.* London, 1633.

Granger, Thomas. *A Familiar Exposition or Commentarie on Ecclesiastes.* London, 1621.

Grierson, Herbert, ed. *Metaphysical Lyrics & Poems of The Seventeenth Century.* Oxford: Clarendon Press, 1921.

Guild, William. *The Throne of David.* Oxford, 1659.

Hall, Joseph. *Heaven vpon Earth and Characters of Vertves and Vices.* Edited by Rudolf Kirk. New Brunswick, N.J.: Rutgers University Press, 1948.

Halliwell, James O., ed. *The Loyal Garland: A Collection of Songs of the Seventeenth Century.* London: The Percy Society, 1850.

Heath, Robert. *Clarastella Together with Poems occasional, Elegies, Epigrams, Satyrs (1650).* Introduction by Frederick H. Candelaria. Gainesville, Fla.: Scholars' Facsimiles & Reprints, 1970.

Herrick, Robert. *The Poetical Works of Robert Herrick.* Edited by L. C. Martin. Oxford: Clarendon Press, 1956.

Heywood, Thomas. *Londoni Status Pacatus: Or, Londons Peaceable Estate.* London, 1639.

Hinds, Allen B., ed. *Calendar of State Papers and Manuscripts . . . in the Archives and Collections of Venice.* Vols. 19–32. London: His Majesty's Stationery Office, 1914–31.

Hobbes, Thomas. *Behemoth: The History of the Causes of the Civil Wars of England.* Edited by William Molesworth. New York: Burt Franklin, 1963.

Horace. *The Complete Works of Horace.* Translated by Charles E. Passage. New York: Frederick Ungar Publishing Co., 1983.

———. *The Odes and Epodes of Horace.* Translated by Joseph P. Chaney. Chicago: The University of Chicago Press, 1960.

———. *The Satires and Epistles of Horace.* Translated by Smith Palmer Bovie. Chicago: The University of Chicago Press, 1959.

———. *Satires, Epistles and Ars Poetica.* Translated by H. Rushton Fairclough. The Loeb Classical Library. Cambridge: Harvard University Press, 1928.

Howell, James. *Dodona's Grove, or the Vocall Forrest.* London, 1644.

———. *England's Tears for the present Wars.* In vol. 5 of *The Somers Collection of Tracts.* London, 1811.

Hughes, John, ed. *The Boscobel Tracts.* Edinburgh: William Blackwood, 1830.

Hutchinson, Lucy. *Memoirs of the Life of Colonel Hutchinson*. Edited by James Sutherland. London: Oxford University Press, 1973.

Jackson, Arthur. *Annotations Upon the Book of Ecclesiastes Or the Preacher*. In *Annotations Upon The five Books*. London, 1658.

Jermin, Michael. *A Commentary, Upon The Whole Booke of Ecclesiastes or the Preacher*. London, 1639.

Johnson, Samuel. "Abraham Cowley." In vol. 1 of *Lives of the English Poets*, edited by George Birkbeck Hill. Oxford: Clarendon Press, 1905.

Jonson, Ben. *Ben Jonson*. Edited by C. H. Herford and Percy and Evelyn Simpson. 11 vols. Oxford: Clarendon Press, 1952–54.

Jordan, Thomas. *A Royal Arbor of Loyal Poesie*. London, 1664. In vol. 3 of *Illustrations of Old English Literature*, reprinted by J. Payne Collier. London, 1866.

Josselin, Ralph. *The Diary of Ralph Josselin, 1616–1683*. Edited by Alan MacFarlane. London: Oxford University Press, 1976.

King, Henry. *The Poems of Henry King*. Edited by Margaret Crum. Oxford: Clarendon Press, 1965.

Langbaine, Gerard. *An Account of the English Dramatick Poets*. Oxford, 1691.

L'Estrange, Hamon. *The Reign of King Charles*. London, 1656.

Lipsius, Justus. *Two Bookes Of Constancie Written in Latine by Iustus Lipsius, Englished by Sir John Stradling*. Edited by Rudolf Kirk. New Brunswick, N.J.: Rutgers University Press, 1939.

Livy. *The History of Rome*. In vol. 1 of *Livy*, translated by B. O. Foster. The Loeb Classical Library. Cambridge: Harvard University Press, 1939.

Lloyd, David. *Memoires of the Lives, Actions, Sufferings & Deaths of those Noble, Reverend, and Excellent Personages*. London, 1668.

Lovelace, Richard. *The Poems of Richard Lovelace*. Edited by C. H. Wilkinson. Oxford: Clarendon Press, 1953.

Luther, Martin. *An Exposition of Salomons Booke, called Ecclesiastes or the Preacher*. London, 1573.

Mackay, Charles, ed. *The Cavalier Songs and Ballads of England from 1642 to 1684*. London: Griffin Bohn and Co., 1863.

Manilius. *Astronomica*. Translated by G. P. Goold. The Loeb Classical Library. Cambridge: Harvard University Press, 1977.

Marbeck, John. *The Holie Historie of King Dauid*. London, 1579.

Marvell, Andrew. *The Poems and Letters of Andrew Marvell*. Edited by H. M. Margoliouth and revised by Pierre Legouis and E. E. Duncan-Jones. 2 vols. Oxford: Clarendon Press, 1971.

Matthews, William, ed. *Charles II's Escape from Worcester*. Berkeley and Los Angeles: University of California Press, 1966.

May, Tom. *The History of the Parliament of England: Which began November the third, M.DC.XL*. London, 1647.

Menander. *Rhetor*. Translated and edited by D. A. Russell and N. G. Wilson. Oxford: Clarendon Press, 1981.

Monro, Robert. *Monro His Expedition*. London, 1637.

Nedham, Marchamont. *A Short History of the English Rebellion*. London, 1661.

North, Dudley. *A Forest Promiscuous*. London, 1659.

Ogilby, John. *The Fables of Æsop*. Introduction by Earl Miner. Los Angeles and Berkeley: University of California Press, 1965.

Orgel, Stephen, and Roy Strong. *Inigo Jones: The Theatre of the Stuart Court*. 2 vols. Berkeley and Los Angeles: University of California Press, 1973.

Peacham, Henry. *Minerva Britanna*. London, 1612.

Pemble, William. *Salomons Recantation and Repentance*. London 1632.

Phillips, Edward. *Theatrum Poetarum*. London, 1675.

Pliny. *Natural History*. Translated by H. Rackham. 10 vols. The Loeb Classical Library. Cambridge: Harvard University Press, 1938–63.

Plutarch. *Plutarch's Morals. Translated from the Greek by Several Hands*. Corrected and revised from the 1684–94 edition by William W. Goodwin. 5 vols. Boston: Little, Brown, and Company, 1878.

Puttenham, George. *The Arte of English Poesie*. Edited by Gladys Doidge Willcock and Alice Walker. Cambridge: Cambridge University Press, 1936.

Quarles, Francis. *The Complete Works in Prose and Verse of Francis Quarles*. Edited by Alexander Grosart. 3 vols. Edinburgh: T. and A. Constable, 1880.

Quarles, John. *Fons Lachrymarum or a Fountayne of Teares*. London, 1649.

Randolph, Thomas. *The Poems of Thomas Randolph*. Edited by G. Thorn-Drury. London: Frederick Etchells & Hugh Macdonald, 1929.

Rollins, Hyder E., ed. *Cavalier and Puritan: Ballads and Broadsides Illustrating the Period of the Great Rebellion, 1640–1660*. New York: The New York University Press, 1923.

Rubens, Peter Paul. *Letters*. Translated and edited by Ruth Saunders Magurn. Cambridge: Harvard University Press, 1955.

*Rump: or an Exact Collection Of the Choycest Poems and Songs Relating to the Late Times*. London, 1662.

Russell, John. *The Two Famous Pitcht Battels of Lypsich, and Lutzen*. Cambridge, 1634.

Saintsbury, George, ed. *Minor Poets of the Caroline Period*. 3 vols. Oxford: Clarendon Press, 1905–21.

Sanderson, William. *A Complete History of the Life and Raigne of King Charles*. London, 1658.

Schloer, Frederick. *The Death of the Two Renowned Kings of Sweden and Bohemia*. London, 1633.

Seneca. *Ad Lucilium Epistulae Morales*. Translated by Richard M. Gummere. 3 vols. The Loeb Classical Library. New York: G. P. Putnam's Sons, 1930–43.

———. *Moral Essays*. Translated by John W. Basore. 3 vols. The Loeb Classical Library. Cambridge: Harvard University Press, 1928–35.

Spingarn, J. E., ed. *Critical Essays of the Seventeenth Century*. 3 vols. Oxford: Clarendon Press, 1957.

Sprigg, Joshua. *Anglia Rediviva*. London, 1647.

Stanley, Thomas. *Excitations Vpon Anacreon*. In *Poems*. London, 1652.

———. *The Poems and Translations of Thomas Stanley*. Edited by Galbraith Miller Crump. Oxford: Clarendon Press, 1962.

Suckling, John. *The Works of Sir John Suckling*. Edited by Thomas Clayton and Lester A. Beaurline. 2 vols. Oxford: Clarendon Press, 1971.

Topsell, Edward, and Thomas Moffett. *The History of Four-Footed Beasts and Serpents and Insects*. Introduction by Willy Ley. 3 vols. New York: Da Capo Press, 1967.

*A Translation Of the Sixth Book of Mr. Cowley's Plantarum*. London, 1680.

Turberville, George. *The Booke of Faulconrie or Hauking*. London, 1575.

Vaughan, Henry. *Poetry and Selected Prose*. Edited by L. C. Martin. Oxford: Clarendon Press, 1963.

Vines, Richard. *The Posture of Davids Spirit*. London, 1644.

Virgil. *Virgil*. Translated by H. Rushton Fairclough. 2 vols. The Loeb Classical Library. Cambridge: Harvard University Press, 1953.

Waller, Edmund. *The Poems of Edmund Waller*. Edited by G. Thorn-Drury. 2 vols. New York: Charles Scribner's Sons, 1901.

Warwick, Philip. *Memoires Of the reigne of King Charles I*. London, 1701.

Weaver, Tom. *Songs and Poems of Love*. London, 1654.

Westmoreland, Mildmay Fane, earl of. *Otia Sacra (1648)*. Introduction by Donald M. Friedman. Delmar, New York: Scholars' Facsimiles & Reprints, 1975.

Whitney, Geoffrey. *A Choice of Emblemes*. Lyden, 1636.

Wilkins, W. Walker, ed. *Political Ballads of the Seventeenth and Eighteenth Centuries*. 2 vols. London: Longmans, Green, Longmans, and Roberts, 1860.

Willan, Leonard. *The Phrygian Fabulist*. London, 1650.

Willet, Andrew. *An Harmonie vpon the First Booke of Samvel*. Cambridge, 1607.

Williams, John. *Great Britains Salomon*. London, 1625.

*Wit and Loyalty Reviv'd*. London, 1682.

Wither, George. *A Collection of Emblemes (1635)*. Edited by John Horden. Menston, England: Scolar Press, 1968.

Wood, Anthony à. *Athenæ Oxonienses*. Edited by Philip Bliss. Vol. 3. London, 1817.

Wright, Thomas, ed. *Political Ballads Published in England During the Commonwealth*. London: Percy Society, 1841.

## Secondary Sources

Adams, Simon. "Spain or the Netherlands? The Dilemmas of Early Stuart Foreign Policy." In *Before the English Civil War,* edited by Howard Tomlinson, pp. 79–101. New York: St. Martin's Press, 1984.

Allen, Don Cameron. *Image and Meaning: Metaphoric Traditions in Renaissance Poetry*. Baltimore: The Johns Hopkins University Press, 1960.

Altieri, Joanne. "Responses to a Waning Mythology in Carew's Political Poetry." *Studies in English Literature* 26 (1986):107–24.

———. *The Theatre of Praise: The Panegyric Tradition in Seventeenth-Century English Drama*. Newark, Delaware: University of Delaware Press, 1986.

Anselment, Raymond A. "Clarendon and the Caroline Myth of Peace." *The Journal of British Studies* 23 (1984):37–54.

———. "The Countess of Carlisle and Caroline Praise: Convention and Reality." *Studies in Philology* 82 (1985):212–33.

———. "The Oxford University Poets and Caroline Panegyric." *John Donne Journal* 3 (1984):181–201.

Ashley, Maurice. *General Monck*. London: Jonathan Cape, 1977.

Ashton, Robert. *The English Civil War: Conservatism and Revolution, 1603–1649*. New York: W. W. Norton, 1979.

————. "From Cavalier to Roundhead Tyranny, 1642–9." In *Reactions to the English Civil War, 1642–49,* edited by John Morrill, pp. 185–207. New York: St. Martin's Press, 1983.

Aylmer, G. E. *The King's Servants.* London: Routledge & Kegan Paul, 1961.

————. *Rebellion or Revolution? England, 1640–1660.* Oxford: Clarendon Press, 1986.

Barton, Anne. "Harking Back to Elizabeth: Ben Jonson and Caroline Nostalgia." *ELH* 48 (1981):706–31.

Baumgartner, Paul R. "Milton and Patience." *Studies in Philology* 60 (1963):203–13.

Berger, Harry, Jr. "The Renaissance Imagination: Second World and Green World." *The Centennial Review* 9 (1965):36–78.

Bone, Quentin. *Henrietta Maria: Queen of the Cavaliers.* Urbana: University of Illinois Press, 1972.

Born, Lester K. "The Perfect Prince According to the Latin Panegyrists." *American Journal of Philology* 55 (1934):20–35.

Braden, Gordon. *Renaissance Tragedy and the Senecan Tradition: Anger's Privilege.* New Haven: Yale University Press, 1985.

Breslow, Marvin A. *A Mirror of England: English Puritan Views of Foreign Nations, 1618–1640.* Cambridge: Harvard University Press, 1970.

Brooks, J. L. "Alexander Brome: Life and Works." Ph.D. diss., Harvard University, 1932.

Brooks-Davies, Douglas. *The Mercurian Monarch.* Manchester: Manchester University Press, 1983.

Bush, Douglas. *English Literature in the Earlier Seventeenth Century, 1600–1660.* New York: Oxford University Press, 1962.

Butler, Martin. *Theater and Crisis, 1632–1642.* Cambridge: Cambridge University Press, 1984.

Capp, Bernard. "The Political Dimension of Apocalyptic Thought." In *The Apocalypse in English Renaissance Thought and Literature,* edited by C. A. Patrides and Joseph Wittreich, pp. 93–124. Ithaca, N.Y.: Cornell University Press, 1984.

Carlton, Charles. *Charles I: The Personal Monarch.* London: Routledge & Kegan Paul, 1983.

Charlton, John. *The Banqueting House Whitehall.* London: Mansell Limited, 1983.

Chernaik, Warren L. *The Poetry of Limitation: A Study of Edmund Waller.* New Haven: Yale University Press, 1968.

Clark, Andrew. "Merry Thoughts in a Sad Place." *Notes and Queries,* 10th ser., 1 (1904):141.

Cliffe, John T. *The Yorkshire Gentry.* London: The Athlone Press, 1969.

Collins-Baker, C. H. *Lely and Kneller.* New York: Frederick A. Stokes Co., 1922.

Cousins, A. D. "The Cavalier World and John Cleveland." *Studies in Philology* 78 (1981):61–86.

Croll, Morris W. *"Attic" & Baroque Prose Style.* Edited by J. Max Patrick, Robert O. Evans, and John M. Wallace. Princeton: Princeton University Press, 1966.

Dahl, Folke. "Amsterdam—Cradle of English Newspapers." *The Library,* 5th ser., 4 (1949–50):166–78.

Davies, Godfrey. *The Restoration of Charles II, 1658–1660.* San Marino: The Huntington Library, 1955.

Dihle, Albrecht. "The Poem on the Cicada." *Harvard Studies in Classical Philology* 71 (1966):107–13.

Dubinski, Roman R. "The Scientific Element in Alexander Brome's Love Poetry." *English Studies in Canada* 2 (1976):8–26.

Eliot, T. S. *Selected Essays. 1917–1932.* New York: Harcourt, Brace and Company, 1932.

Elliot, J. H. "England and Europe: A Common Malady?" In *The Origins of the Civil War,* edited by Conrad Russell, pp. 246–57. New York: Barnes and Noble, 1973.

Elton, G. R. *Parliament/Political Thought.* In vol. 2 of *Studies in Tudor and Stuart Politics and Government.* Cambridge: Cambridge University Press, 1974.

Erksine-Hill, Howard. *The Augustan Idea in English Literature.* London: Edward Arnold, 1983.

Evans, Willa McClung. "Richard Lovelace's 'Mock-Song.' " *Philological Quarterly* 24 (1945):317–28.

Firth, C. H. "The Reign of Charles I." *Transactions of the Royal Historical Society,* 3d ser., 6 (1912):19–64.

———. "The Royalists Under the Protectorate." *English Historical Review* 52 (1937):634–48.

Firth, Katharine R. *The Apocalyptic Tradition in Reformation Britain, 1530–1645.* Oxford: Clarendon Press, 1979.

Fletcher, Anthony. *The Outbreak of the English Civil War.* New York: New York University Press, 1981.

Frank, Joseph. *The Beginnings of the English Newspaper, 1620–1660.* Cambridge: Harvard University Press, 1961.

———. *Hobbled Pegasus: A Descriptive Bibliography of Minor English Poetry, 1641–1660.* Albuquerque: The University of New Mexico Press, 1968.

Gardiner, Samuel R. *History of England from the Accession of James I. to the Outbreak of the Civil War, 1603–1642.* 10 vols. London: Longmans, Green, 1884.

———. *History of the Great Civil War, 1642–1649.* 4 vols. London: Longmans, Green, 1893–94.

Garrison, James D. *Dryden and the Tradition of Panegyric.* Berkeley and Los Angeles: University of California Press, 1975.

Gordon, D. J. *The Renaissance Imagination.* Edited by Stephen Orgel. Berkeley and Los Angeles: University of California Press, 1975.

Greene, Thomas M. "Ben Jonson and the Centered Self." *Studies in English Literature* 10 (1970):325–48.

Gregg, Pauline. *King Charles I.* Berkeley and Los Angeles: University of California Press, 1984.

Guibbory, Achsah. "The Poet as Myth Maker: Ben Jonson's Poetry of Praise." *Clio* 5 (1976):315–29.

Hardacre, Paul H. *The Royalists During the Puritan Revolution.* The Hague: Martinus Nijhoff, 1956.

Harris, R. W. *Clarendon and the English Revolution.* Stanford: Stanford University Press, 1983.

Hearnshaw, F. J. C. "Court and Parliament, 1588 to 1688." In no. 4 of *English History in Contemporary Poetry.* London: The Historical Association, 1926.

Henderson, Sam H. "Neo-Stoic Influence on Elizabethan Formal Verse Satire." In

*Studies in English Renaissance Literature,* edited by Waldo F. McNeir, pp. 56–86. Baton Rouge, La.: Louisiana State University Press, 1962.

Herendeen, W. H. "Like a Circle Bounded in Itself: Jonson, Camden, and the Strategies of Praise." *Journal of Medieval and Renaissance Studies* 11 (1981):137–67.

Hibbard, Caroline M. *Charles I and the Popish Plot.* Chapel Hill: The University of North Carolina Press, 1983.

Hill, Christopher. *The Experience of Defeat: Milton and Some Contemporaries.* New York: Viking Penguin, 1984.

Hinman, Robert B. *Abraham Cowley's World of Order.* Cambridge: Harvard University Press, 1960.

———. "'The Pindarique Way': Abraham Cowley's 'Character of His Own Thoughts' in His *Essays,* Particularly 'Of My Self.'" In *Der Englische Essay,* edited by Horst Weber, pp. 82–94. Darmstadt: Wissenschaftliche Buchgesellschaft, 1975.

Hirst, Derek. *Authority and Conflict: England, 1603–1658.* Cambridge: Harvard University Press, 1986.

———. "Revisionism Revised: The Place of Principle." *Past and Present* 92 (1981):79–99.

Holland, Norman N. "Literary Value: A Psychoanalytic Approach." *Literature and Psychology* 14 (1964):43–55.

Holmes, Clive. "The Country Community in Stuart Historiography." *Journal of British Studies* 19 (1980):54–73.

Howat, G. M. D. *Stuart and Cromwellian Foreign Policy.* London: Macmillan, 1974.

Hutton, Ronald. "The Structure of the Royalist Party, 1642–1646." *The Historical Journal* 24 (1981):553–69.

James, Marvyn. *English Politics and the Concept of Honour, 1485–1642.* Supplement 3. The Past and Present Society, 1978.

Jones, George Fenwick. "Love'd I not Honour More: The Durability of a Literary Motif." *Comparative Literature* 11 (1959):131–43.

Jones, Richard F. "The Originality of *Absalom and Achitophel.*" *Modern Language Notes* 46 (1931):211–18.

Jose, Nicholas. *Ideas of the Restoration in English Literature, 1660–71.* Cambridge: Harvard University Press, 1984.

Judson, Alexander C. "Who Was Lucasta?" *Modern Philology* 23 (1925):77–82.

Kearney, Hugh F. *The Eleven Years' Tyranny of Charles I.* London: Routledge & Kegan Paul, 1962.

Kenyon, J. P. *Stuart England.* New York: St. Martin's Press, 1978.

Keough, James G. "Cowley's Brutus Ode: Historical Precepts and the Politics of Defeat." *Texas Studies in Literature and Language* 19 (1977):382–91.

Kermode, Frank. "The Date of Cowley's *Davideis.*" *Review of English Studies* 25 (1949):154–58.

King, Bruce. "The Grasse-hopper and Allegory." *Ariel* 1 (1970):71–82.

———. "Green Ice and a Breast of Proof." *College English* 26 (1964–65):511–15.

Knights, L. C. "The Social Background of Metaphysical Poetry." In *Further Explorations,* pp. 99–120. London: Chatto and Windus, 1965.

Kogan, Stephen. *The Hieroglyphic King: Wisdom and Idolatry in the Seventeenth-*

*Century Masque*. Rutherford, New Jersey: Fairleigh Dickinson University Press, 1986.

Korshin, Paul J. *From Concord to Dissent: Major Themes in English Poetic Theory, 1640–1700*. Menston, England: Scolar Press, 1973.

Langley, T. R. "Abraham Cowley's 'Brutus': Royalist or Republican?" *Yearbook of English Studies* 6 (1976):41–52.

Leinwand, Theodore B. "London Triumphing: The Jacobean Lord Mayor's Show." *Clio* 11 (1982):137–53.

Lewalski, Barbara K. *Milton's Brief Epic: The Genre, Meaning, and Art of Paradise Regained*. Providence: Brown University Press, 1966.

Lindley, David, ed. *The Court Masque*. Manchester: Manchester University Press, 1984.

Logan, George M. *The Meaning of More's Utopia*. Princeton: Princeton University Press, 1983.

Long, A. A. "Freedom and Determinism in the Stoic Theory of Human Action." In *Problems in Stoicism,* edited by A. A. Long, pp. 173–99. London: The Athlone Press, 1971.

Long, Ada, and Hugh Maclean. " 'Dear *Ben*,' 'Great DONNE,' and 'my *Celia*': The Wit of Carew's Poetry." *Studies in English Literature* 18 (1978):75–94.

Low, Anthony. *The Georgic Revolution*. Princeton: Princeton University Press, 1985.

McGaw, William D. "The Civil War in Cowley's *Destinie*." *English Language Notes* 14 (1977):268–70.

MacGillivray, Royce. *Restoration Historians and the English Civil War*. The Hague: Martinus Nijhoff, 1974.

McGuire, Mary Ann C. "The Cavalier Country-House Poem: Mutations on a Jonsonian Tradition." *Studies in English Literature* 19 (1979):93–108.

Manning, Brian. *The English People and the English Revolution, 1640–1649*. New York: Holmes & Meier Publishers, Inc., 1976.

———. "What Was the English Revolution?" *History Today* 34 (March 1984):18–21.

Margoliouth, H. M. "*The Poems of Richard Lovelace*. Edited by C. H. Wilkinson. 1925." *Review of English Studies* 3 (1927):89–95.

Martz, Louis L. *The Wit of Love*. South Bend, Ind.: University of Notre Dame Press, 1969.

Mathew, David. *The Social Structure in Caroline England*. Oxford: Clarendon Press, 1948.

Maus, Katharine Eisaman. *Ben Jonson and the Roman Frame of Mind*. Princeton: Princeton University Press, 1984.

Millar, Oliver. *Rubens: The Whitehall Ceiling*. London: Oxford University Press, 1958.

Miner, Earl. *The Cavalier Mode from Jonson to Cotton*. Princeton: Princeton University Press, 1971.

———. "Patterns of Stoicism in Thought and Prose Styles, 1530–1700." *PMLA* 85 (1970):1023–34.

Morrill, John. "The Church in England, 1642–9." In *Reactions to the English Civil War, 1642–1649,* edited by John Morrill, pp. 89–114. New York: St. Martin's Press, 1983.

———. "The Religious Context of the English Civil War." *Transactions of the Royal Historical Society,* 5th ser., 34 (1984):155–78.

————. *The Revolt of the Provinces*. London: Allen and Unwin, 1976.

————. "What Was the English Revolution?" *History Today* 34 (March 1984):11–16.

————, ed. *Reactions to the English Civil War, 1642–1649*. New York: St. Martin's Press, 1983.

Nethercot, Arthur H. *Abraham Cowley: The Muses's Hannibal*. Oxford: Clarendon Press, 1931.

Nevo, Ruth. *The Dial of Virtue: A Study of Poems on Affairs of State in the Seventeenth Century*. Princeton: Princeton University Press, 1963.

Norbrook, David. *Poetry and Politics in the English Renaissance*. London: Routledge & Kegan Paul, 1984.

O Hehir, Brendan. *Harmony from Discords: A Life of Sir John Denham*. Berkeley and Los Angeles: University of California Press, 1968.

O'Loughlin, Michael. *The Garlands of Repose: The Literary Celebration of Civic and Retired Leisure*. Chicago: The University of Chicago Press, 1978.

Oman, Carola. *Henrietta Maria*. London: Hodder and Stoughton Limited, 1936.

Orgel, Stephen. *The Illusion of Power: Political Theater in the English Renaissance*. Berkeley and Los Angeles: University of California Press, 1975.

————. *The Jonsonian Masque*. Cambridge: Harvard University Press, 1965.

Palme, Per. *Triumph of Peace*. Stockholm: Almqvist and Wiksell, 1956.

Palmer, Paulina. "Lovelace's Treatment of Some Marinesque Motifs." *Comparative Literature* 29 (1977):300–12.

————. "Thomas Carew's Reference to 'The Shepherd's Paradise.'" *Notes and Queries*, n.s., 13 (1966):303–4.

Palomo, Dolores. "The Halcyon Moment of Stillness in Royalist Poetry." *Huntington Library Quarterly* 44 (1981):205–21.

Parry, Graham. *The Golden Age Restor'd: The Culture of the Stuart Court, 1603–42*. New York: St. Martin's Press, 1981.

Parker, Michael P. "Carew's Politic Pastoral: Virgilian Pretexts in the 'Answer to Aurelian Townsend.'" *John Donne Journal* 1 (1982):101–16.

————. " 'To my friend *G. N.* from *Wrest*': Carew's Secular Masque." In *Classic and Cavalier*, edited by Claude J. Summers and Ted-Larry Pebworth, pp. 171–91. Pittsburgh, Pa.: University of Pittsburgh Press, 1982.

Partridge, Edward. "Jonson's *Epigrammes:* The Named and the Nameless." *Studies in the Literary Imagination* 6 (1973):153–98.

Patterson, Annabel M. *Marvell and the Civic Crown*. Princeton: Princeton University Press, 1978.

Pebworth, Ted-Larry. "Cowley's *Davideis* and the Exaltation of Friendship." In *The David Myth in Western Literature*, edited by Raymond-Jean Frontain and Jan Wojcik, pp. 96–104. West Lafayette, Ind.: Purdue University Press, 1980.

Peck, Linda Levy. " 'For a King not to be bountiful were a fault': Perspectives on Court Patronage in Early Stuart England." *Journal of British Studies* 25 (1986):31–61.

Pennington, Donald. "The War and the People." In *Reactions to the English Civil War, 1642–1649*, edited by John Morrill, pp. 115–35. New York: St. Martin's Press, 1983.

Peterson, Richard S. *Imitation and Praise in the Poems of Ben Jonson*. New Haven: Yale University Press, 1981.

Pickel, Margaret Barnard. *Charles I as Patron of Poetry and Drama*. London: Frederick Muller Ltd., 1936.

Rawlinson, David. "Cowley and the Current Status of Metaphysical Poetry." *Essays in Criticism* 13 (1963):323–40.

Richards, Judith. "'His Nowe Majestie' and the English Monarchy: The Kingship of Charles I before 1640." *Past and Present* 113 (1986):70–96.

Richardson, R. C. *The Debate on the English Revolution*. New York: St. Martin's Press, 1977.

Richmond, H. M. "A Note on Professor Holland's Psychoanalytic Approach to Lovelace." *Literature and Psychology* 14 (1964): 125–27.

Rivers, Isabel. *Classical and Christian Ideas in English Renaissance Poetry*. London: George Allen & Unwin, 1979.

———. *The Poetry of Conservatism, 1600–1745*. Cambridge, England: Rivers Press, 1973.

Roberts, Michael. *Gustavus Adolphus: A History of Sweden, 1611–1632*. 2 vols. London: Longmans, Green, 1953–58.

Røstvig, Maren-Sofie. *The Happy Man*. 2 vols. Oslo: Norwegian Universities Press, 1954, 1962.

Roy, Ian. "The English Civil War and English Society." In *War and Society*, edited by Brian Bond and Ian Roy, pp. 24–43. New York: Holmes and Meier Publishers, Inc., 1975.

Russell, Conrad. "The Nature of a Parliament in Early Stuart England." In *Before the English Civil War*, edited by Howard Tomlinson, pp. 123–50. New York: St. Martin's Press, 1984.

———. *Parliaments and English Politics, 1621–1629*. Oxford: Clarendon Press, 1979.

———. "Why Did Charles I Fight the Civil War?" *History Today* 34 (June 1984):31–34.

———, ed. *The Origins of the English Civil War*. New York: Barnes and Noble, 1973.

Sadler, Lynn Beach. "Lovelace's 'A Fly Caught in a Cobweb.'" *Literatur in Wissenschaft und Unterricht* 6 (1973):23–30.

———. *Thomas Carew*. Boston: Twayne Publishers, 1979.

Sams, Henry W. "Anti-Stoicism in Seventeenth- and Early Eighteenth-Century England." *Studies in Philology* 41 (1944):65–78.

Saunders, Jason Lewis. *Justus Lipsius: The Philosophy of Renaissance Stoicism*. New York: The Liberal Arts Press, 1955.

Schiffhorst, Gerald J., ed. *The Triumph of Patience*. Orlando, Fla.: University Presses of Florida, 1978.

Scoular, Kitty W. *Natural Magic: Studies in the Presentation of Nature in English Poetry from Spenser to Marvell*. Oxford: Clarendon Press, 1965.

Seaton, Ethel. *Literary Relations of England and Scandinavia in the Seventeenth Century*. Oxford: Clarendon Press, 1935.

Sharpe, Kevin. "Faction at the Early Stuart Court." *History Today* 33 (October, 1983):39–46.

———. "The Personal Rule of Charles I." In *Before the English Civil War*, edited by Howard Tomlinson, pp. 53–78. New York: St. Martin's Press, 1984.

Slack, Paul. "Books of Orders: The Making of English Social Policy, 1577–1631." *Transactions of the Royal Historical Society*, 5th ser., 30 (1980):1–22.

Smart, Ian Michael. "An Interim Period in Royalist Political Writing, 1647–48." *Durham University Journal,* n.s., 45 (1983):25–30.

———. "Francis Quarles: Professed Royalist and 'Puritanical Poet.'" *Durham University Journal,* n.s., 39 (1978):187–92.

Smuts, [R.] Malcolm. "The Political Failure of Stuart Cultural Patronage." In *Patronage in the Renaissance,* edited by Guy Fitch Lytle and Stephen Orgel, pp. 165–87. Princeton: Princeton University Press, 1981.

———. "The Puritan Followers of Henrietta Maria in the 1630s." *English Historical Review* 93 (1978):26–45.

Stone, Lawrence. *The Causes of the English Revolution, 1529–1642.* London: Routledge & Kegan Paul, 1972.

Strong, Roy. *Van Dyck: Charles I on Horseback.* New York: The Viking Press, Inc., 1972.

Stroup, Thomas B. "George Daniel: Cavalier Poet." *Renaissance Papers* 4 (1957):39–51.

Summers, Claude J. "Herrick's Political Counterplots." *Studies in English Literature* 25 (1985):165–82.

Taaffe, James G. *Abraham Cowley.* New York: Twayne Publishers, 1972.

Teunissen, John J. "The Book of Job and Stuart Politics." *University of Toronto Quarterly* 43 (1973):16–31.

Thomas, Peter W. "Charles I of England: The Tragedy of Absolutism." In *The Courts of Europe,* edited by A. G. Dickens, pp. 191–211. New York: McGraw-Hill, 1977.

———. *Sir John Berkenhead, 1617–1679.* Oxford: Clarendon Press, 1969.

———. "Two Cultures? Court and Country under Charles I." In *The Origins of the English Civil War,* edited by Conrad Russell, pp. 168–93. New York: Barnes and Noble, 1973.

Thomason, T. Katharine. "The Stoic Ground of Marvell's 'Garden.'" *Texas Studies in Literature and Language* 24 (1982):222–41.

Thorn-Drury, G. "Response to 'Merry Thoughts in a Sad Place.'" *Notes and Queries,* 10th ser., 1 (1904):250.

Tomlinson, Howard. "The Causes of War: A Historiographical Survey." In *Before the English Civil War,* edited by Howard Tomlinson, pp. 7–26. New York: St. Martin's Press, 1984.

———, ed. *Before the English Civil War.* New York: St. Martin's Press, 1984.

Trevor-Roper, H. R. *Archbishop Laud, 1573–1645.* Hamden, Ct.: Archon Books, 1962.

———. "The General Crisis of the Seventeenth Century." In *Religion, The Reformation and Social Change,* pp. 46–89. London: Macmillan, 1972.

Trotter, David. *The Poetry of Abraham Cowley.* Totowa, N.J.: Rowman and Littlefield, 1979.

Turner, James. *The Politics of Landscape: Rural Scenery and Society in English Poetry, 1630–1660.* Cambridge: Harvard University Press, 1979.

Underdown, David. *Pride's Purge: Politics in the Puritan Revolution.* Oxford: Clarendon Press, 1971.

———. *Revel, Riot, and Rebellion: Popular Politics and Culture in England, 1603–1660.* Oxford: Clarendon Press, 1985.

————. *Royalist Conspiracy in England, 1649–1660.* New Haven: Yale University Press, 1960.

————. "What Was the English Revolution?" *History Today* 34 (March 1984):22–25.

Veall, Donald. *The Popular Movement for Law Reform, 1640–1660.* Oxford: Clarendon Press, 1970.

Veevers, Erica. "A Masque Fragment by Aurelian Townshend." *Notes and Queries,* n.s., 12 (1965):343–45.

Verbeke, Gerard. *The Presence of Stoicism in Medieval Thought.* Washington, D. C.: The Catholic University of America Press, 1983.

Wadsworth, Randolph L., Jr. "Comment and Rebuttal." *College English* 31 (1970):637–40.

————. "On 'The Snayl' by Richard Lovelace." *Modern Language Review* 65 (1970):750–60.

Waite, Arthur E. "Lovelace." *The Gentleman's Magazine* 257 (1884):459–77.

Wallace, John M. "*Coopers Hill:* The Manifesto of Parliamentary Royalism, 1641." *ELH* 41 (1974):494–540.

————. *Destiny His Choice: The Loyalism of Andrew Marvell.* Cambridge: Cambridge University Press, 1968.

Walpole, Horace. *Anecdotes of Painting in England.* London: A. Murray, 1872.

Waterhouse, Ellis. *Painting in Great Britain, 1530–1790.* London: Penguin Books, 1953.

Wedgwood, C. V. "Cavalier Poetry and Cavalier Politics." In *Velvet Studies,* pp. 15–31. London: Jonathan Cape, 1946.

————. "The Last Masque." In *Truth and Opinion: Historical Essays,* pp. 139–56. New York: Macmillan, 1960.

————. *Oliver Cromwell and the Elizabethan Inheritance.* London: Jonathan Cape, 1970.

————. *Poetry and Politics under the Stuarts.* Cambridge: Cambridge University Press, 1960.

Weidhorn, Manfred. *Richard Lovelace.* New York: Twayne Publishers, 1970.

Whinney, Margaret, and Oliver Millar. *English Art, 1625–1714.* Oxford: Clarendon Press, 1957.

Withington, Eleanor. "The 'Fugitive Poetry' of Mildmay Fane." *Harvard Library Bulletin* 9 (1955):61–78.

————. "Mildmay Fane's Political Satire." *Harvard Library Bulletin* 11 (1957):40–64.

Woolrych, Austin. "Court, Country and City Revisited." *History* 65 (1980):236–45.

Wortham, C. J. "Richard Lovelace's 'To Lucasta, Going to the Warres': Which Wars?" *Notes and Queries,* n.s., 26 (1979):430–31.

Wright, Herbert G. "The Theme of Solitude and Retirement in Seventeenth Century Literature." *Études Anglaises* 7 (1954):22–35.

Wrightson, Keith. *English Society, 1580–1680.* New Brunswick, N.J.: Rutgers University Press, 1982.

Wykes, David. "Ben Jonson's 'Chast Booke'—The *Epigrammes.*" *Renaissance and Modern Studies* 13 (1969):76–87.

Zagorin, Perez. *The Court and the Country: The Beginning of the English Revolution.* New York: Atheneum, 1970.

# Index

Abraham, 168, 169
Adams, Simon, 189n.17
Aelian, 112, 121
Aeneas, 125, 168, 179
Aesop, 105, 107, 112, 119
Allen, Don Cameron, 200nn. 28, 32, and 33
Altieri, Joanne, 33, 190n.28, 191n.38, 192n.44, 193n.55
Anacreon, 105, 106, 107, 128, 136–37
Anne, Princess, 50
Anne of Denmark, 26–27
Anselment, Raymond A., 188n.3, 194n.2, 196n.25
Arminius, Jacobus, 57
Ashford, Mrs., 63
Astraea, 66, 77, 102, 103
Aubrey, John, 111, 123
Aubrey, Richard, 152
Aylmer, G. E., 25, 188n.41, 188–89n.7, 189n.11, 205n.38, 206n.16

Bacon, Francis, 32–33
Balcarres, Alexander Lindsay, earl of, 178
Barish, Jonas, 52
Barksdale, Clement, 167
Bayning, Paul, 64
Beaumont, Francis, 60, 70
Behn, Aphra, 209n.49
Berger, Harry, Jr., 186n.18
Berkenhead, John, 145
Bible: Genesis, 162; 1 Samuel, 166, 167, 168–69, 170–71, 172; 2 Samuel, 167; Kings, 168; Chronicles, 168; Proverbs, 112; Ecclesiastes, 134, 139, 141, 142, 153, 154; Ecclesiasticus, 72–73, 95
Bishops' Wars, 19, 39, 44, 51, 65, 72, 76, 157
Blount, Thomas, 209n.52

Boethius, 13, 14, 16, 19, 70, 134; *The Consolation of Philosophy,* 13, 72
Bold, Henry, 135, 152, 204n.20
Booth, George, 145
Bourne, Nicholas, 28
Braden, Gordon, 14, 186nn. 15 and 26
Brome, Alexander, 17, 19, 20, 84, 127–54, 155, 156, 160, 165, 173, 177, 184, 202nn. 2, 4, and 5; and anacreontics, 128, 136–37; and detachment, 134, 138–39, 153; and indifference, 129, 130, 137–38, 140–42, 143, 149, 149–51, 154; and sequestration, 137, 142–43; and steadfast service, 150–54; and stoic self-sufficiency, 138–42, 147, 154. Works: "The Advice," 141, 142; "Advice to *Caelia,*" 129, 203n.10; "The Answer," 128; "The Antipolititian," 138; "The Cavalier," 148; "The Cheerful heart," 139; "The Clown," 133; "The Club," 135; "Come let us be merry," 137; "The Commoners," 133; "The Companion," 136; "Content. Out of *Anacreon,*" 136; "The Contrary," 203n.10; *"Copernicus,"* 136; "The Counsel," 203n.10; "The Cure of Care," 136; "An Essay of the Contempt of Greatnesse," 134, 138, 153; "For General *Monk,*" 146; "For the Generalls entertainment," 146; "A funeral Elegy on Mr. *Aubrey,*" 152; "The Good-fellow," 135–36; "The Holy Pedler," 131; "The Indifferent," 129, 203n.10; "The Independants resolve," 132; "The Lamentation," 204n.26; "The Leveller," 138–39, 140; "The Levellers rant," 131; "The Libertine," 203n.10; "Loves Anarchy," 129; "Mirth. Out of *Anacreon,*" 136–37; "The Murmurer," 143; "A New Bal-

lad," 128, 148–49; "The New-Courtier," 136; "The New Gentry," 140, 143; "The New Knight Errant," 144; "The New Mountebanck," 131; "An Ode. Written in 1643," 132; "On the Kings death," 141; "On the loss of a Garrison," 141; "On . . . *The Passionate lovers*," 152; "On Sir G. B. his defeat," 145; "On the death of King CHARLES," 151; "The Painters entertainment," 135; "A paraphrase upon the first Chap. of *Ecclesiastes*," 134, 154; "Plain Dealing," 203n.10; "The Polititian," 134, 138, 138–39; "The Prodigal," 134; "The Reformation," 143, 144; "The Riddle," 132, 133; "The Royalist," 129–30, 134, 136; "The Royalists Answer," 138–39; "The safe Estate," 140; "The Safety," 139–40; "The Saints Encouragement," 130–31, 132; "Satisfaction," 140, 142; "The Satyr of Money," 144; "A Satyre on the Rebellion," 133; "The *Scots* Curanto," 131; "A Serious Ballade," 132; "A speech made to the Lord General *Monck*," 146–47; "Though *Oxford* be yielded," 203n.9; "To a coy Lady," 203n.10; "To C. C. Esquire," 128; "To Colonel *Lovelace*," 128; "To C. S. Esquire," 149–50, 150–51; "To his Friend C. S. Esquire," 154; "To his Friend T. S.," 150; "To his ingenious *FRIEND* Mr. *Henry Bold*," 152; "To his ingenuous Friend Mr. IZAAK WALTON," 152–53; "To his Mistres affrighted in the wars," 129, 203n.9; "To his Mistress," 195; "To his reverend Friend Dr. S.," 153; "To the Kings most Sacred Majesty," 147–48; "To the Meritoriously Honorable Lord Chiefe Justice," 151; "To the Reader," 130; "The Trouper," 137; "Upon the Cavaleers departing out of *London*," 142; "Upon the Kings imprisonment," 140. *See also* Charles I; Wine and mirth

Brome, Richard, 127, 152

Brooks, J. L., 202n.2

Browne, Thomas, 70, 84, 88

Bruno, Giordino, 34

Brutus, 114, 174–76, 208n.38

Buckingham, George Villiers, first duke of, 24

Buckingham, George Villiers, second duke of, 178

Bush, Douglas, 198n.2

Butler, Martin, 188n.41

Butter, Nathanial, 28

*Calendar of State Papers . . .* , *Venice*, 22, 24, 28, 37

Camden, William, 53

Camerarius, Joachim, 106–7, 107, 116, 117, 117–18, 118, 119, 121

Carew, Thomas, 18–19, 28–36, 41–44, 48, 73, 74, 75, 103, 148. Works: *Coelum Britannicum*, 34–36, 43, 44, 74; "An Elegie upon . . . Iohn Donne," 29, 32; "In answer of . . . *Aurelian Townsend*," 28–34, 43, 44, 74, 191n.38, 192nn. 44 and 48, 192–93n.54; "A New-yeares gift. To the King," 32; "To Ben. Iohnson," 34; "To my friend *G. N.* from *Wrest*," 41–43, 44, 108, 194n.72; "To my worthy Friend, M. *D'avenant*," 32; "To the Queene," 30. *See also* Halcyon era

Carlisle, Lucy Hay, countess of, 59–60, 196n.25

Cartwright, William, 17, 19, 45, 46–68, 69, 73, 75, 110, 128, 152, 154, 155, 157, 164, 165, 178, 184, 194n.1, 195nn. 7 and 20, 198n.2; elegies of, 62–66; and inner nobility, 46, 49, 58–59, 62, 63–64; his links with Jonson, 47, 48, 49, 53, 54, 56, 59, 60, 62, 64, 67; and literary criticism, 60–62; and self-sufficient and gathered self, 46, 51–52, 55–56, 57, 59, 62–67; and steadfast service, 52–53, 55–58, 60; and university commemorative verse, 46–48. Works: "An Epitaph on Mr. *Poultney*," 64; "In the memory of . . . *Beniamin Iohnson*," 60, 61–62; "A New-years Gift," 58; "A New-years-gift to a Noble Lord. 1640," 57–58; "A New-years-gift to *Brian* Lord Bishop of *Sarum*," 56–57; "On Mrs *Abigall Long*," 63; "On the Birth of the Duke of *York*," 48–50; "On the Birth of the King's fourth Child. 1635," 50; "On the Death of the most vertuous Gentlewoman, Mrs *Ashford*," 63; "On the Death of . . . Lord Viscount *Bayning*," 64; "On the Lady *Newburgh,* 62; "On the *Queens* Return from the Low Countries," 66–67; "A Panegyrick to the most Noble *Lucy* Countesse of *Carlisle,*" 59–60; "To Dr *Duppa*," 53–54; "To Mrs *Duppa,*" 55–56; "To My Honovr'd Friend Mr. Thomas Killigrew," 60–61; "To *Philip,* Earl of Pembroke," 60; "To the King, On His Majesties Return from *Scotland,*" 47–48; "To the King, on the Birth of the Princess *Anne,*" 50–51; "To the Memory of . . . *Henry Spelman,*" 64; "To the Queen after her dangerous Delivery. 1638," 51; "To the Right Reverend Father in God, *Brian,* Lord Bishop of *Chichester,*" 54–55; "A Translation of *Hugo Grotius's* Elegy on Arminius," 57; "Vpon the Birth of the Kings sixth Child. 1640," 51–52; "Vpon the Death of . . . Lord *Stafford,*" 63–64; "Vpon the death of . . . Sir *Bevill Grenvill,*" 64–66; "Vpon the Dramatick Poems of Mr John Fletcher, 61. *See also* Charles I; Halcyon era; Virgilian irony

Catherine, Princess, 51

Cavendish, William, 162–63

Charles, Prince (later Charles II), 27, 45, 46, 53–54, 54–55, 94, 108–9, 147–48, 167, 179, 180, 183–84, 208n.47

Charles I., 17, 18, 19, 21–45, 54, 69, 97, 144, 148, 187n.34, 189nn. 10, 13, and 19, 190nn. 26, 28, and 30, 191n.34, 193nn. 44 and 50, 193n.62, 197nn. 7 and 12, 198n.18, 200n.33; celebrated in masques, 25–28, 34–36, 38–39, 40–41, 162; his death, 92–93, 98, 110, 119, 141, 151, 169, 199n.5, 200n.32, 201n.38; and Gustavus Adolphus, 28; and patient fortitude, 18–19, 41, 44, 51, 52, 55, 92–93, 108–9, 125, 140, 151. Works about: by Brome, 129, 131, 132, 136, 140, 141, 151; by Cartwright, 46–47, 47–49, 49–53, 58; by Cowley, 156–47, 157–58, 160–65, 173, 175, 179, 182, 183; by Daniel, 73–77, 84–87, 88–89, 90–93; *Eikon Basilike,* 21, 22, 23, 41, 93, 151; by Lovelace, 100–102, 102, 104, 108–9, 114, 116, 117,

119, 120, 124. *See also* Halcyon era

Charlton, John, 193n.57

Chaucer, Geoffrey, 60, 70

Christ, 41, 166, 168, 172, 178

Cicero, 14, 15, 158–59, 176, 206n.5; *De Officiis,* 14, 15, 64, 110, 160

Clarendon, Edward Hyde, first earl of, 74, 90, 100, 148, 175; *History of the Rebellion,* 22, 23; *The Life,* 22, 23, 33, 125. *See also* Virgilian irony

Clayton, Thomas, 100, 197n.5, 201nn. 38 and 44, 202n.62

Cleveland, John, 86, 198nn. 18 and 21, 206n.16

Cliffe, John T., 197n.6

Coningsby, Harry, 13, 16, 70, 185n.1

Coningsby, Thomas, 13, 16, 70, 185n.1

Cook, Thomas, 208n.39

Cotton, Cassandra, 109

Cotton, Charles (the elder), 105–7

Cotton, Charles (the younger), 98, 123, 128, 149, 204n.20

Cousins, A. D., 186n.28

Cowley, Abraham, 17, 19, 23, 105, 155–84, 187n.39, 206nn. 2 and 4, 207n.21, 208n.39; and Cromwell, 165, 169, 175, 182, 207n.32, 208n.38; Falkland as ideal of, 157, 159, 164, 172, 180; and retirement, 155, 157, 181, 206n.3; and stoic self-sufficiency and patient fortitude, 156, 157, 158–60, 165, 167, 168–69, 170, 171–72, 174–77, 178, 179, 181, 183–84; and tyranny, 160, 162, 169–70, 170, 170–71, 175, 176, 182. Works: "Brutus," 173, 174–77, 208n.38; *The Civil War,* 160–65, 166, 171–72, 180; *The Davideis,* 165–72, 173, 174, 176, 180, 207nn. 21 and 32; "Destinie," 173–74, 177; *A Discourse By way of Vision,* 170, 176, 208n.47; "The Extasie," 177, 178; "The Grashopper," 105; "In imitation of *Martials* Epigram," 157; "Life," 177, 178; "Life and Fame," 177–78; *Miscellanies,* 157–60, 165; "The Motto," 157; "Ode V," 156; "Of Agriculture," 182; "Of My self," 155, 156; "On his Majesties returne out of *Scotland,*" 156–58; "On the Death of Mr. *Crashaw,*" 165, 207n.21; "On the Death of Mr. *Jordan,*" 157, 159; "On

the Death of Mrs. *Katherine Philips*," 178; "On the Death of Sir *Henry Wootton*," 157; "On the praise of Poetry," 156; "On the Queens Repairing *Somerset* House," 180; "On the uncertainty of Fortune," 156; *Pindarique Odes,* 172–78; "The Plagues of *Egypt*," 173; *Plantarum,* 180, 181–84, 209 nn. 49 and 53, 209–10 n.54; *Poetical Blossoms,* 156; "Preface of the Author," 19, 160–61, 165, 166, 174, 208 n.39; *The Puritan and the Papist,* 160, 162, 197 n.12, 206 n.16; *Several Discourses by way of Essays,* 155, 156, 181, 182; *Sylva,* 156–57, 157, 159, 181; "The 34. Chapter of the Prophet *Isaiah*," 173; "To Dr. *Scarborough*," 173, 177; "To Mr. *Hobs*," 174, 177; "To Sir *William Davenant*," 165, 207 n.21; "To the Bishop of *Lincoln*," 158–60; "To the Duke of *Buckingham*," 178; "To the Lord Falkland," 157; "To the New Year," 177, 178; "To the *Royal Society*," 180; "*Upon* Dr. *Harvey*," 178; "Upon His Majesties Restoration and Return," 178–80, 205 n.35; "Upon the Death of the Earl of *Balcarres*," 178; "Upon the shortnesse of Mans life," 156; *Verses Lately Written upon Several Occasions,* 178–80; "A Vote," 156. *See also* Charles I; Halcyon era; Virgilian irony
Crashaw, Richard, 165, 207 n.21
Creed, William, 167
Crompton, Hugh, 135, 204 n.20
Cromwell, Oliver, 79, 114, 144, 146, 155, 192 n.46, 198 n.16. *See also* Cowley, Abraham
Cromwell, Richard, 144, 150

Dahl, Folke, 191 n.34
Daniel, George, 17, 19, 20, 69–96, 97, 98, 103, 110, 122, 128, 134, 141, 154, 156, 163, 165, 170, 178, 180, 184, 197 n.8; and literary criticism, 70–72, 87–88; and rural solitude and withdrawal, 69–70, 70–72, 77–78, 87; and stoic contemplation, 72, 73, 78, 84, 95–96; and solitary recreation, 77, 78–82, 87; and stoic self-containment, 73, 78, 81, 82, 92, 95–96. Works: "An Addresse," 73; "After a

storme, going a hawking," 77; "The Author," 87; "Crastini Animarum," 93–94; Ecclesiasticus, 72–73, 95; "An Epode," 70–71; "An Essay; Endevouring to ennoble our English Poesie," 70; "Freedome," 77–78; "The Genius of this Great and glorious Ile," 73–75; "Idyllia," 94–96; "An Ode Upon . . . *The Temple*," 70, 87–88; "A Pastorall Ode," 70; "Royall Expedition against the Scotts," 76; *Several Ecloges,* 71–72, 83–86, 95: "An Ecloge Spoken by *Amintas* and *Strephon*," 71–72; "An Ecloge Spoken by *Damon* and *Amintas*," 84–85; "An Ecloge Spoken by *Halon* and *Eudoemon*," 84; "An Ecloge Spoken by *Hilas* and *Strephon*," 85–86, 90; "An Ecloge Spoken by *Maelibeus* and *Dorilus*," 83–84; *Scattered Fancies,* 78–83: "Ode III," 81; "Ode V," 80; "Ode VII," 79, 81; "Ode VIII," 81; "Ode IX," 81; "Ode XI," 80; "Ode XXII," 81–82; "Ode XXIII," 78, 80; "Ode XXXII," 79–80; "Ode XXXIII," 78; Ode XXXIV," 83; "Ode XXXVI," 82; "Ode XXXIX," 82; "Ode LVII," 81; "Ode XLVIII," 78–79; "A Strange Maye," 76–77; *Trinarchodia,* 88–94, 95; "Upon . . . *Religio Medici*," 70, 88; "Vanitie," 77; *Vervicensis,* 75–76; "A Vindication of Poesie," 70; "Vpon a Reviewe of Virgil, translated by Mr. Ogilby," 70, 88; "When the Cloud of Calamitie," 77. *See also* Charles I; Halcyon era; Virgilian irony; Wine and mirth
Daniel, Samuel, 88
Davenant, William, 32, 165, 207 n.21. Works: *Britannia Triumphans,* 38; "Epitaph. On Mr. John Sturmy," 196 n.30; *Gondibert,* 165; *Luminalia,* 38–39; *Salmacida Spolia,* 40–41, 42, 43, 52, 194 n.72
David, 79, 165–72, 176, 178, 180, 183
Davies, John, 22, 23
D'Ewes, Simonds, 28, 32
Diogenes Laertius, 14
Dobson, William, 108
Donne, John, 14, 29, 32, 46, 63, 70, 99, 194 n.1
Drummond, William, 146

Drury, Elizabeth, 63
Dubinski, Roman R., 202 nn. 2 and 4, 203 nn. 10 and 12
Dunlap, Rhodes, 192 n.48
Duppa, Brian, 47, 53, 53–57, 59
Du Vair, Guillaume, 15, 186 n.15; *The Moral Philosophy of the Stoics,* 14, 15, 201 n.54

Ebsworth, J. Woodfall, 204 n.20
Elizabeth, Princess, 53
Elizabeth I, 27, 33, 73, 74, 75
Elizabeth of Bohemia, 24, 27, 37
Elton, G. R., 188 n.41
Elyot, Thomas, 186 n.15
Epictetus, 14
Epicurean, 73, 105, 108, 200 n.34
Erasmus, 49, 186 n.15
Erskine-Hill, Howard, 34
Evans, G. Blakemore, 194 n.1
Evans, Willa McClung, 199 n.5, 201 n.44

Falkland, Lucius Cary, Viscount, 70, 125. *See also* Cowley, Abraham
Farley, Robert, 120
Felltham, Owen, 205 n.39
Firth, C. H., 204 n.27
Flatman, Thomas, 204 n.20
Fletcher, Anthony, 16, 18
Fletcher, John, 60, 61, 62, 70
Fletcher, Robert, 203–4 n.16
Forbes, Walter, 37
Foster, Robert, 151
*Foure Ages of England, The,* 18, 187 n.39
Frank, Joseph, 191 n.32, 203 n.12, 204 n.19
Franz, Wolfgang, 115, 122
Frederick V, 24, 28, 37
Fuller, Isaac, 108

Garrison, James D., 195 n.7
Gauden, John, 44–45
George, Saint, 25, 36, 41, 49, 115, 147, 178
Gill, Alexander, 28
Glapthorne, Henry, 45
Goring, George, 97, 110
Gouge, William, 28
Granger, Thomas, 139
Greene, Thomas M., 195 n.20
Grenville, Sir Bevil, 64–66, 67, 164

Grey, Henry de, 42
Grierson, Herbert, 198 n.2
Grosart, Alexander, 197 n.6
Grotius, Hugo, 57
Guild, William, 167
Gustavus Adolphus, 28–34, 37, 41, 191 nn. 32 and 34, 192 nn. 44 and 46. *See also* Charles I

Habington, William, 197 n.8
Halcyon era, 18–19, 21–28, 37–38, 39–40, 44–45, 50, 189 nn. 11 and 13; and Carew, 29, 32, 33–34, 35; and Cartwright, 48, 58; and Charles I, 21, 33; and Cowley, 156, 161, 180, 182, 183–84; and Daniel, 73–75, 76–77, 81, 83, 84–85; and Lovelace, 103–4
Hall, John, 123
Hall, Joseph, 201 n.54; *Heaven vpon Earth,* 14; *Characters of Vertves and Vices,* 13–14, 184
Hampden, John, 162
Hardacre, Paul H., 204 nn. 19 and 27
Harvey, William, 178
Haselrig, Arthur, 150
Hearne, Thomas, 151
Hearnshaw, F. J. C., 202 n.5
Heath, Robert, 203 n.16
Henrietta Maria, 25–26, 27, 28, 30, 33, 35, 36, 38, 40–41, 45, 47, 47–48, 50, 51, 51–52, 53, 66–67, 75, 102, 108, 114, 155, 162, 179, 180, 182, 183–84, 190 nn. 26 and 28
Henry, Prince, 51–52
Henry IV, 88, 91–93
Henry V, 75, 88, 93–94
Henry VI, 76, 93
Henry VIII, 73, 197 n.12
Henry IV of France, 49
Herbert, George, 70, 88
Herrick, Robert, 97
Heywood, Thomas, 39–40
Hierocles, 123
Hill, Christopher, 188 n.44
Hinman, Robert B., 181, 206 n.2, 208 n.44
Hirst, Derek, 128, 187–88 n.41, 189 n.10, 197 n.7
Hobbes, Thomas, 138, 154, 175, 177, 205 n.28
Holland, Henry Rich, earl of, 59
Holles, Denzil, 160

Holmes, Clive, 197n.7

Homer, 174, 179

Horace, 16, 34, 55, 56, 61, 69, 70, 72, 77, 88, 127, 155, 156, 178, 181, 186n.26, 197n.8. Works: "Epistle II. 2," 87, 198n. 19; "Ode II. 10," 123–24; "Ode IV. 9," 75; "Satire II. 7," 56, 195n.19

Horatius, 51

*Horti Carolini Rosa Altera,* 51

Howell, James, 32, 203n.15

Hutchinson, Lucy, 22

Isaac, 168, 172

Isaiah, 172–73, 173

Jackson, Arthur, 141

James, Prince (later James II), 46, 48–50, 108–9

James I, 23–24, 25, 26–27, 33, 37

Jeremiah, 204n.26

Jermin, Michael, 139

Jermyn, Henry, Lord, 155, 163, 164, 165

Jesus or Ben-Sira, 72

Job, 107, 183, 209n.52

John I, 161

Johnson, Samuel, 170

Jonathan, 167, 171–72, 176, 180

Jones, George Fenwick, 199n.10

Jones, Inigo, 28, 34, 36, 42, 52

Jonson, Benjamin, 14, 19, 34, 45, 46, 47, 48, 49, 53, 55, 56, 60, 61–62, 62, 68, 70, 71, 86, 125–26, 174, 186n.18, 194n.1, 195n.11, 195–96n.20, 196n.26, 197n.8. Works: *Chloridia,* 25–26, 28, 48; *Love's Triumph through Callipolis,* 25–26, 28, 48; "A New-yeares-Gift sung to King *Charles,*" 54; "Ode to Himself," 62; "A Panegyre, on the Happy Entrance of James," 48; *Timber: or, Discoveries,* 53, 70; "To Penshurst," 64; "To Sir Iohn Radcliffe," 56; "To Sir Robert Wroth," 77; "To Sir Thomas Roe," 56; "To Sir William Iephson," 49; "To William Roe," 125. *See also* Cartwright, William

*Jonsonus Virbius,* 60, 61

Jordan, John, 157, 159

Jordan, Thomas, 135, 205nn. 34 and 36

Jose, Nicholas, 155, 206n.3, 208nn. 33, 38, and 42

Josselin, Ralph, 198n.18

Kenyon, J. P., 22, 188n.41

Keough, James G., 208nn. 38 and 42

Kermode, Frank, 207n.21

Killigrew, Thomas, 60, 62

King, Bruce, 115, 199n.4, 200n.33

Kirk, Rudolph, 185nn. 12 and 13

Knights, L. C., 29

Kogan, Stephen, 190n.28, 191n.38, 193n.55

Korshin, Paul J., 208n.38

Kynaston, Francis, 60

Lambert, John, 150

Langbaine, Gerard, 127

Langley, T. R., 208nn. 38, 42, and 44

Laud, William, 158

Lely, Peter, 108, 119, 123

Lenton, Francis, 98

L'Estrange, Hamon, 22

L'Estrange, Roger, 104

Lipsius, Justus, 13, 15, 16, 70, 134, 186n.15, 201n.54, 208n.44; *Two Bookes Of Constancie,* 13, 14, 15, 19, 78, 95–96, 176–77, 186n.15

Livy, 51

Lloyd, David, 22, 23, 47, 189n.13

Lockey, Thomas, 47

Lodge, Thomas, 14

Logan, George M., 185n.11, 186n.18

Long, Abigail, 63

Lovelace, Dudley Posthumous, 111

Lovelace, Francis, 110, 123–25

Lovelace, Richard, 17, 19, 77, 78, 84, 97–126, 127, 128, 129–30, 135, 136, 140, 147, 152, 154, 156, 165, 173, 183, 184, 198n.2, 199nn. 8 and 10; and anacreontics, 105–6; Lucasta as symbol in, 19, 99, 101–2, 103–4, 112, 113; and retirement, 103–4, 107–8; and self-containment and stoic tranquillity, 98, 99, 104–5, 106–7, 108–11, 115–17, 123–25, 126; and victory in defeat, 117–21. Works: "Advice to my best Brother. Coll: *Francis Lovelace,*" 123–25; "*Amyntor* from beyond the Sea," 101, 102; "Amyntor's Grove," 107–108,

200 n.34; "Another," 116–17; "The Ant," 112–13, 115, 117, 119; "Aramantha," 98, 102–3, 124; "Calling *Lucasta* from her Retirement," 98, 102; "An Elegy. On the Death of Mrs. *Cassandra Cotton*," 109–10; "The Falcon," 117–19, 121; "A Fly caught in a Cobweb," 119–21; "The Grasshopper," 104, 105–7, 112, 113, 138, 200 nn. 32 and 33; "A Guiltlesse Lady imprisoned," 109; "Her Reserved looks," 111; "The Lady *A. L.*," 109; "A Lady with a Falcon on her fist," 117; "A loose Saraband," 113–14, 115, 119, 128, 130; *Lucasta*, 97, 98–110, 112, 199 n.5, 200 n.32; "Lucasta laughing," 111–12; *Lucasta Posthume*, 98, 110–26; "*Lucasta*, taking the waters at Tunbridge," 100; "*Lucasta* Weeping," 100; "*Lucasta's Fanne*," 100; "*Lucasta's* World," 100; "A Mock Charon," 125; "A Mock-Song," 114–15, 125, 128, 201 n.44; "Night. To *Lucasta*," 112; "On *Sanazar's* being honoured," 125–26; "Peinture," 123; "The Rose," 99; "The Snayl," 115–16, 117, 119; "The *Toad* and *Spyder*," 121–23; "*To Althea*, From Prison," 104–5, 129; "To Generall *Goring*," 110; "To his Deare Brother Colonel *F. L.*," 110; "To *Lucasta*," 114; "*To Lucasta*. From Prison," 100–102; "*To Lucasta*, Going beyond the Seas," 98, 99, 124; "*To Lucasta*, Going to the Warres," 98, 99; "*To Lucasta*. Ode Lyrick," 99; "To my Dear Friend Mr. *E. R.*," 123; "To my Worthy Friend Mr. *Peter Lilly*," 108–9, 119; "To the Genius of Mr. *John Hall*," 123; "The *Triumphs* of PHILAMORE and AMORET," 123. *See also* Charles I; Halcyon era; Virgilian irony
Lovelace, William, 110
Lucian, 80, 134, 138, 139, 142, 153
Lucretius, 107
Luther, Martin, 139, 154

MacGillivray, Royce, 209 n.50
McGuire, Mary Ann C., 200 n.34
Manilius, 174, 177–78
Marbeck, John, 167

Marcus Aurelius, 14, 73
Margoliouth, H. M., 199 n.5, 200 n.34
Martial, 121, 155, 157, 181
Martz, Louis L., 191 n.38, 192 n.48
Marvell, Andrew, 20, 45, 97, 119
Matthew, Toby, 31
Maus, Katharine Eisaman, 186 n.18, 195 n.11
May, Tom, 22
Mayne, Jasper, 47, 48
Menander, 195 n.7
Millar, Oliver, 29
Milton, John, 20, 45, 167, 206 n.16
Miner, Earl, 16, 186 n.28, 200 n.33
Moab, 169–70
Moffett, Thomas, 106
Monck, George, 145–47, 180
Monro, Robert, 28
Montague, Walter, 32, 192 n.48
Morrill, John, 187 n.34, 187–88 n.41, 189 n.10
Moseley, Humphrey, 47, 59, 60, 152, 194 n.1
Moses, 28, 169
Mytens, Daniel, 108

Napier, Robert, 128
Nethercot, Arthur H., 158, 160, 206 n.16, 207 nn. 21 and 32, 208 n.38
Nevo, Ruth, 155, 206 n.3, 208 n.38
Newburgh, Lady, 63
Newcourt, Richard, 128
North, Dudley, 29

Ogilby, John, 70, 88, 119–20, 122, 124
O Hehir, Brendan, 197 n.12
Oldis, Valentine, 128
O'Loughlin, Michael, 186 n.26
Orgel, Stephen, 190 n.30
Ormonde, James Butler, earl of, 208 n.41
Orpheus, 87
Osbaldeston, Lambert, 158
Ovid, 116, 122

Palmer, Paulina, 192 n.48, 199 n.4
Parker, Michael P., 191 n.38, 192–93 n.54, 194 n.72
Parry, Graham, 21
Peacham, Henry, 119, 121, 125
Pebworth, Ted-Larry, 207 n.21
Pembroke, Philip, earl of, 60

Pennington, Donald, 204 n.22
Persius, 116
Peterson, Richard S., 195 n.20
Philips, Katherine, 178
Phillip IV of Spain, 24
Phillips, Edward, 127
Philostratus, 106
Pinchbacke, John, 98
Pindar, 172–73
Pliny, 78, 112, 121
Plutarch, 14
Porter, Endymion, 108, 200 n.34
Poultney, Mr., 64
Pride, Thomas, 144–45
Pritchard, Allan, 161, 200 n.38
Puttenham, George, 48–49
Pym, John, 79, 160

Quarles, Francis, 29, 83, 134, 192 n.44, 198 n.17
Quintilian, 206 n.5

Randolph, Thomas, 196 n.20, 197 n.8
Revett, Eldred, 111, 123
Rhymer, Thomas, 166–67
Richard II, 88, 89–93, 161
Richards, Judith, 192 n.50
Rivers, Isabel, 185 n.13, 187 n.28
Roberts, Michael, 192 n.46
Røstvig, Maren-Sofie, 16, 186 n.28, 197 n.8
Rubens, Peter Paul, 24–25, 26; Works: Banqueting House ceiling, 36–37, 52, 193 n.57; *The Horrors of War,* 38; *Landscape with St. George and the Dragon,* 36; *War and Peace,* 25
Russell, Conrad, 16, 23, 188 n.41
Russell, John, 29

Sadler, Lynn Beach, 191 n.38, 202 n.62
Saltmarsh, John, 29
Samuel, 169, 170, 207 n.32
Sanazar (Jacobus Sannazarius), 125
Sanderson, William, 22
Sandys, George, 125
Sarbiewski, Casimire Mathias, 88
Satan, 162, 163, 166, 167
Saul, 165–72, 183
Saunders, Jason Lewis, 185 n.13
Scarborough, Charles, 177
Schiffhorst, Gerald J., 186 n.15
Schloer, Frederick, 28

Scoular, Kitty, W., 201 n.57
Seaton, Ethel, 29
Seneca, 14, 15, 73, 118. Works: "Epistle XCII. On the Happy Life," 104, 178; "Epistle CXXIV. On the True Good," 108; "On Leisure," 15, 44, 69–70; "On Providence," 98, 159; "On the Happy Life," 13, 70, 105, 109, 184; "On Tranquillity of Mind," 15, 69, 73, 98, 104, 116; "To Helvia His Mother," 116–17
Shakespeare, William, 14, 61, 70, 88
Sharpe, Kevin, 188 n.41
Shirley, James, 34, 152
Shute, Josias, 152
Sidney, Philip, 70, 71
Slack, Paul, 25
*Solis Britannici Perigaevm,* 47
Solon, 15
Sparke, Edward, 153
Spelman, Henry, 64
Spenser, Edmund, 70, 71, 87, 155
Sprat, Thomas, 175, 207 n.21, 208 n.39
Sprigg, Joshua, 22
Stafford, Henry, Lord, 63–64, 64
Stanley, Thomas, 105–6, 136–37, 152
Steynings, Charles, 149, 150, 154
Stokes, William, 60
Strafford, Thomas Wentworth, earl of, 85
Strong, Roy, 190 nn. 26 and 30
Stroup, Thomas B., 197 n.6, 198 n.16
Suckling, John, 39, 70, 86, 129, 197 n.5, 203 n.10

Taaffe, James G., 206 n.4, 207 nn. 21 and 32, 208 n.38
Terrent, Jeremy, 47
Thirty Years' War, 18, 21, 23, 24, 27, 28, 31, 74
Thomas, Peter W., 17, 21, 29, 46, 60, 145
Thomason, George, 206 n.16
Thorn-Drury, G., 199–200 n.17
Thynne, Richard, 128
Tomlinson, Howard, 188 n.41
Topsell, Edward, 121–22
Townshend, Aurelian, 32–34, 44, 192 n.48. Works: *Albion's Triumph,* 27–28, 50; "Aurelian Tounsend to Tho: Carew vpon the death of the King of Sweden," 28, 29, 31; "On

hearing her Majesty sing," 192 n.48
Trotter, David, 155, 161, 171, 207 n.21, 207–8 n.32
Turberville, George, 117, 201 n.55
Turner, James, 194 n.76
Tyler, Wat, 88, 90

Underdown, David, 175, 187 n.34, 204 n.27, 205 n.29, 208 n.42

Van Dyck, Anthony, 36, 108
Vane, Henry, 31
Vaughan, Henry, 86, 197 n.18
Veall, Donald, 204–5 n.28
Veevers, Erica, 192 n.48
Verbeke, Gerard, 185 n.11
Virgil, 34, 72, 73, 87, 88, 179, 181. Works: *The Aeneid,* 118; "Eclogue VI," 71; "Eclogue VIII," 73; *Georgics,* 23, 25, 34, 52, 180, 181. *See also* Virgilian irony
Virgilian irony, 23, 24–25, 29, 34, 38–39, 189 n.13; in Cartwright, 51–52; in Cowley, 180, 181, 182; in Daniel, 74; in Lovelace, 119
*Voces Votivae,* 47

Wadsworth, Randolph L., Jr., 199 n.4, 201 nn. 48 and 53

Wallace, John M., 187 n.40
Waller, Edmund, 196 n.20, 205 n.35
Walton, Izaak, 128, 152
Warwick, Philip, 22, 23
Warwick, Richard Neville, earl of, 75–76
Weaver, Tom, 204 nn. 20 and 23
Wedgwood, C. V., 17, 21, 130, 202 nn. 4 and 5
Wenman, Francis, 125
Wesley, Samuel, 117
Westmoreland, Mildmay Fane, earl of, 97, 198 n.20
Weston, Richard, 37
Whinney, Margaret, 29
Whitney, Geoffrey, 104
Wilkinson, C. H., 200 n.34
Willet, Andrew, 167, 176
Williams, John, 158–60, 165, 206 n.9
Wine and mirth: in Brome, 128, 129–30, 134–37, 139, 149, 154; in Daniel, 73, 84; in Lovelace, 98, 104, 105, 107
*Wit and Loyalty Reviv'd,* 158
Wither, George, 70, 115
Wood, Anthony à, 97, 111, 123
Woolrych, Austin, 193 n.62
Wortham, C. J., 199 n.8
Wortley, Francis, 204 n.20
Wotton, Henry, 157

Zagorin, Perez, 21